# CITIZENSHIP
## FOR THE 21st CENTURY

# CITIZENSHIP

## FOR THE 21ST CENTURY

*An International Perspective on Education*

John J Cogan • Ray Derricott

**KOGAN PAGE**

First published 1998
Reprinted with revisions 2000

Kogan Page Limited
120 Pentonville Road
London
N1 9JN
UK

Stylus Publishing Inc.
22883 Quicksilver Drive
Sterling
VA 20166-2012
USA

---

**British Library Cataloguing in Publication Data**

A CIP record for this book is available from the British Library.

ISBN 0 7494 3201 2

---

Typeset by JS Typesetting, Wellingborough, Northants
Printed and bound by Creative Print and Design, Wales

To Grace and Margaret,
the two best teachers we know, and the
twenty-six CEPS researchers without whom
this book would not be possible.

# CONTENTS

# CONTRIBUTORS

Roland Case is Professor of Education in the Faculty of Education, Simon Fraser University, Burnaby, British Columbia, Canada. He is a co-director of Research and Development in Global Studies, a multi-university project to promote global education. Critical thinking is an area of particular current interest. He has written widely in all these areas.

John J Cogan, Professor of Education, University of Minnesota, Minneapolis, MN, USA. Director of the Citizenship Education Policy Study (CEPS) project. Scholarly work in the areas of citizenship and global/environmental education. Co-author of three books and more than seventy-five journal publications. He is the US member of a research initiative in the Pacific Rim focusing upon the development of civic values in six societies in this region. He is also the Co-Director (with David Grossman, below) of a USIA College and University Affiliation Programme project that will link the Hong Kong Institute of Education with the University of Minnesota in the areas of civic, environmental and values/moral development education over a three-year period.

Raymond Derricott, Reader and Director of Continuing Education, University of Liverpool, UK. He has long experience in teacher education, curriculum development and research and evaluation. He has conducted evaluation projects for the Department of Employment, Government Office Merseyside and LEAs. He is currently conducting research and evaluation on a project with educators from the UK and Scandinavia. He has written extensively about the social subjects and the management of change in books, contributions to books and journal articles.

Athan Gotovos is a Professor in the Department of Philosophy, Education and Psychology at the University of Ioannina, Ioannina, Greece where he specializes in intercultural education and educational theory.

David L Grossman, Head, Department of Social Sciences, Hong Kong Institute of Education. He is an internationally known specialist in the areas of global and citizenship education and has published in these areas. He is the Director of the Centre for Citizenship Education at HKIEd, which is engaged in research and development activities with respect to furthering the concept of civil society throughout the Asia Pacific region. He is also the Co-Director with John Cogan of a USIA College and University Affiliation Programme project that will link HKIEd with the University of Minnesota in the areas of civic, environmental and values/moral development education over a three-year period.

Sjoerd Karsten is Director of the Centre for the Study of Educational Policy and Administration, University of Amsterdam, Amsterdam, NL. He has published on school choice, local governments, the teaching profession, ethnic segregation, and comparative education. He is also the European CEPS research team leader.

Patricia K Kubow, Assistant Professor of Educational Foundations and Inquiry in the School of Leadership and Policy Studies at Bowling Green State University, Bowling Green, OH, USA. She was the Research Coordinator on the CEPS project and her own current research is focused upon democratic citizenship education with special attention to the impact of these changes upon teachers and those in teacher education programmes.

# Contributors

Ruthanne Kurth-Schai, Associate Professor and Chair, Education Department, Macalester College, St Paul, MN, USA. She is a specialist in Delphi research and other qualitative methodologies. Current research projects include philosophic and policy analyses centred on the role of public education in addressing social justice and environmental issues.

Zsuzsa Matrai, Director, Assessment and Evaluation Section, National Institute for Public Education, Budapest, Hungary. She is a specialist in social science education with special interest in the major changes taking place in core curricular areas in Eastern/Central European states. She is currently involved as the Hungarian representative to the Second IEA study on civic education.

Shuichi Nakayama, Professor and Dean, Graduate School for International Development and Cooperation, Hiroshima University, Hiroshima, Japan. He is a geographer who has spent many years working in the Social Studies Education Division of the Faculty of Education at Hiroshima. He was asked to move to the new Graduate School because of his thirty years' experience working and researching in rural villages in India. He was also the co-director of a bilateral geographic education curriculum project between the US and Japan that resulted in the production of materials for the classroom.

Akira Ninomiya, Professor of Comparative Education and Director of the Center for the Study of International Cooperation in Education, Hiroshima University, Hiroshima, Japan. He is the Japanese CEPS research team leader and his special scholarly interests lie in the areas of school reform and the problems surrounding these changes. He has conducted and published numerous cross-national studies. He is also the Japanese Director of the OECD project on 'Schooling for Tomorrow'.

Kenneth Osborne, Professor Emeritus, University of Manitoba, Winnipeg, Canada. He is a recognized authority in North America in the areas of history education, global education and citizenship education and has written widely in these areas.

Kazuko Otsu, Professor of Education, Hokkaido University of Education, Sapporo, Japan. Her areas of specialization are in citizenship and global education. She has studied recently in these areas at the University of York in the UK and is the Japanese representative to a major new study of civic education practices in the Pacific Rim. She is also part of a major Japanese government initiative in education in Africa.

Walter Parker, Professor of Education, University of Washington, Seattle, WA, USA. He is a specialist in history/social studies curriculum and education for democratic citizenship and has researched and published widely on these topics, including several recent books. He is also a member of the US team to the Second IEA civic education study.

Somwung Pitiyanuwat, Professor and former Dean of the Faculty of Education, Chulalongkorn University, Bangkok, Thailand. He is an acclaimed scaling methodology specialist in SE Asia and was one of the three consulting methodology specialists to the CEPS project. In 1997, he was honoured by the King of Thailand as the Outstanding Educational Researcher in Thailand. He is also the leader of the Thai CEPS research team.

Chumpol Poolpatarachewin, Professor of Educational Philosophy in the Faculty of Education at Chulalongkorn University, Bangkok, Thailand. He is a specialist in the philosophy of education with a special focus upon the impact of Buddhism on educational structures and programmes. He is also the creator of the Educational Delphi Futures Research methodology from which the adaptation for use in the CEPS project was drawn.

## Contributors

Chanita Rukspollmuang, Professor of Educational Foundations in the Faculty of Education, Chulalongkorn University, Bangkok, Thailand. She is a specialist in the areas of comparative and international development education. She is a member of the Thai CEPS research team.

Kathryn Skau is an administrator with Century College, Vancouver, British Columbia, Canada. Previously she was Professor of Education at the University of Calgary, Calgary, Alberta, Canada, where she specialized in social studies and teacher education.

# PREFACE TO THE PAPERBACK EDITION

In the two years since the first publication of this book, a number of significant developments with respect to what it means to be a citizen have occurred across the planet. Nationalism is on the rise in parts of Europe, Asia and Africa. As new states emerge, or old ones remake themselves following years of totalitarian rule, the tendency to reassert one's national identity, or *identities* in some cases, is at the same time freeing and problematic. The situation in the former Yugoslavia is the best-known example but there are many others, eg Indonesia and former Soviet republics.

As a result, global peacekeeping efforts have risen sharply and the debate is on as to whether the UN should become, or even can afford to become, primarily a global peace officer. Member states are reluctant to put their young men and women in harm's way in situations that don't directly impact upon their nations or their national interests. Ethnic and political groups within the nation in turmoil are often suspicious of having someone from the outside come in to assume control, even if only temporary, of their civil affairs. Human rights issues often become central in these situations, as they are generally fraught with ethnic conflicts internal to the particular nation-state.

This has led to increased tensions between some of the peacekeeping states themselves, given their differing perspectives on situations, historical alliances and preferred ways of handling conflict. This has also raised tensions once again between the former superpowers, and to some extent China, in recent conflicts in Europe. Taking the recent conflict in Kosovo as an example, Russia and the United States had very different perspectives on who the perpetrators were and how to resolve the situation. It also brought the North Atlantic Treaty Organization (NATO) into a peacekeeping situation in a major way for the first time. Finally, the bombing of the Chinese Embassy compound in Belgrade, accidental or otherwise, brought the Beijing regime into the situation. As a result, there were charges of increased hegemony on the part of the United States and Britain in particular, raising new fears in some parts of the world of global military expansion.

The economic collapse in East and South-east Asia beginning in the summer of 1997 also led to flare-ups of nationalism in the region. South Korea, Hong Kong (SAR), Thailand, Malaysia and Indonesia were perhaps the most notable examples, with the latter still embroiled in turmoil over East Timor as we write. These economic crises led members of those societies to reflect upon the meaning of citizen in an increasingly interdependent world. Identity became defined in a national, regional and global sense as a result.

Globalization has also impacted the meaning of the term 'citizen'. Moisi (1999) suggests that there are four key concepts that are useful in grasping the revolutionary nature of this global age: complexity, vulnerability, identity and responsibility. He goes on to suggest that in today's transnational world, traditional '[d]istinctions between private and public sectors, between private and public activities, and even between civil and international wars, have become blurred'.

Further, 'fear of globalization also brings fragmentation. In a world that is increasingly homogenized, a person's search for identity rests only in the marginal difference he or she makes to society'.

With respect to the third concept, Moisi notes that '[g]lobalization may erode the authority of the state, alter the meaning of sovereignty and nationality, but it increases the importance of identity. The more global our world, the more vital the search for identification'.

Finally, he suggests that:

> we have lost the privilege of ignorance since the Internet and instant information networks have taken away our ability to pretend we are not aware of what happens in the world. At this point, the notion of sovereignty becomes irrelevant. . . This is not a new form of neo-colonialism; it is responsible universalism. In this context, democracy becomes an essential value that must be promoted and defended.

'Citizenship' takes on new meaning in this context. It must, of necessity, become *multidimensional* in that one must hold multiple identities. Within this phenomenon of globalization we are also witnessing an unprecedented period of global movement. Some have described the late 20th century as 'the age of migration'. Numbers of people are moving across borders, making virtually every country more multiethnic in composition.

Migration movements are becoming one of the biggest world order problems. They endanger peace in and between states and severely test human rights. The social gap between islands of prosperity and regions of poverty is growing and many developing countries are becoming less and less able to provide their ever younger, fast growing populations with work and food. That builds up migration pressure across frontiers, regions and continents (Hauchler and Kennedy, 1994, p123).

As these pressures increase, more racial, ethnic and national groups throughout the world are asserting their identity. As a result, the settled rules of political life in many countries are being challenged by a new 'politics of cultural difference' (Kymlicka, 1995; West, 1993; Ladson-Billings and Tate, 1995).

These parochial allegiances were supposed to fade as the world becomes increasingly integrated, both economically and politically. In reality, 'globalization' has often created more room for minorities to maintain a distinct identity and group life. Globalization has made the myth of a culturally homogeneous state even more unrealistic, and has forced the majority within each state to be more open to pluralism and diversity. The nature of ethnic and national identities is changing in a world of free trade and global communications, but the challenge of multiculturalism is here to stay (Kymlicka, 1995, p9).

## GLOBAL DEVELOPMENTS WITH RESPECT TO CITIZENSHIP EDUCATION

The past decade has seen perhaps more attention to democratization and the development of civil society worldwide than at any time in recent memory, certainly since the end of the Second World War. Everywhere one turns, be it Asia, Europe, Latin America and even parts of Africa, there is renewed emphasis upon civic and citizenship education as a part of the formal school curriculum.

Australia has developed the first ever set of guidelines (*Whereas The People*, Civics Expert Group, 1994) in civic education as a means of providing direction to schools regarding how they should proceed in educating for citizenship. Nearby, Indonesia, as an outgrowth of economic and political collapse in late 1997 and 1998, has established a national centre for civic education and held the first ever national conference in this area in March 1999, in Bandung. Recent elections have served to stimulate a democratic feeling and a hopeful perspective on the future. In Thailand, one of the participant nations in the CEPS project reported on in this book, there is a new constitution and a new education law that place strong emphasis upon citizenship education.

In Hong Kong, SAR, China, they are now engaged in an experiment that will continue over at least a fifty-year period as this Special Administrative Region of China operates under the 'one nation, two systems' approach as outlined in the Basic Law. Books, journal and newspaper articles, academic forums and even educational centres have been established to study what it means to be 'citizen'. At the Hong Kong Institute of Education, the tertiary institution responsible for the preparation of all the SAR's primary, and most junior, secondary teachers, a Centre for Citizenship Education (CCE) has been established to work with schools, teachers in service, policy makers and related education officials to focus upon the area of democratic citizenship. In addition, the CCE has established an Asian network of citizenship educators who meet annually to discuss issues of mutual concern and develop projects that will result in benefiting specific nation-states as well as the region as a whole. The Centre's governing board has also taken the original CEPS model and enhanced it to reflect the local Hong Kong and Asian regional situation. This is an example of the dynamic that was intended *vis-à-vis* the original *multidimensional citizenship* model.

In Japan the new curriculum syllabus has placed a renewed emphasis upon the areas of civic and moral education as a means towards developing more democratic and participatory citizens. There is similar interest in Taiwan.

In Europe, the Council of Europe has embarked upon a multi-year project called 'Education for Democratic Citizenship' (Web site: culture.coe.fr/-postsummit/ citizenship). Launched in February 1997, the project focuses upon a reassessment of the meaning of participatory democracy and the status of citizen within a united Europe. Three primary questions guide the work:

● What values and skills will individuals require in order to be full citizens of Europe in the 21st century?
● How can these values and skills be acquired?
● How can citizens learn to pass them on to others; to children, young people and adults?

There are other related movements throughout the continent as well, eg Open Society fellowships and seminars focusing on democratization, and Uppsala University's multi-year series of symposia on citizenship education supported jointly by the Council of Europe and the Swedish government. But none are as striking as the impact of the follow-on from the Crick Report in Britain and one of the main reasons for the revision of this book at this particular point in time. In the Foreword to this document, *Education for Citizenship and the Teaching of Democracy in Schools* (DfEE, 1998), the Speaker of the House of Commons, The Right Honourable Betty Boothroyd, comments on the urgent need for attention to citizenship:

Like my immediate predecessor as Speaker, I have become increasingly concerned that Citizenship as a subject appeared to be diminishing in importance and impact in schools – this despite a number of non-governmental initiatives over a long period of years. This area, in my view, has been a blot on the landscape of public life for too long, with unfortunate consequences for the future of our democratic processes. (p3)

Our guess is that one could take the Speaker's concern and place it in numerous documents in various nations around the world and it would be equally supported. Everywhere we travel these days, the topic of developing 'civil society' and the role of citizenship education in doing so is paramount. We are hopeful that this revised edition of our work will help teachers, policy makers and ultimately students in classrooms to understand what it means to be a citizen in the world of the new millennium in a way that is personal and social, spatial and temporal. We believe that the *multidimensional* model presented in these pages is one way to achieve the Speaker's goal of eliminating this 'blot' on the landscape of public life.

## References

DfEE (1998) *Education for Citizenship and the Teaching of Democracy in Schools*, (The Crick Report), QCA, London.

Civics Expert Group (1994) *Whereas the People*, Government of Australia, Canberra.

Hauchler, I and Kennedy, P M (1994) *Global Trends: The world almanac of development and peace*, Continuum, New York.

Kymlicka, W (1995) *Multicultural Citizenship*, Clarendon Press, Oxford.

Ladson-Billings, G and Tate, W F (1995) Toward a critical race theory of education, *Teachers College Record* (Fall 97), pp47–68.

Moisi, D (1999) Universal truths, *Financial Times*, Monday 27 September.

West, C (1993) The new cultural politics of difference, in *Race, Identity and Representation in Education*, ed C McCarthy and W Crichlow, pp11–23, Routledge, London.

# PREFACE

As editors of this book we have had the advantage of working together for over twenty-five years on projects and topics related to the social subjects and citizenship. With one of us living and working in Minnesota and the other in Liverpool we have watched the 4000 miles between us shrink over the years due to both the strength of our friendship and the changes in technology which have eased our collaboration. Almost all of the Citizenship Education Policy Study research team was already known to at least one of us. The project therefore had the advantage of building onto an existing North American–European and Asian network.

Working in an international group such as this offered many challenges. As we worked through the English language, we became increasingly aware of the differences of nuance and meaning between British and American English. We also came fully to appreciate the efforts, abilities and perspectives of many of our colleagues who were working, in a concentrated way, in their second, third and in some cases, their fourth language. We pay our tribute to their dedication and perseverance.

The project researchers used modern electronic means of communication to reduce the time and distance between us but in truth it was the periodic face-to-face contact which renewed our energies and encouraged us to continue when situations became difficult. The various international meetings in Minnesota, Hawaii, Bangkok, Hiroshima, Sydney and Amsterdam were anticipated with the joy of working and socializing with one another. Together in these groups the cross-cultural problems were eased and we became hard-working professionals totally dedicated to the tasks in hand. The diverse ways we had been socialized, trained and educated added to our similar and different experiences. Education and training had produced a powerful cocktail for work and to work towards changes in educational policy in our various nations. At each of the international meetings we suspended for just a few hours our research focus and took time to appreciate geographical, cultural and value differences and learnt to share our different senses of fun and humour. In the end it is these personal relationships which shall bond us for ever as a very special group.

All these experiences were made possible by the generous support of the Sasakawa Peace Foundation, Tokyo, Japan. The Foundation always kept in touch with the progress of the project through the annual reports submitted to it and also through the presence at each of our international meetings by the Project Officer Mr Tomoatsu Shibata. We wish to recognize as well that without Mr Masafumi Nagao, Vice-President of the Foundation, whose initial vision of what this project could be and his faith in seeing that we got the necessary resources to do it, the study could never have been completed. To both these gentlemen we are deeply indebted. We express the gratitude of all members of the Project for this crucial help in our work.

Thanks also to the panel of experts and our universities and colleges for making space for our involvement, and to the Project's administrative, financial and secretarial staff from our various locations who all gave us their support.

Special mention must go to three people whose help at the end brought this project to a much earlier closure than we thought possible. First, to Ken Osborne, Professor Emeritus, University of Manitoba, Winnipeg, Canada, for his superb review and critique of the manuscript before we made the final copy, we owe a great debt. His keen eye and sharp pen have improved the manuscript immeasurably. And to Jen Lawton Williams and Cathy Zemke whose knowledge of word processing and graphics – to say nothing of converting disks and files across the Atlantic in forms that were compatible with our different systems – made the completion of the final manuscript possible, we are greatly indebted as well.

# Citizenship Education for the 21st Century: Setting the Context

## John J Cogan

As we approach the end of this turbulent century and prepare to meet the challenges of the next, the question of what constitutes education for citizenship in various nations appropriate to the demands and needs of a rapidly changing global community is critical in both national and international contexts. The planet and the human family are facing an unprecedented set of challenges including the globalization of the economy, a significant level of deterioration in the quality of the global environment, rapidly changing technologies and the uses of same, loss of a sense of community and shared belief in the common good, ethical questions regarding the use of genetic engineering, large-scale migration both within and between nations and rising crime. How does one respond to these challenges both as a member of a particular nation-state as well as a member of the global community of nations in a manner that is thoughtful, active, personal and yet with a commitment to the common good? This was the underlying question faced by the Citizenship Education Policy Study project (CEPS), an international research network project designed to examine the changing character of citizenship over the next twenty-five years and the implications of these changes for educational policy for the nine participating nations and beyond.

Formal education programmes have traditionally been assigned, as one of their duties, the preparation of citizens, primarily within the social subjects' area of the curriculum. Citizenship education has typically been an important goal in courses of study in history and civics in most nations and has, for the most part, focused upon developing knowledge of how government and other institutions in any given state work, of the rights and duties of citizens with respect to the state and to the society as a whole and has been oriented largely towards the development of a sense of national identity. At one point, when the world was a simpler place, this conceptualization of citizenship may have served us well; but this is no longer the case. The complexity, scale and interconnectedness of the challenges facing us at the close of this century and the dawn of the next simply cannot be met through conventional means. What is called for is a new conception of citizenship education, one in which both schools and the communities they serve and are a part of, are equal partners in the education of each new generation of citizens. This calls for an approach to citizen education which is *multidimensional* in nature; which, while including personal development, also includes a commitment to thinking and acting in ways that take account of local, national and global communities and their concerns. It is a conception which is based on dimensions of time, that is, it takes account of present problems in ways that respect the heritage of the past while also protecting the interests of the future. It is also spatial in nature in that it acknowledges the different levels of community which must be taken into account as we face and attempt to resolve global problems and issues which are manifested in regional, state, provincial, and most certainly, local circumstances.

This new conceptualization of citizenship education was, for us, arrived at through the assistance of policy shapers and scholars who had examined global trend data and had a vision about what the near-term future might hold. A total of 182 policy shapers from across the broad range of fields noted below participated in this study, either through interviews designed to generate survey questionnaire items and/or two subsequent survey iterations over an eighteen-month period. The goal was to use policy experts and scholars from politics and government; business, industry and labour; science and technology; health and education; and cultural and academic fields as the informants in the study which was conducted across nine nations in Asia, Europe and North America. These were the fields of endeavour which emerged as being significant in the near-term future, ie, the next twenty-five years, as derived from the background reading carried out by the researchers before launching the study, particularly in the area of emerging global trends.

This book is about this endeavour, its process, its findings, the recommendations emerging from the findings, and especially the development of a new model of citizen education which we term *multidimensional citizenship*, and the challenges that educators and policy makers face in implementing this model. Before proceeding with a detailed account of the study, it is important to examine and reflect upon what we know about citizenship and citizenship education as well as what futurists and others tell us about emerging global trends which will set the context for the world in which children and youth now in their formative years will live and work.

## THE FIVE ATTRIBUTES OF CITIZENSHIP

Modern political systems depend for their successful functioning upon a conception of citizenship. It can be explicitly spelt out in a constitution, a bill of rights or some similar document, or it can be left implicit within national traditions and institutions. Usually it is a combination of both: explicit prescription and implicit practice. But whichever is the case, any conception of citizenship contains a sense of the knowledge, skills, values and dispositions that, ideally, citizens should possess.

These attributes of citizenship will vary according to the nature of the political system of which they are a part, but in general terms they can be classified into five categories:

- a sense of identity
- the enjoyment of certain rights
- the fulfilment of corresponding obligations

- a degree of interest and involvement in public affairs, and
- an acceptance of basic societal values.

All five are conveyed through a wide variety of institutions, both governmental and non-governmental, including the media, but they are usually seen as a particular responsibility of the school. Citizenship education, in the broadest sense, is an important task in all contemporary societies.

## A sense of identity

The first element of citizenship – a sense of identity – is usually defined in national terms, though not necessarily exclusively so, since most countries acknowledge the existence of multiple and overlapping identities, be they local, ethnic, cultural, religious or whatever. This is obviously especially the case in societies that are multicultural in their make-up, though even in the most homogeneous society citizens will usually possess an attachment to more than one identity. None the less, a sense of national identity and patriotism is usually seen as an essential ingredient of citizenship, though some commentators argue that national citizenship alone will not be enough to meet the challenges of the 21st century as the world becomes ever more interconnected and interdependent.

There are those who reject national citizenship as obsolete and even dangerous and argue instead for a globally oriented cosmopolitan citizenship that cuts completely across national loyalties (Nussbaum, 1996). More usually, however, it is argued that the demands of national citizenship should not be denied, but must be combined with a realization that no nation can operate in isolation in today's world, so that citizenship must contain both national and multinational dimensions (Boulding, 1990; Commission on Global Governance, 1995; Ramphal, 1991; World Commission on Environment and Development, 1987). This interest in combining the national and multinational dimensions of citizenship is clearly reflected in the data emerging from CEPS and is one of the reasons why later in this book we speak of the concept of multidimensional citizenship.

## Rights and entitlements

The second element of citizenship consists of the enjoyment of certain rights or entitlements. To be a citizen is to be a member of a group and thus to be entitled to the benefits that group membership confers. Citizens, for example, are entitled to the protection of their government when they are travelling outside their own country. They are entitled to the protection of the law and to whatever rights their constitution and political system guarantee them.

The British sociologist, T H Marshall, has argued that in the Western world citizenship rights can be classified into three categories, listed in the order in which they were won historically. The first are legal rights, such as freedom from arbitrary arrest and imprisonment, and the entitlement to a fair trial and due process if charged with a crime. The second are political rights, consisting primarily of the right to vote, to run for public office, and to participate in public affairs. The third are economic and social rights, as in the case of the right to organize trade unions, to attend school, to obtain social security and so on (Barbalet, 1988; Marshall, 1950; Turner, 1986, 1989). There is obviously a good deal of debate about rights such as these. How extensive should they be? What is the appropriate balance between public and private provision? How much should be the responsibility of the individual citizen and how much of society as a whole? These and other questions remind us that citizenship is not a static, once and for all, set of practices, but rather a continuing process of debate and often a subject of political disagreement and dispute. This is another reason why, in this book, we argue for what we describe as multidimensional citizenship.

## Responsibilities, obligations and duties

The third element of citizenship consists of responsibilities, obligations and duties. Some commentators, especially in the Western world, argue that the pursuit of individual rights has overshadowed the performance of the duties of citizenship, which have been unduly neglected (Gwyn, 1995). Indeed, some political theorists argue that liberal democracy, as practised in Europe and North America, contains a built-in tendency to emphasize the maximization of individual rights and to minimize the pursuit of the public interest. This charge, for example, is at the heart of the continuing debate between so-called liberals and communitarians (Barber, 1984; Bell, 1993; Etzioni, 1993; Galston, 1991; Holmes, 1993; Macedo, 1990).

In any event, though practice is not always consistent with theory, it is universally accepted that citizenship carries with it the obligation to perform certain duties, including the responsibility to obey the law, to pay one's taxes, to respect the rights of other people, to fight for one's country and generally to fulfil one's social obligations. Some commentators go further than this and insist that the most pressing duty of all is participation in public affairs. As in the case of citizenship rights, the duties and obligations of citizenship are also subject to debate and discussion, thus leading us again in this book to argue for what we describe as multidimensional citizenship in which the 21st-century citizens' responsibilities, obligations and duties are viewed within a more global context.

## Active in public affairs

The question of the duties of citizenship introduces the fourth element of citizenship, consisting of the responsibility to play some part in public affairs. There is a long tradition, dating back to the ancient Greeks, that distinguishes between a good person and a good citizen. A good person lives his or her life virtuously and honourably, but without any involvement or interest in public affairs. A good citizen, by contrast, not only lives decently in his or her private life, but is also committed to participation in public life; at the very least to taking an informed interest in public affairs and, ideally, playing an active part in them. Again, as with citizenship rights and duties, involvement in public affairs is not a matter for prescriptive command, but rather for deliberation and debate. The readiness to engage in this debate constitutes an important facet of what we describe in this book as multidimensional citizenship.

## Acceptance of basic societal values

The fifth element of citizenship is the acceptance of basic societal values. These will obviously vary from country to country and they are often the subject of debate in which honest and principled differences of opinion reveal themselves. They are sometimes described, directly or indirectly, in constitutional documents and sometimes left more or less unstated, but they always exist. Examples include trust, cooperation, respect for human rights, non-violence and so on. Such societal values are seen as helping to constitute the distinctive identity of a country and as making social living possible. They are also seen as an important ingredient of good citizenship, and, as with the other elements of citizenship, can pose problems which citizens must be ready and able to resolve for themselves while at the same time respecting the viewpoints, interests and rights of others. This interplay between the priorities of the individual citizen, those of his or her fellow citizens, of citizens of other societies, and even of citizens yet unborn, constitutes another reason for this book's insistence on what we call multidimensional citizenship.

As already noted, all five elements or attributes of citizenship can and do give rise to debate and dispute. Rights can conflict with each other. The interpretation of rights and duties is not always clear-cut. Citizens can differ with each other over solutions to public issues. Political change can lead to accepted definitions of citizenship coming into question. Certain groups can be denied the benefits of citizenship, as happened historically in the case of women and racial and ethnic minorities. Citizens can honestly and honourably place claims of principle and conscience above those of citizenship as conventionally defined. In all such cases, and others like them, citizenship is not a matter of unquestioned obedience to whomever is in power or to the forces of tradition. Nor is it conformity to majority opinion or passive acceptance of conventional wisdom. Rather, citizenship involves thinking for oneself, while at the same time listening to and respecting the viewpoints of other people, in order to become personally engaged with the problems and issues that confront one's society. Some commentators speak of deliberative citizenship, arguing that citizens must be able to think, to reflect, to discuss and to act in ways that are rational, reasonable and ethically defensible (Cohen, 1989; Mathews, 1996; Miller, 1993). We include this concept of deliberation, of reflective action, in the concept of multidimensional citizenship that forms the main theme of this book.

All five elements of citizenship have obvious implications for and application to education. Historically, compulsory public education has always been assigned an important role in the preparation of citizens. Schools were intended to give the young citizens a sense of identity, and often of national pride; and to teach them the rights and duties of citizenship as officially defined. There is research to indicate that the schools have not been as effective in this role as the proponents of citizenship education have hoped (Hodgetts, 1968; Oppenheim *et al.*, 1975). For example, the view of citizenship taught in the schools has often been unduly passive and conformist, and it has discriminated against girls and minority students (Anyon, 1980; Crick and Porter, 1978; Curtis *et al.*, 1992; Hess and Torney, 1968; Oakes, 1985; Phillips, 1989, 1993). It has also often reflected the interests of those in power in a particular society and thus has been a matter of indoctrination and the establishment of ideological hegemony rather than of education (Apple, 1979, 1982; Bourdieu and Passeron, 1977; Snyders, 1976; Whitty, 1985).

Recent years have seen a wide variety of proposals for the strengthening of citizenship education in the schools (Center for Civic Education, 1991; Crick and Heater, 1978; Engle and Ochoa, 1988; Ichilov, 1990; Janowitz, 1983; Newmann, 1970, 1975; Osborne, 1994; Parker, 1996; Shaver, 1977) and the concept of multidimensional citizenship that is described later in this book reflects much of this debate.

Recent years have also seen increasing attention given to the subject of citizenship by political theorists and philosophers. Some have approached it directly, examining the strengths and weaknesses of current conceptions of citizenship, its present practice and its historical development (Andrews, 1991; Beiner, 1995; Heater, 1990; Kaplan, 1993; Kymlicka, 1992, 1995; Pocock, 1992; Riesenberg, 1992; Shklar, 1991). Feminist scholars have drawn attention to the biases of citizenship theory and practice (Elshtain, 1981; Frazer and Lacey, 1993; Okin, 1992; Phillips, 1989, 1993; Young, 1990). Advocates of multiculturalism have argued for a more inclusive approach to citizenship (Banks, 1996; Kymlicka, 1995; Taylor, 1992) and have provoked counter-arguments from those who worry that their proposals might be unduly divisive (Bissoondath, 1994; Schlesinger, 1991).

Others have placed citizenship in a broader context, looking at ways of reshaping and strengthening democratic institutions so as to produce a richer and deeper sense of citizenship than now often exists (Held, 1993). In this vein, there have been proposals for strong democracy (Barber, 1984); for radical democracy (Mouffe, 1992; Trend, 1996); for deliberative democracy (Cohen, 1989; Mathews, 1996; Miller, 1993); for participatory democracy (Gould, 1988; Pateman, 1971); for associational democracy (Hirst, 1994); for discursive democracy (Drysek, 1990); for dialogic democracy (Giddens, 1994); all of which have clear implications for citizenship. There is also an increasing literature that argues for a global conception of citizenship in which people will identify less with their own nations and more with the planet as a single entity. This is not, of course, a new concept. In this century it received some attention after both the First and Second World Wars and formed part of the educational agenda of both the League of Nations and the United Nations. However, it is now receiving a new emphasis as it becomes more and more obvious that the world's problems and the solutions to them can be dealt with only on a multinational basis (Boulding, 1990; Ramphal, 1991).

The five elements of citizenship outlined above depend heavily for their support upon European and North American research and scholarship. However, these elements, as described, are generally acceptable and applicable to the two Asian nations participating in this study as well. There are differences to be sure. For example, in Japan, while all five of these elements are seen as important constituents of citizenship and civic education, family membership and harmonious social relationships are seen as equally, and perhaps even more, important. In addition, citizenship education programmes tend to emphasize the concept of 'nation' more than that of 'citizen'. Moral aspects of citizenship are nearly always included in the concept of being a 'good citizen'.

In Thailand, the conceptualization of citizenship includes, in addition to the family and human relationships that are valued in Japan, a religious definition of the good citizen. Spiritual and moral development are seen as important elements of citizenship. In this predominantly Buddhist society, these are very important and are both explicit in curricula and implicit in educational policies and the preparation of teachers.

In both Japan and Thailand, there is an explicit attempt to educate 'globally oriented' citizens who have both international perspectives and a strong national sense of identity. But the basic five elements, as described in the main body of this section, apply across the Asian and Western nations participating in this study.

Regardless of country, citizenship and citizenship education, whether defined in national, multinational, or global terms, have attracted considerable attention in recent years, and this book should be read in the context of this overall debate as well as within the context of the global trends that will characterize the near-term future.

## THE GLOBAL TRENDS LITERATURE

During the past decade or more, there have been a number of published works forecasting likely global trends as we approach the turn of the century (Brown, 1996; Brown and Kane, 1994; Drucker, 1994; Hauchler and Kennedy, 1994; Kaplan, 1994; Kennedy, 1993; Kidder, 1987, 1989, 1994; McRae, 1995; Naisbitt, 1982, 1996; Ohmae, 1987, 1990; Reich, 1992; Snyder, 1995; World Commission on Environment and Development, 1987). As one reads the work of these scholars several themes begin to emerge, notably, economic developments, technology and communication, and population and the environment. These are not seen as mutually exclusive, but as interwoven and linked to one another.

### The global economy

While opinions differ on the desirability of a global economy, as well as the speed with which it will come about, all writers agree that this is where we are headed. It will take the next twenty-five years for this trend to fully emerge but its momentum will ensure its realization. Perhaps Robert Reich describes it best in his book, *The Work of Nations*.

> We are living through a transformation that will rearrange the politics and economics of the coming century. There will be no *national* products or technologies, no national corporations, no national industries. There will no longer be national economies, at least as we have come to understand that concept. All that will remain within national borders are the people who comprise a nation. Each nation's primary assets will be its citizens' skills and insights. Each nation's primary political task will be to cope with the centrifugal forces of the global economy which tear at the ties binding citizens together – bestowing ever greater wealth on the most skilled and insightful, while consigning the less skilled to a declining standard of living. As borders become ever more meaningless in economic terms, those citizens best positioned to thrive in the world market are tempted to slip the bonds of national allegiance, and by doing so disengage themselves from their less favored fellows. (Reich, 1992, p3)

Japanese commentator Ohmae Kenichi states it even more simply: 'Words such as overseas operations, affiliates, and subsidiaries are disappearing. Nothing is "overseas" any longer' (Ohmae, 1990, pviii).

Within this global economy, a major shift in emphasis is taking place. It is the move, gradually, away from the production of manufactured goods to services. Associated with this move to globalization, other economic transformations will occur, as the global distribution of the production of goods and services, and the balance between them shifts. A British commentator, Hamish McRae, offers this forecast in his recent book, *The World in 2020.*

> During the next century, the gradual shift away from the production of manufactured goods towards the production of services in industrial countries will not happen suddenly or swiftly, and it will not happen at all for the newly industrialized countries, so for the rest of the twentieth century and the first years of the twenty-first, it will remain vitally important to be good at making things. But gradually the comparative advantage will be won by being good at producing services. (McRae, 1995, pp11–12)

The movement away from many individual national economies to a global one does not come easily. People's sense of identity is in many fundamental ways tied to the nation-state. Nevertheless, signs that a global economy is emerging can be seen in the movement, especially in the industrialized world, to regional trading zones or blocs, eg, the European Community (EC), the North American Free Trade Association (NAFTA), the Association of Southeast Asian Nations (ASEAN) and others. Many commentators believe that these are but transitional groupings while nations position themselves to take full advantage of the global trade potential. In some respects this represents a last attempt to hold on to what *was* rather than accepting what *will be*. That is to say that many nations are simply moving from bilateral trading mechanisms and frameworks to regional groupings or blocs in an attempt to solidify their comparative advantage, while in point of fact the transnational corporations conducting the actual business of manufacture, trade and the production and delivery of services have moved considerably beyond this point to a totally global operation which transcends national borders and even national sovereignties with increasing frequency. Thus, rather than taking the truly big leap from national to global economic activity, nation-states are lagging further and further behind. Transnational corporations may come to see the nation-state as superfluous and move ahead without their involvement.

## Technology and communication

Technology is the second global trend area which receives a great deal of attention in the media. Technological change has affected nearly every activity in which people are engaged on a daily basis, eg, in the workplace, the home, at school, at leisure; yet it is probably the computer and electronics revolutions which have most noticeably touched our lives directly. People are increasingly 'online' to the entire world with instant access to so much information we don't even know where to begin to sort it all out.

The key element, however, is access. Proponents of 'on-line access' claim that this will level the playing field; that everyone will have access to the same information, and will accordingly be more empowered. But information is a commodity as we enter the 21st century; it represents wealth and power. Snyder warns of the potential dangers:

> Since information is a key economic asset and speed in moving information gives an economic edge, wealth increasingly means access to information. The global gap between the 'haves' and 'have-nots' is increasingly a question of the information access that makes material wealth possible. (Snyder, 1995, p43)

Hauchler and Kennedy, in their recent book, *Global Trends*, also raise questions about the impact of the new technologies:

> In many parts of the world, technological innovations are gaining influence over economic, social and cultural development. New technologies promise solutions to global problems such as hunger, environmental destruction, and disease; but they also harbor a host of risks that have as yet been scarcely explored, and they raise questions about the ethical and social problems associated with an automated world. In addition, they widen the technological gap between industrial and developing countries. Attempts at formulating a responsible technology policy geared to global considerations are almost non-existent. Up to now, this area has been dominated by 'strategic alliances' between large-scale technology-intensive enterprises based in the industrial countries. (Hauchler and Kennedy, 1994, p15)

Another aspect of technology that will be of increasing importance in the future is genetic engineering, which though rooted in basic science, is brought to reality through technology. This raises many ethical and moral questions and would bring about major changes in the societies.

Technological change will continue and probably occur at an ever-increasing rate well into the next century. In many ways it will make people's daily lives easier. But there is a potential negative side to this trend which bears careful attention to avoid the pitfalls noted by McRae, Hauchler and Kennedy, and Snyder above.

Another aspect to this development which needs to be addressed, especially within the context of education and schooling, is the tendency for these new technologies to be utilized in a very passive manner. This presents a major challenge for educators regarding the intelligent and active use of technology.

## Population and environment

The third and fourth most prevalent trends discussed in the literature involve population and the environment. There is considerable disagreement over what the real issues are. But at the same time, there is increasing agreement that these two areas are closely interrelated and, if left unchecked, could be the undoing of the planet. The planet's population continues to rise, currently at 6 billion and, barring a major global disaster, will continue to rise by most estimates to nearly 8 billion by 2025. This exerts enormous pressures upon the environment. All of these new humans need to be fed, sheltered, able to find work, and try to achieve some decent quality of life.

The list of problems facing the planet is enormous. They include, but are not reserved to, desertification, destruction of arable lands, depletion of major aquifers, acid rain, the disposal of nuclear and chemical waste, resource depletion, endangered species, erosion, rainforest destruction, salination due to poor irrigation practices, poisoning of the atmosphere, ozone depletion and climate change, and critically short supplies of fresh water. The latter will very likely be the most serious resource problem facing the world in the next twenty-five years.

McRae comments that the freshwater problem is not one of uneven distribution inasmuch as three-quarters of the planet's fresh water supply is contained in polar icecaps and glaciers and thus unavailable for use, at least utilizing current technologies. The real problem is that 'where water is plentiful, people are frequently few, and vice-versa' (McRae, 1995, p124). The problem is so serious that, 'Water will become a political issue in much the same way that oil has been for much of the period after the Second World War' (McRae, 1995, p127).

Howard Snyder describes what he terms the 'lethal spiral' linking population growth, the ecological crisis and social conflict. It is a dangerous cycle which must be broken for us to survive through the next century.

> Each of these factors affects the others, and together they form a cycle. *Population growth*, concentration, or displacement put new burdens on the environment. These burdens take various forms: pollution, depletion of water, deforestation as people cut down forests for firewood. The result is *ecological crisis*. . .Environmental crisis in turn increases social conflict. Disease, famine, and resulting migrations of people add to existing political, ethnic and religious tension. When the physical environment goes bad, social conflict easily leads to complete social breakdown. The social environment reflects the physical environment. Even if chaos is averted, ecological crisis aggravates social tensions. It is now clear that social conflict in turn stimulates further population growth, thus completing the lethal cycle. (Snyder, 1995, p85)

Robert D Kaplan argues forcefully in his article entitled 'The Coming Anarchy' that the environment will be 'the national security issue of the early twenty-first century', unless the spiral described above is broken:

> The political and strategic impact of surging populations, spreading disease, deforestation and soil erosion, water depletion, air pollution, and, possibly, rising sea levels in critical, overcrowded regions like the Nile Delta and Bangladesh – developments that will prompt mass migrations and, in turn, group conflicts – will be the core foreign-policy challenge from which most others will ultimately emanate. (Kaplan, 1994, p46)

The link between environment and population is strong, and the interrelationships are clear. Changing demographic patterns have powerful and long-lasting effects. One of the key problems, of course, is that population growth is not evenly distributed. Most of it will take place in the non-industrialized world, about 95 per cent by most estimates. This means that the industrial world will grow older and will have to learn to adapt. This will have major social, economic and political consequences.

The future could well see increased tensions between the 'have' and 'have-not' nations. Immigration pressures will increase as a result of population growth, thus raising tensions between the industrialized and non-industrialized worlds. It is a natural response. People on the fringes of the rich industrial nations will continue to seek to get into them. None the less, even if immigration quotas were dramatically increased in the industrialized world, this would not in any significant way alleviate the pressures of population in the non-industrialized world. Hauchler and Kennedy cite that only 'if extreme poverty is eliminated, health and education improved, and the social status of women enhanced will it be possible to put a brake on the growth in population' (Hauchler and Kennedy, 1994, p12).

But McRae warns that we are a long way from the resolution of the population–environment issue. Indeed, he forecasts that this will be with us for some time to come:

> The degradation of the environment will be a greater preoccupation in the year 2020 than it is in the early 1990s. The industrialized countries, and increasingly the middle-income countries, will be spending a greater proportion of their resources to try to correct the damage, and as a result will be cleaner and in many ways nicer places to live. The present generation of newly industrialized countries will be working hard to improve the quality of their environment, and will be achieving much higher standards of air and water quality and solid waste disposal in their cities. They will have the advantage of the technologies developed in the rich countries under the influence of their tough environmental controls. But other countries (or regions) at the earliest stages of industrialization will be struggling with even more serious problems than they do at present. (McRae, 1995, p137)

## GLOBAL MOVEMENT: MIGRATION, DIVERSITY AND REFUGEES

Some have described the late 20th century as 'the age of migration'. Numbers of people are moving across borders, making virtually every country more multi-ethnic in composition. More racial, ethnic and national groups throughout the world are asserting their identity. As a result, the settled rules of political life in many countries are being challenged by a new 'politics of cultural difference'.

Kymlicka, in his book *Multicultural Citizenship* (1995), suggests that:

> These parochial allegiances were supposed to fade as the world becomes increasingly integrated both economically and politically. In reality, 'globalization' has often created more room for minorities to maintain a distinct identity and group life. Globalization has made the myth of a culturally homogeneous state even more unrealistic, and has forced the majority within each state to be more open to pluralism and diversity. The nature of ethnic and national identities is changing in a world of free trade and global communications, but the challenge of multiculturalism is here to stay. (Kymlicka, 1995, p9)

As the reader can see, these trends closely parallel the four areas of the futurists we noted above. Even though these trends in no way constitute a Pollyannaish view of the future, some critics of globalization go further, questioning both the inherent nature of globalization and its impact. Summarizing some of these critical views, Baylis and Smith (1997) remind us that:

- globalization is often equated with a stage of capitalism or western imperialism, and as such carries a lot of baggage with it;
- globalization is uneven in its effects, producing both winners and losers, the latter especially amongst the poor;
- globalization obscures accountability in that it is difficult to trace and specify responsibility;
- globalization gives rise to paradox and even processes of counter-globalization, eg, more global homogeneity engenders fierce reactions that strengthen local identities, be they religious, ethnic or national (Baylis and Smith, 1997, pp9–11).

Most experts agree that the global trends we have described are the kinds of global realities that will shape the world of the early 21st century. If so, then what kinds of citizens are needed to function in this world? What kind of knowledge, skills and behaviours will they need to exhibit? What kind of education and schooling will be needed to develop these citizens? It is our belief that one way to address these questions is through the model of *multidimensional citizenship*.

## MULTIDIMENSIONAL CITIZENSHIP

These global trends predictions of leading scholars, policy experts and futurists, together with the findings of this study, strongly suggest that current modes of educating for citizenship will not be sufficient as we enter a new century. They require that citizens be able to focus upon many diverse elements, issues and contexts simultaneously. Thus, the central recommendation emerging from this study is that future educational policy must be based upon a conception of what we describe as *multidimensional citizenship* appropriate to the needs and demands of the early part of the 21st century. This conception must permeate all aspects of education, including curriculum and pedagogy, governance and organization, and school–community relationships. This can be achieved only if schools and other key elements and agencies of society work together. The four dimensions embodied in our conceptualization of *multidimensional citizenship* are personal, social, temporal and spatial. These will be explained and examined in more depth later in Chapter 5. Suffice to say, however, that these four dimensions must be present and in harmony for the citizen of the next century to be a contributing, effective member of her or his society.

## OVERVIEW OF THE STUDY

### How the study began

This project first began to take shape in 1991 when the Project director approached various colleagues with the idea of investigating the ways in which citizenship education could effectively respond to the challenges of the next twenty-five years. The Project director, based at the University of Minnesota in the United States, made use of a network of partner universities located in Europe, Japan and Thailand, with the idea of organizing a multinational research project. After a number of meetings, agreement was reached and Minnesota was designated as the secretariat for the project.

The Project director then developed a research proposal and circulated it to the appropriate faculty at the partner institutions, ie, Amsterdam in the Netherlands, Chulalongkorn in Thailand, and Hiroshima in Japan, for comment and feedback before submitting it to a possible funding agency. Several foundations expressed some interest but in the end it was the Sasakawa Peace Foundation, Tokyo, Japan, which committed the financial resources necessary to conduct the study.

## Selection of research team leaders

Once project funding was secured, the next step was to select a research team leader from each of the four partner universities to guide the project activities. The criterion for the selection of these individuals was:

- demonstrated expertise in either citizenship education and/or research methodology
- a future-oriented vision
- interest in the study and
- a commitment to remain with the project throughout the entire period of its existence.

This last criterion was very important as this was to be a commitment of four years, endless meetings, coordination of one's national and regional team activities, making very meagre budgets stretch to the limit to accomplish the work, preparing a regular series of reports on the progress of their team, preparing team members for each of the three international meetings which were to take place over the course of the life of the project, and all without any financial remuneration. In each instance, the team leaders did this willingly and without complaint.

Four research teams, one each from Japan, Thailand, the European region including England, Germany, Greece, Hungary, and the Netherlands and from the North American region, including Canada and the United States, carried out the study. The latter two were treated as regions given that they included multiple nations. However, there is no intent here to suggest that these were inclusive, ie, that they represented all of the remainder of European or North American nations. The project was guided by a steering committee made up of the Project director, a graduate student Project coordinator, the four team leaders and one associate from each of the four teams and a Delphi methodology specialist. This committee totalled nine persons and met at least twice annually throughout the project.

## Working definitions

In a cross-national, cross-cultural study such as this, there are many nuances with respect to concepts and the definition of terms. Accordingly, at the first meeting of the project steering committee in September 1993, held in Hiroshima, Japan, both general and working definitions were established for the project to guide the inquiry over the next four years. These were not necessarily optimal definitions in the eyes of each participating research team but they were acceptable for the purposes of launching the study. The discussion of and consensus reached upon these signalled from the outset the collaborative nature of this project.

The steering committee first developed a set of general definitions and then a working definition of citizenship. The general definitions included the following:

> A *citizen* was defined as 'a constituent member of society'. *Citizenship*, on the other hand, was said to be 'a set of characteristics of being a citizen'. And finally, *citizenship education*, the underlying focal point of the study, was defined as 'the contribution of education to the development of those characteristics of being a citizen'.

It should be further noted that education is defined here in its broadest sense, including formal, meaning primarily schooling; non-formal, meaning educational programmes which are outside the context of formal schooling, eg, adult and continuing education programmes, special educational programmes for children and youth, etc; and informal, which consist of those learnings acquired almost unconsciously in a variety of settings both in school and in the wider community.

These general definitions then led to the working definition of citizenship established for this study.

> *Citizenship* is a set of characteristics of the citizen of the 21st century, given and agreed upon by a panel of experts, including educational, political, socio-cultural and economic dimensions at the local, national and international levels.

Once the research teams were established, the first task of their members was to carry out an extensive programme of background reading in both the citizenship education and emerging global trends literature. This was deemed necessary to ensure that each of the twenty-six researchers from the four teams had the requisite foundation in these areas before going into the research process over the next several years. This was a very time-consuming but necessary part of the initial phase of the study.

## Development of research teams

The next step was to select and organize the project research teams. These were made up of between five and ten persons. In each instance the research team leaders took responsibility for selecting their team members based upon the criteria established at the initial steering committee meeting in Hiroshima in September 1993. The research team members, like their leaders, were required to meet the same criteria. Initially twenty-eight individuals met and agreed to these criteria. However, very early into the first year of work, two individuals, one from each of the Japanese and North American teams had to withdraw due to work and health problems. The remaining twenty-six continued with the project throughout the four-year period.

It can reasonably be asked why these particular nine nations were chosen, especially since most are considered members of the industrialized world. Why, for example, were no African, South Asian, Middle Eastern or Latin American countries included? The answer is that the research network was based upon the working educational exchange agreements between the four partner universities, Minnesota, Hiroshima, Chulalongkorn and Amsterdam. In the case of the North American region, several Canadian scholars agreed to participate and a number of attempts were made to include Mexican scholars but unfortunately without success, so the North American region includes only Canada and the United States.

In Europe, the possibilities were, of course, much wider and the difficulties of choosing scholars from member European states was a major task. The limited funding for the project determined in large part how many nations would be included. In the end, the research team leader for the European region, from the University of Amsterdam, elected to select persons from nations with whom he had good working relationships from the past. Scholars from several additional nations were invited to participate but they could not meet the conditions set forth and thus declined. The European region also had to face the task of working across five different language groups, to say nothing of cultural traditions, and this added to the difficulty of the work.

The selection and composition of the research teams were also limited by the funding available. The supporting foundation had a limited amount of funding available for this project, and there were times when the project secretariat and the steering committee questioned whether we had attempted more than we could realistically achieve.

A second stage of the project is currently under way. It involves the use of the research questionnaire as a survey to be utilized with college and university-level students from England, The Netherlands, Canada, the United States, Japan, Taiwan, Hong Kong (SAR), China, Thailand and Singapore. These findings will be compared with those of the policy experts in the initial study, as well as analysed within the groups of students themselves. Publication of this second stage is expected in late 2000. A third stage involving secondary school teachers and their students is in the early planning phase at the time of this publication.

## Background reading and case studies

In the first year of the project, each of the four research teams carried out an extensive programme of background reading in the area of citizenship education, both generally and specifically, related to their nations, as well as in the area of future global trends in order to develop the kinds of key questions necessary to elicit information from policy shapers. This background reading was essential to build the necessary foundation to begin framing possible questions for the initial interview round as well as the subsequent survey rounds. The several teams undertook the reading independently and then met to discuss and debate the import and relevance of the readings for the forthcoming tasks.

The teams also developed summary reports of the 'state of citizenship education' in their respective nations and regions. These descriptions of citizenship education in the respective nations and regions were important in giving all of the twenty-six researchers a sense of what was taking place in the other eight nations as a basis for discussion at the first international meeting held in Bangkok, Thailand, in June 1994. These cases are included in Chapters 2 and 3. A further task during the first year of the project was for each research team to develop lists of key policy shapers representing the broad range of fields noted above from which the study participants would ultimately be drawn.

## The cultural futures Delphi method

The methodology employed in this study was a cross-cultural adaptation of an Ethnographic Delphi Futures Research (EDFR) model. This research method is based upon the Delphi method (Linstone and Turoff, 1975). It is a method commonly used by governments and businesses to make long-term projections in order to develop appropriate policy directives. The methodology is explained in depth in Chapter 3 along with an interesting set of issues which arose over the course of the study in terms of conducting cross-cultural, cross-national research.

## The policy expert panellists

A total of 182 policy experts and scholars from across a broad range of fields participated in this study, either in the interview round and/or the subsequent two survey rounds over an eighteen-month period. Policy shapers were selected from politics and government, business, industry and labour, science and technology, health and education, and cultural and academic fields as the informants in the study across the nine nations, as these were the fields of endeavour which emerged as important from the background reading, particularly in the area of emerging global trends. Each team was asked to identify a pool of potential experts from across these fields to be considered as panellists for both the interview and survey rounds. Many more were identified than could be included and so decisions were made as to who should be the first choice in a given category and so on. Without fail, however, each of the potential panellists had to meet each of the following criteria in order to be eligible for inclusion:

- *future orientation* as demonstrated by the ability to envision changes and opportunities in the future
- *leadership* in one's field of expertise as demonstrated through public addresses, published remarks and the level of esteem amongst their peers
- *interest in the areas of civic and public affairs* as demonstrated by writings, speeches, policies implemented, or participation in civic and other public groups; and
- *knowledge of global trends and issues* as demonstrated by writings, speeches or policies.

In addition, it was determined by the steering committee that the final selection of expert panellists should also reflect as much as possible, and where applicable, balance in gender, ethnicity, and between policy shapers and scholars.

The composition of the expert pool who participated in either the interview and/or survey rounds of the study was indeed rich. The policy makers and scholars who made up the 182 responding expert panellists come from government ministries, elected representative bodies, non-governmental organizations in a variety of areas including the environment and human rights, trade unions, business and industry, media and journalism, health, religion and ethics, a variety of academic fields including science and technology, the arts and humanities and professional schools, as well as writers and artists. The majority were in their 40s, 50s and 60s in terms of the age span. And they were diverse in their backgrounds. All met each of the four selection criteria noted above.

The 182 panellists responding to the interview and survey rounds included a total of 43 female and 139 male respondents. While these figures were representative of the respective percentages of women and men in leadership and policy positions in the nine participating nations, they were none the less disappointing.

Clearly, we fell short of our goal of balance or parity in gender representation. A re-analysis of the data indicates that there was initially a general balance with respect to the number of female and male panellists in the original selection pool. But for some reason, women declined to participate in the final two survey rounds at a much higher rate than did men. This held true across all four teams but was especially true in the two Asian nations participating in the study. There are perhaps many explanations for this, eg, multiple responsibilities in both the workplace and the home, excessive expectations in the workplace and thus no time to give to a study such as this, timing of the survey periods, etc. Without a follow-up, however, we shall never know the real reasons for this drop-off in participation. Still, it is troubling to us as we had hoped to have a much better gender balance represented in the final panel of experts even though the final totals were representative of the respective percentages of women and men in leadership and policy positions in the nine participating nations.

**Table 1.1** Distribution of panellists by team

| Research Teams | Female | Male | Total |
| --- | --- | --- | --- |
| Japan | 3 | 40 | 43 |
| Thailand | 11 | 40 | 51 |
| Europe | 10 | 33 | 43 |
| North America | 19 | 26 | 45 |
| Total | 43 | 139 | 182 |

## THE ORGANIZATION OF THE BOOK

In the remainder of this book we shall examine background Case Studies of Citizenship Education in several of the participating nations (Chapters 2 and 3); carry out an in-depth examination of the Delphi Cultural Futures research method utilized in conducting the study (Chapter 3); summarize the study findings based upon the opinions of the panel of policy experts and scholars (Chapter 4); discuss in depth the multidimensional citizenship model which has been developed as a result of the study findings (Chapter 5); examine possible applications of the findings and recommendations of the study for schools and other educational agencies (Chapter 6); and finish with (Chapter 7) a discussion of the challenges facing educators and policy makers as a result of the findings of this study as we enter the 21st century.

## REFERENCES

NOTE: There is a vast and increasing literature on the subjects of citizenship and citizenship education and global trends. The references listed here form only a small part of what is available but were the specific resources utilized in compiling this report.

Andrews, G (ed) (1991) *Citizenship*, Lawrence & Wishart, London.

Anyon, J (1980) 'Social Class and the Hidden Curriculum of Work', *Journal of Education*, **162,** pp 67–92.

Apple, M (1979) *Ideology and Curriculum*, Routledge, New York.

Apple, M (1982) *Education and Power*, Routledge, New York.

Banks, J A (1996) *Multicultural Education: Transformative knowledge and action*, Teachers College Press, New York.

Barbalet, J M (1988) *Citizenship: Rights, struggle and class inequality*, University of Minnesota Press, Minneapolis.

Barber, B (1984) *Strong Democracy: Participatory politics for a new age*, University of California Press, Berkeley.

Baylis, J and Smith, S (1997) *The globalization of world politics*, Open University Press, Oxford.

Beiner, R (ed.) (1995) *Theorizing Democracy*, State University of New York Press, Albany.

Bell, D (1993) *Communitarianism and its Critics*, The Clarendon Press, Oxford.

Bissoondath, N (1994) *Selling Illusions: The cult of multiculturalism in Canada*, Penguin, Toronto.

Boulding, E (1990) *Building a Global Civic Culture: Education for an interdependent world*, Syracuse University Press, Syracuse.

Bourdieu, P and Passeron, J C (1977) *Reproduction in Education, Society and Culture*, Sage, London.

Brown, L (1996) *State of the World*, W W Norton, New York.

Brown, L and Kane, H (1994) *Full House: Reassessing the earth's population*, W W Norton, New York.

Center for Civic Education (1991) *CIVITAS: A framework for civic education*, Center for Civic Education, Calabasas, California.

Cohen, J (1989) 'Deliberation and Democratic Legitimacy', in A Hamlin and P Pettit (eds), *The Good Polity*, Blackwell, Oxford.

Commission on Global Governance (1995) *Our Global Neighbourhood*, Oxford University Press, New York.

Commonwealth of Australia (1991) *Active Citizenship Revisited: A report by the Senate Standing Committee on employment, education and training*, Parliament of the Commonwealth of Australia, Canberra.

Crick B and D B Heater (1978) *Essays on Political Education*, Falmer Press, Ringmer.

Crick, B and Porter, A (eds) (1978) *Political Education and Political Literacy*, Longman, London.

Curtis, B, Livingstone, D W and Smaller, H (1992) *Stacking the Deck: The streaming of working class kids in Ontario schools*, Our Schools Ourselves, Toronto.

Drucker, P F (1994) *The New Realities*, HarperCollins, New York.

Drysek, J (1990) *Discursive Democracy*, Cambridge University Press, Cambridge.

Elshtain, J B (1981) *Public Men, Private Women: Women in social and political thought*, Princeton University Press, Princeton.

Engle S and Ochoa, A (1988) *Education for Democratic Citizenship: Decision making in the social studies*, Teachers College Press, New York.

Etzioni, A (1993) *The Spirit of Community: The reinvention of American society*, Simon & Schuster, New York.

Frazer, E and Lacey, N (1993) *The Politics of Community: A feminist critique of the liberal-communitarian debate*, University of Toronto Press, Toronto.

Galston, W A (1991) *Liberal Purposes: Goods, virtues and diversity in the liberal state*, Cambridge University Press, Cambridge.

Giddens, A (1994) *Beyond Left and Right: The future of radical politics*, Polity Press, Cambridge.

Gould, C (1988) *Rethinking Democracy: Freedom and social cooperation in politics, economy and society*, Cambridge University Press, Cambridge.

Gutmann, A (1987) *Democratic Education*, Princeton University Press, Princeton.

Gwyn, R (1995) *The Unbearable Lightness of Being Canadian*, McClelland & Stewart, Toronto.

Hauchler, I and Kennedy, P M (eds) (1994) *Global Trends: The world almanac of development and peace*, Continuum, New York.

Heater, D B (1990) *Citizenship: The civic ideal in world politics, history and education*, Longman, London.

Held, D (ed.) (1993) *Prospects for Democracy*, Stanford University Press, Stanford.

Hess, R D and Torney, J V (1968) *The Development of Political Attitudes in Children*, Aldine Press, Chicago.

Hirst, P (1994) *Associative Democracy: New forms of economic and social governance*, Polity Press, Cambridge.

Hodgetts, A B (1968) *What Culture? What Heritage?*, Ontario Institute for Studies in Education, Toronto.

Holmes, S (1993) *The Anatomy of Illiberalism*, Harvard University Press, Cambridge.

Ichilov, O (ed.) (1990) *Political Socialization, Citizenship Education, and Democracy*, Teachers College Press, New York.

International Commission on Education for the Twenty-first Century (1996) *Learning: The treasure within*, Paris, UNESCO.

Janowitz, M (1983) *The Reconstruction of Patriotism: Education for civic consciousness*, University of Chicago Press, Chicago.

Kaplan, R D (1994) 'The Coming Anarchy', *The Atlantic Monthly*, **274**(8) p76.

Kaplan, W (ed.) (1993) *Belonging: The Meaning and Future of Canadian Citizenship*, McGill-Queen's University Press, Montreal.

Kennedy, P M (1993) *Preparing for the Twenty-first Century*, Random House, New York.

Kidder, R M (1987) *An Agenda for the 21st Century*, MIT Press, Cambridge.

Kidder, R M (1989) *Reinventing the Future: Global goals for the 21st century*, MIT Press, Cambridge.

Kidder, R M (1994) *Shared Values for a Troubled World: Conversations with men and women of conscience*, Jossey-Bass, San Francisco.

Kymlicka, W (1992) *Recent Work in Citizenship Theory*, Government of Canada, Department of Multiculturalism and Citizenship, Ottawa.

Kymlicka, W (1995) *Multicultural Citizenship*, The Clarendon Press, Oxford.

Linstone, H and Turoff, M (eds) (1975) *The Delphi Method: Techniques and applications*, Addison-Wesley, Reading, MA.

Macedo, S (1990) *Liberal Virtues*, The Clarendon Press, Oxford.

Marshall, T H (1950) *Citizenship and Social Class*, Cambridge University Press, Cambridge.

Mathews, D (1996) 'Reviewing and Previewing Civics', in W C Parker (ed.), *Educating the Democratic Mind*, State University of New York Press, Albany.

McRae, H (1995) *The World in 2020*, HarperCollins, New York.

Miller, D (1993) 'Deliberative Democracy and Social Choice', in D Held (ed.), *Prospects for Democracy*, Stanford University Press, Stanford.

Mouffe, C (ed.) (1992) *Dimensions of Radical Democracy*, Verso, London.

Naisbitt, J (1982) *Megatrends*, Warner, New York.

Naisbitt, J (1996) *Megatrends Asia*, Nicholas Brealey, London.

Newmann, F (1970) *Clarifying Public Controversy*, Little, Brown, Boston.

Newmann, F (1975) *Education for Citizen Action*, McCutchan, Berkeley.

Nussbaum, M (1996) *For Love of Country: Debating the limits of patriotism*, Beacon Books, Boston.

Oakes, J (1985) *Keeping Track: How schools structure inequality*, Yale University Press, New Haven.

Ohmae, K (1987) *Beyond National Borders: Reflections on Japan and the world*, Kodansha International, Tokyo.

Ohmae, K (1990) *The Borderless World*, HarperCollins, New York.

Okin, S M (1992) 'Women, Equality and Citizenship', *Queen's Quarterly*, **99**(1), pp 56–71.

Oppenheim, A, Torney, J V and Farnan, R F (1975) *Civic Education in Ten Countries*, Wiley, New York.

Osborne, K W (1994) *Teaching for Democratic Citizenship*, Our Schools Ourselves, Toronto.

Parker, W (ed.) (1996) *Educating the Democratic Mind*, State University of New York Press, Albany.

Pateman, C (1971) *Participational Democratic Theory*, Cambridge University Press, Cambridge.

Phillips, C (1989) *Engendering Democracy*, University of Pennsylvania Press, University Park.

Phillips, C (1993) *Democracy and Difference*, University of Pennsylvania Press, University Park.

Pocock, J G A (1992) 'The Ideal of Citizenship since Classical Times', *Queen's Quarterly*, **99**(1), pp 33–55.

Ramphal, S (1991) *Our Country the Planet: Forging a partnership for survival*, Island Press, Washington, DC.

Reich, R B (1992) *The Work of Nations*, Vintage, New York.

Riesenberg, P (1992) *Citizenship in the Western Tradition*, University of North Carolina Press, Chapel Hill.

Schlesinger, A M (1991) *Disuniting America: Reflections on a multicultural society*, Norton, New York.

Senate of Canada (1993) *Canadian Citizenship: Sharing the responsibility*, Senate of Canada Standing Committee on Social Affairs, Science and Technology, Ottawa.

Shaver, J (ed.) (1977) *Building Rationales for Citizenship Education*, National Council for the Social Studies, Washington.

Shklar, J (1991) *American Citizenship: The quest for inclusion*, Harvard University Press, Cambridge.

Snyder, H A (1995) *EarthCurrents*, Abingdon, Nashville.

Snyders, G (1976) *Ecole, classe, et lutte des classes*, Les Presses Universitaires de France, Paris.

Taylor, C (1992) *Multiculturalism and the Politics of Recognition*, Princeton University Press, Princeton.

Trend, D (ed.) (1996) *Radical Democracy*, Routledge, London.

Turner, B S (1986) *Citizenship and Capitalism*, Sage, London.

Turner, B S (1989) 'Outline of a Theory of Citizenship', *Sociology*, **24**, pp 189–217.

Whitty, G (1985) *Sociology and School Knowledge: Curriculum theory, research and politics*, Methuen, London.

World Commission on Environment and Development (1987) *Our Common Future*, Oxford University Press, New York.

Young, I M (1990) *Justice and the Politics of Difference*, Princeton University Press, Princeton.

Zhou N (1996) 'Implications of the Delors' Report "Learning: The Treasure Within for Re-engineering Education: An Asia-Pacific Perspective"', Keynote Address of the 2nd International UNESCO-ACEID Conference on Re-engineering Education for Change, 12 December.

# 2

# NATIONAL CASE STUDIES OF CITIZENSHIP EDUCATION

## *Ray Derricott*

## INTRODUCTION

This chapter contains case studies of the position of Citizenship Education (CE) in the nine participating nations. These position papers were starting points for the research. Ideas and practices exist in CE, Civic Education or Civics in all nine nations and any recommendations from the CEPS project have to build onto these practices. The ideas put forward in each of the studies are in no way official statements but represent personal perspectives.

## CITIZENSHIP: A EUROPEAN PERSPECTIVE

The European aspect of this chapter is difficult to draw. The CEPS Project worked in only England, Germany, Greece, Hungary and the Netherlands. This can hardly be called a spectrum of contemporary Europe. There is no Scandinavian perspective, no French perspective and no Iberian perspective. The chapter therefore draws together a series of issues from the case studies of the five participating European nations. The concept of Citizenship and Citizenship Education (CE) is influenced by general political, economic and social movements and changes across the continent of Europe and particular problems emerging in the individual countries. Both these things do and should have serious effects on curricular practices in each country. The chapter therefore begins with an attempt to paint a backcloth of change at the macro socio-political level before returning to the case studies of the individual countries. Curricular issues will be introduced but these are the subject of Chapter 6, where the practical implications of the work of the CEPS project are elaborated.

Changes at the macro socio-political level have swept across Europe particularly since 1989. Within the European Union (EU), following the Maastricht Treaty, monetary union and political union have come to the top of the agenda. The concept of monetary union with a single currency used throughout the EU makes considerable economic sense. The use of the Euro will avoid the inconveniences and expense of constantly having to change from one currency to another. The criteria for entry to the monetary union have been laid down and many of the member states have been working hard to manipulate their economies so that they satisfy these criteria. Germany and France are leading proponents of European

Monetary Union (EMU). Major doubts have been expressed in the UK and some commentators on the results of the General Election of May 1997 have claimed that the overwhelming defeat of the Conservatives was due to the growth and influence of those Members of Parliament who had come to be known as Euro-sceptics. The UK Government of John Major had refused to commit itself in advance to joining EMU. Their wait and see tactics appear more popular in Denmark and Sweden. Even in Germany where unemployment has risen sharply and in France where the economy has remained relatively stagnant, there is growing fear that even the two strongest advocates of EMU will not meet the criteria for joining the system. In southern Europe the Italians, the Greeks, the Spanish and the Portuguese are all striving to meet the criteria for EMU and suspicions are that each of these economies is being artificially 'laundered' to meet the economic targets.

Political union for members of the EU is further down the agenda but for some this horizon is nearer than it is for others. Again, for some countries in the EU, such as Germany, there seems to be an enthusiasm for this concept and, as usual, the UK finds itself at the sceptical end of the spectrum. The Maastricht Treaty introduced the idea of a federal Europe. To some leading politicians in the UK the use of the word federal is synonymous with the loss of sovereignty for individual states and conceding power to a transnational authority. In other states, such as Germany which is a federal state, the notion of federalism means giving as much power as possible to a local form of government. The term 'subsidiarity' is the one favoured in the UK which can be interpreted as allowing decisions to be taken at the lowest possible level in any political system. This debate is likely to run beyond the millennium.

Within the EU there is also an intention to extend membership to the nations of central and eastern Europe. According to the Dutch presidency (1997) this remains a priority for the EU but extension of membership is not likely to be accomplished until after the year 2000 when the Czech Republic, Hungary and Poland will be invited to become members. There is a tension between the desire to meet the criteria for EMU and the intention to extend membership eastwards. Many of the potential new member states do not have economies strong enough to meet the financial targets set for EMU. This illustrates the tension between the economic objectives of the Union and their political objectives.

At the level of macro socio-political change there is another potential tension. Within the member states of the existing EU there is a propensity to move towards a single united states of Europe. Since 1989 in central and eastern Europe there has been a breaking-up of unions such as the former Soviet Union and the former Yugoslavia. Political unrest in Albania also signals potential turbulence in the Balkans. All of these events have resulted in the emergence of a plethora of single nation-states and the rise of nationalistic feelings and direct confrontation. Thus we have a movement to larger political/economic blocs in western Europe and the movement to single nation-states in the east. Spreading eastwards in Europe is the impact of the market economy.

There is, of course, a military dimension to the potential expansion of the EU into central and eastern Europe. Before the demise of the former Soviet Union and its combined military might, the major interface between east and west was that between the North Atlantic Treaty Organization (NATO) and the Soviet bloc. Since the political changes of 1989 there has been a rethinking of the place of

NATO in Europe. Like the EU, NATO has plans to change its affiliations by moving eastwards. In May 1997 a new agreement was signed with Russia which gave that country a place in the meetings of NATO. Membership of the Treaty was extended to Poland, Hungary and the Czech Republic. Slovenia, Bulgaria and Romania are also potential new members. There is still considerable suspicion within Russia about the extension of NATO. In an attempt to ease this suspicion at a conference in Paris in May 1997 between the NATO allies and the Russian Federation, a Founding Act was signed, pledging a lasting and inclusive peace.

All the developments outlined above and all at the macro political, social and economic levels have an impact on what is meant by Europe, what is meant by European, what is meant by nationship and citizenship. All have important implications for educational practice and those organizations that are given the responsibility of preparing citizens for the 21st century.

After this painting of the backcloth to a European perspective on Citizenship Education there follow short case studies from England and Wales, Germany, Greece, Hungary and the Netherlands. The second part of this chapter then includes case studies from Canada, Japan, Thailand and the USA. The final section of the chapter identifies common themes and issues which are relevant to the preparation of programmes in CE for the 21st century.

## ENGLAND AND WALES
## RAY DERRICOTT

This case study focuses on England and to some extent on Wales because in law both of these parts of the UK share the same legal and educational systems. Scotland has its own educational system; that of Northern Ireland is directed from the Department of Education (Northern Ireland) which has its own variants of education practice which make generalizations about Citizenship in the six northern counties of the Island of Ireland inappropriate in the present context. It is also difficult to give a perspective from the UK because of the devolution of power to Scotland and Wales in the form of a regional parliament for these two parts of the UK. The perspective given here is therefore from England and by an Englishman.

Any study of the history of the idea of education for citizenship in the UK and which is best covered by Heater (1990), and perhaps also by Dufour (1990), will show peaks and troughs in interest in the topic over the past fifty to sixty years. Focus on citizenship education has usually been initiated by a government or an officially backed association. In the 1930s the advocacy for citizenship education in schools came from the Association for Citizenship Education and was essentially an appeal for schools to combat the rise of Fascism in Germany. After the 1939–1945 War the government issued a document entitled *Citizens Growing Up* (1949) which, again, emphasized the important role to be played by schools in encouraging citizenship and raising awareness about the use of education as a way of combating the persuasive messages of extreme political thinking. This paper looked back at the dangers of Fascism but also warned about the potential spreading of communism. Reflecting the mood of the immediate post-war years, and the perceived need to reconstruct society, the paper advocated an active role for schools in building an understanding of community and the workings of local and national government and the duties and responsibilities of 'good' citizens.

These official initiatives to encourage education for citizenship had little impact on the schools. With no statutory framework for a curriculum, schools in the UK were highly resistant to change.

All the above is well documented. The more recent history of UK citizenship education is less well covered. The past twenty years have seen the emergence and subsequent fading of the political literacy movement. The leading proponents of political literacy were Crick and Porter (1978), Brennan (1981), Stradling and Noctor (1981) and Lister (1989) who from 1974 to the period before the advent of the Education Reform Act of 1988 developed the Programme for Political Education. This aimed to change patterns of teaching and learning about political life with an emphasis on the development of political skills rather than on the learning of knowledge content. The programme was issues-based and made full use of discussion and debate, problem-solving and games and simulations.

The use of the literacy metaphor assumed that there existed a state of political illiteracy and a basic level of literacy could be developed through a school programme. The Political Education Programme attracted the attention of Her Majesty's Inspectorate who legitimated the approach by featuring the aim of political literacy in an influential review of the curriculum of secondary schools which was published in 1977 (DES). In this report HMI indicated that as a nation the UK suffered from being politically illiterate and saw any treatment of this condition to be a major task for secondary schools.

The Programme for Political Education was subjected to research and evaluation by Stradling and Noctor (1981) and Lister (1989). These studies found a number of impressive courses but indicated that the issues-based approach was presenting teachers with problems. The researchers found that teachers were not skilled at presenting alternative interpretations of political situations to students and that rarely was any reference made to other political systems other than the British. Much of the issues-based work 'encouraged contemplation rather than participation-politics as a spectator sport' (Lister, 1989). In addition, the studies found the usual examples of students' misconceptions about political ideas, concepts and situations.

The Programme for Political Education was not intended to promote international and global perspectives. These were the focus of related movements which developed in the UK during the 1970s and 1980s. Some of these were World Studies, Peace Studies, Development Studies, Multicultural Education and Human Rights Education. All these movements, as in the cases of Citizenship and Political Education, had to fight for space at the margins of an already cluttered curriculum. There was no way in which any of these movements could succeed in a general and national sense. Their success depended on the presence of enthusiastic and highly motivated individuals who found themselves with enough professional space and power to influence the programmes in their own schools. Coalition with history and geography was sometimes the tactic employed but these two traditional subjects were themselves fighting to assert their own places in the curriculum. Then, as the 1980s progressed, HMI, in prescient mood in preparation for the coming of a National Curriculum, issued a series of discussion documents (DES, 1986) which provided powerful structures and frameworks for the teaching of traditional curriculum subjects from ages 5 to 16. These documents had the effect of encouraging teachers of the social subjects (history and geography) away from integrated or inter-disciplinary courses and into concentrating on teaching the traditional content of their subjects.

In the period between 1974 and 1988 in the UK the Programme for Political Education and the projects to establish contemporary studies, as defined above, developed in parallel. The explicit purposes of the former were to develop political skills with which to analyse social issues in a context which encouraged the consideration of a wide range of different interpretations. In contrast, contemporary studies often aimed at the fostering of attitudes and values towards international, global and environmental issues. These differences between the two separate movements were often so subtle that they escaped the perceptions and thinking of many educators. They were often totally unappreciated by the political establishment, especially by the Radical Right (Scruton *et al.*, 1986, O'Keeffe, 1986) which distrusted both movements as dangerous, unnecessarily subversive and being guilty of indoctrination. Such arguments added in a small way to the effects of fundamental changes in East–West relationships and debates about national sovereignty within the European Community to bring the notion of citizenship back to the forefront of the UK's agenda.

In a style typical of the UK, two reports were published by official (establishment) bodies within months of each other. The first was the Speaker's Commission on Citizenship, *Encouraging Citizenship* (1990) which was followed by the National Curriculum Council's *Education for Citizenship* (1990).

*Encouraging Citizenship* was written after taking evidence from distinguished academics, lawyers and politicians. The Commission also made use of two pieces of research: one on the views of young people and the second a survey of citizenship in schools. The former showed the notion of citizenship was frequently vague in the minds of young people. It appeared to be an idea to which little systematic thought had been given. When probed, many young people thought that citizenship should have been included in their own education. There is some correlation between the findings in this survey and one conducted in Liverpool and in three other locations in the UK with a sample of 16 to 19 year olds (Derricott and Parsell, 1990). This showed that after the compulsory school years, young people expressed low levels of interest in political and societal issues, claimed that their schooling had not covered such issues and as they grew older their levels of political cynicism increased as did their negative attitudes towards their own possible role in changing society. For the Commission, Fogelman's (1990) survey on citizenship in schools came to the unsurprising finding that overt teaching of citizenship was hard to find in the UK and that there was little evidence of planned, systematic approaches to the teaching. This is confirmed by research conducted in English schools and recently reported by an American researcher (Hahn, 1993, 1998). Hahn, in comparing the teaching of citizenship in the UK, Denmark, The Netherlands and Germany, shows UK students coming consistently at the negative side of her scales on interest and attitude to Europe and related citizen topics. She also reports that during her observations she found little or no evidence of the teaching of citizenship in UK schools. She concludes, agreeing with Lister, that in the UK, 'citizenship is *caught* and not *taught*'.

The Speaker's Commission, like many before them, had difficulty in coming to agreement on a definition of citizenship but returned to Marshall's (1950) definition in which there are three key elements: civil, political and social. The Commission then set out its perspectives on Rights, Duties and Obligations. The Report was discussed at conferences and in the media. Its critics saw too much emphasis being put by a right-wing government on duties and obligations rather than on rights; too much, it was claimed, was being given to conformity and lip-service was being paid to development of critical factors.

At this stage, the NCC's document, *Education for Citizenship*, was published. The 1988 Education Reform Act had established, for 5 to 16 year olds, a statutory entitlement for a National Curriculum. The NCC was the statutory body set up to advise the Secretary of State for Education on the implementation of the National Curriculum. The curriculum is subject-based and includes three core subjects, English, Maths and Science, and seven more foundation subjects, History, Geography, Technology, Music, PE, Art and a Modern Foreign Language. Other aspects of the curriculum were to be included in Themes and Dimensions, although the distinction between these two categories has eluded academic and philosophical analysis. The Themes are: economic and industrial understanding, health education, careers education and guidance, environmental education and education for citizenship. The Dimensions are: multicultural education, gender issues and special educational needs. Thus, students between the age of 5 and 16 have a statutory entitlement to education for citizenship as a cross-curricular theme. The document, *Education for Citizenship*, is intended to offer guidance to teachers on the teaching of Citizenship and to provide examples of how the theme can be integrated into subject area work. The document reminds schools that it is their legal responsibility to provide citizenship education. Referring to Fogelman's (1990) survey, it is claimed that 43 per cent of all schools surveyed indicated that they had a policy in this area of their work. No mention is made that there is evidence to suggest that these policies are being implemented. The central concept of the publication is defined thus:

Education should and must develop pupils' potential to the full and prepare them for the world in which they live. Education for citizenship embraces both responsibilities and rights in the present and preparation for citizenship in adult life. . . Schools must lay the foundations for positive, participative citizenship in two important ways:

- by helping pupils to acquire and understand essential information and
- by providing them with opportunities and incentives to participate in all aspects of school life.

The document then lays out eight essential components for citizenship education. These are three broad areas:

- the nature of community
- roles and relationships in a pluralist society
- the duties, responsibilities and rights of being a citizen.

Then there are five everyday contexts for citizenship, present and in the future. These are:

- the family
- the citizen and the law
- work, employment and leisure

- public democracy in action
- services.

For each of these components a suggested framework for planning and teaching is provided.

This document is open to criticism on four counts in terms of its adequacy as a set of guidelines for teachers, and also in terms of its status in relation to the rest of the National Curriculum.

First, as a set of guidelines for teachers the document contains a set of untried ideas which have not been tested in school contexts. The areas and the contexts overlap with other cross-curricular themes and dimensions such as those for Health Education, Economic and Industrial Understanding and work on multiculturalism and equal opportunities. The specific links between these themes, dimensions, areas and context as they relate to citizenship are not made clear. At all times, duties and responsibilities are emphasized before rights. The document in this sense is about citizenship as conformity and many of the lessons the development of political skills established through the work on political literacy is ignored. Citizenship exists in a political context and in these sets of guidelines the political seems to have been removed. One of the characteristics of citizenship education in the UK is that it has usually been associated with political education. The latter has always been low status and been seen as a risk-taking activity by many teachers and educational decision makers. The citizenship education proposed by the NCC has been emasculated and turned into a risk-free activity. As both Fogelman and Hahn (referred to above) have indicated, citizenship education in practice in UK schools is hard to find. British teachers have no tradition in teaching in this area. The legal obligation to provide citizenship education makes heavy demands upon training and staff development programmes in order to prepare teachers for this task. In an educational system which is suffering from 'initiative strain' it is easy to predict that teachers in the UK will resist this additional task. The National Curriculum may be enshrined in the law but UK teachers since 1988 have proved that they are not powerless, easy to manipulate and open to any kind of change; they have used their power, through passive resistance, to slow the pace of change and in some cases (over aspects of national assessment) to change the direction of change (Cogan and Derricott, 1996).

Second, the treatment of citizenship education within the National Curriculum is related to its status as a cross-curricular theme. The National Curriculum is an assessment-led curriculum with students being continuously assessed by their teachers and being subject to national assessment at ages 7, 11, 14 and 16. Cross-curricular dimensions and themes are not to be assessed and therefore their status is immediately reduced in the eyes of students, parents and teachers. In an assessment-led curriculum that which is not assessed is ignored or neglected. Left out in the cold, this is what will probably happen to citizenship.

Third, the National Curriculum requires citizenship education to be given to pupils in primary schools. If there is little tradition of teaching this area in secondary schools, the tradition in primary schools is almost non-existent. Over the past twenty years there have been national initiatives, mainly through the efforts of the now defunct Schools Council, to introduce environmental education, world studies and development studies to primary school pupils and also to tackle sensitive social issues in this age group. But there is very little evidence of attempts to introduce citizenship education at this stage. If the National Curriculum is to be fully implemented, a major teacher training programme is needed to support it. To overstretched primary school teachers, citizenship will figure low in their professional priorities.

Post-16 there is no entitlement to a national curriculum and citizenship has not figured in the debate about core skills for the 16 to 19 age group or any plans to develop a broader set of curricular experiences for students at this stage. The emphasis here has been on attempts to vocationalize the curriculum.

Fourth, there is considerable confusion about the meaning and feasibility of making the teaching of citizenship *active* and *participative*. With these two terms in mind, the NCC document's rhetoric is considerably stronger than its suggestions for practice; it could almost be said to be proposing a form of pseudo-participation. Most of the recommendations for active participation on the part of students are suggested as being confined to the classroom, the school group or the school. Here are some examples:

*At Key Stage 1 (5 to 7)* 'Opportunities for pupils to participate in decision-making abound, eg, identifying jobs that need to be done. . .'

*At Key Stage 2 (7 to 11)* 'They may become involved in enterprises such as running the school shop'.

*At Key Stage 3 (11 to 14)* '. . .assuming collective responsibility for an aspect of school or community life, eg, keeping the school litter free'.

*At Key Stage 4 (14 to 16)* '. . .projects about and placements within the community, eg, painting and decorating, carrying out environmental improvements, gardening, work experience with young children, the elderly, the handicapped, the disabled and the disadvantaged'.

Such school and community-based voluntary service activities are popular with members of the Conservative Party. The Ex-Foreign Secretary Douglas Hurd made his own contribution to this debate in a newspaper article entitled 'Freedom flourishes where the citizen takes responsibility'. The voluntary principle has a long and positive history in the UK. Over the years philanthropists, both individual and in groups, have been responsible for significant social change in society. As a nation the British value voluntarism and it is natural that this should be encouraged in the schools. All the official documents on citizenship, however, hide or purposely ignore, a crucial issue for the educator. The suggested citizen's activities can be seen as patronizing youth if such activities are assumed to be naturally good and capable of producing 'good citizens' unless they are accompanied by a programme which dares to ask probing questions such as: Why has the environment been left to deteriorate? Why is it necessary for us to help care for the old/the disabled? Who has the responsibility to provide adequate resources to support these services? Wringe, in his paper on active citizenship, puts this point more eloquently:

Unless personal ministration is backed by political action, the old and the disabled remain insecure and dependent on gratuitous acts of kindness or arbitrary enthusiasms while the powerful remain free to trample over what has been lovingly preserved. (Wringe, undated)

## Developments in the late 1990s

The late 1990s saw many significant events, both nationally and internationally, that brought the importance of citizenship to the top of the agenda for educational debate in England and Wales. Once more the notion of the education of citizens was re-visited.

The general election of May 1997 saw a New Labour government returned with the biggest majority of any British political party since 1945. The New Labour government began immediately to set the scene for what was called the Third Way. While this concept remains obscure to many, it is based on ideas put forward by Anthony Giddens in his book entitled *The Third Way* (Giddens, 1998). Giddens reviews and analyses the social democracy movement in Europe, especially since the fall of the Berlin wall, and gives the analysis a global perspective. The Third Way, according to Giddens, is not about the fight to take over the centre ground of the political spectrum. It belongs to the ground left of centre and he sees it as a reaction to or readjustment against the radical right or Thatcherist Conservativism that dominated British politics for almost twenty years, through the 1980s to 1997, and the ideas of the old left and traditional socialism. The Third Way is seen as the renewal of social democracy. The debate on it is permeated with five dilemmas, which are:

1. globalization;
2. individualism;
3. Left and Right in political terms and whether these terms are redundant;
4. political agency;
5. ecological problems (Giddens, 1998, pp27–28).

Giddens sees globalization as:

> a complex range of processes, driven by a mixture of political and economic influences. It is changing everyday life, particularly in the developed countries, at the same time as it is creating new transnational systems and forces. . . .globalization is transforming the institutions of the societies in which we live. It is certainly directly relevant to the rise of the 'new individualism' that has figured large in social democratic debates. (Giddens, p33)

From this it can be seen that the five dilemmas cannot be taken separately: they are interrelated. Giddens sees the dilemmas acting upon the lives of citizens. He sees the aim of Third Way politics as helping citizens to understand and cope with what he calls 'the major revolutions of our time: globalization, transformations in personal life and our relationship to nature' (p64). At the core of Third Way politics are social justice and equality. In this sense, the Third Way is a reworking of the dilemmas that are the major concern of Rousseau's Social Contract when considering the conflict between individual rights and the General Will.

The Third Way is governed by two maxims. The first of these is that there are no rights without responsibilities – which also contains echoes of Marshall as discussed above. Under the Third Way, individual rights have conditions attached to them. For example, in the UK today, welfare benefits are often paid on the condition that the recipient is actively seeking work and, much more controversially, single parents are being encouraged into work. However, the balancing of rights with responsibilities is a maxim that applies to not just the under-privileged, but to all members of a society.

The second maxim is that there should be no authority without democracy. As Giddens puts it, 'In a society where tradition and custom are losing their hold, the only route to the establishing of authority is through democracy' (Giddens, 1998, p66). It is easy to see the appeal of these ideas to contemporary, reforming politicians such as Tony Blair. The rhetoric of the Third Way permeates his speeches. In his speech to the 1999 Labour Party conference Blair indicated that he was aiming to oppose the conservatism of both the political right and left; his emphasis was on equality and ending political discussion that used the traditional notion of class. He even used the old cliché, 'Set our people free!'. Blair's self-confessed modernization includes a moral and ethical dimension. In a society in which two out of five marriages end in divorce, New Labour rhetoric places family values in the context of marriage. Much is also made of the ethical foreign policy that takes into account the human rights reputation of foreign powers when considering economic and aid arrangements. This notion resulted in strong debate during and after the visit of the Chinese President to the UK in 1999.

Through the ideas of the Third Way, New Labour has tried to redefine a view of society. These ideas pose the question of the type of citizenry needed to bring about this modernization. In turn this raises the issue of the type of schooling and education that is likely to support and enhance these views.

There are, of course, alternative views. David Alton brings a different perspective to the debate (1999). The former Liberal Democrat MP, now Lord Alton, a Life Peer who sits in the House of Lords as an Independent, has resurrected the classical notion of virtue by providing an analysis of the virtues needed by citizens in contemporary society. Alton comes to the debate from the left of centre and as a committed Christian. At times Alton's analysis of the political, economic and social elements of UK society during the last twenty years has similar starting points as those of Blair. Both men see the 1980s as 'a decade of unrestrained individualism' (Alton, 1999, p5), which can be taken as one of the usual attacks on Thatcherism. The pursuit of the common good (whatever that is) is seen as being replaced by materialism. Blair talks about a stakeholder society and Alton welcomes this if it means placing less emphasis on the market and taking a more responsible view of personal and corporate citizenship. Alton, however, does not believe that this is the case.

> So what is the situation today? The unrestrained liberal economics of the right have converged with the liberal social theories of the left. . . . Both endanger the already fragile balance of civil society. . . . When. . . the economically disadvantaged and the stability of the community are doubly threatened often the same people are hit twice. (Alton, 1999, p7)

Both Alton and Blair believe that the electorate has lost its trust in politicians and government. Blair was elected pleading with the electorate to trust him and trust Labour. It was the previous Conservative Government and party, and not John Major, that had lost the trust of citizens. Blair, by redrawing the estate of New Labour, has tried to restore the citizenry's trust. Since 1997 there has been considerable action on the part of the government to begin to redraw the structures through which the political system of the UK functions.

The devolution issue, which was on the agenda of the previous government, has been moved from debate to action. Referenda on devolution were held in Scotland and Wales. The Scots voted heavily for a form of devolved government, which gave them an elected Scottish Parliament with the limited right to raise revenue from tax. A Scottish Parliament was established in Edinburgh. The first election for the parliament brought to an end the Act of Union of 1707. For the first time in an internal UK election a form of proportional representation was used. This was a significant feature in its own right. The Scottish National Party had a successful election. Some leaders of this party are openly in favour of Scottish independence but for the time being, although Scotland has more control over many fields of activity than it did before the election, it remains a member of the UK. The First Minister of the Parliament is Donald Dewar, who was a minister in Blair's first Cabinet.

In Wales, the referendum produced a smaller majority than that of the Scots in favour of devolution. A Welsh Council was set up in Cardiff with the former Welsh Secretary, Alun Michael, as First Secretary. As in Scotland, the Welsh National vote was significant and Plaid Cymru hold the balance of power and share power with Labour. The Welsh national chamber has the status of a Council and does not have tax-raising powers.

The Good Friday agreement of 1998 was an attempt to set up a council to handle affairs in Northern Ireland. The implementation of this idea was continually held up by disputes between Unionists and Nationalists over the end of sectarian violence in Ulster and the decommissioning of arms. However, if the agreement can be made to work, there will be cross-border groups that will consider political, social and economic problems in Northern Ireland and the Irish Republic.

Developments in devolution have changed, in some ways fundamentally, the structure of the political system of the UK. Already there are signs that policy and political decision making in Scotland and Wales will challenge or conflict with UK law legitimized in the Parliament in Westminster. The Scottish Parliament is at odds with the UK Government over the contribution that students in higher education make towards the cost of their tuition. The Scots would like all student contributions to be abolished. This may seem to be a relatively minor point but perhaps it points to many more major conflicts in the future. There is also what has been called 'the English backlash' to events following the setting up of devolved chambers. Some English MPs have challenged the right of Scottish MPs to vote on issues that relate to England. At the extremes some people have called for the setting up of an English parliament. The road to devolution is far from smooth. The fundamental question that the development raises is what being British means. Consideration of this question has to be included in any attempts to educate future citizens. At the start of a new century, Britain cannot be looked upon as a nation – it is a collection of nations.

The restructuring of the political map in Scotland, Wales and Northern Ireland has been accompanied by consideration of potential changes in the English regions. Under the previous Conservative Government a select committee under the chairmanship of Lord Hunt investigated the relationships between central and local government and published its report called *Rebuilding Trust* (DETR, 1996). This supported the need for change and experimentation in the political organization of local government. Suggestions of this kind represented a change of tide at the end of over sixteen years in which the power of local government had been eroded. Successive Conservative governments had restricted operations in major areas such as housing and education by capping any expense it thought to be prodigal. Some thought that this capping policy was being targeted at the overspending of mainly Labour-controlled councils. In 1997 a series of Acts of Parliament loosened the reins on local government by making it possible to release local finance for new initiatives. In 1998 the Government suggested through a White Paper that an elected Assembly should govern Greater London. The Assembly was to be presided over by a separately elected Mayor. This idea was heavily endorsed through a referendum. Also in 1998 the Government issued its White Paper on the modernization of local government. The title of the White Paper is itself a symbol of what was being widely conceived within and outside government as the major need to reorganize the way in which democracy was being conducted in the UK. Entitled *Modern Local Government: In touch with the people* (DETR, 1998), it recognizes that democratic processes and citizens' participation in them were in need of a significant overhaul and that the British electorate have shown clear signs of political indifference or alienation.

A table included in the White Paper (DETR, 1998, p14) shows the average percentage turnout at local elections in countries in the European Union. The average British turnout at 40 per cent places the country at the bottom of a league table in comparison to ten other countries. Denmark, Germany and France, where voting, as in Britain, is not compulsory, have average turnout figures of between 67 and 80 per cent. British indifference to European Parliament elections is well documented. The European Elections of June 1999 produced a turnout figure in Britain of 23 per cent. These figures, taken with the traditional low turnout at by-elections, especially when the party in power has a large majority, indicate that the citizens of Britain need to be persuaded that involvement and participation in the political system is worthwhile and necessary in promoting a healthy democracy.

*Modern Local Government* analyses what are seen as the inadequacies of the local government system. The basic structure of local government in England and Wales was laid down mainly through 19th-century legislation and consequential amendments. It is seen as in need of change to face the challenges of the 21st century. The local government committee structure is seen as opaque and paternalistic, and as remote from the electorate. The system for the registration of voters and the conduct of elections is also seen as needing some changes. The Nolan committee report on *Standards of Conduct in Local Government in England, Scotland and Wales* (DETR, 1997) questioned the standards of councillors and council employers and concluded that the profusion of rules had led to a growing lack of clarity in standards of personal conduct. Procedures in local government were seen to be weak and inadequate in terms of quality assurance. The growth of participation initiatives in local government, which allowed consultation with local groups and communities, were seen as too diverse and uncoordinated. In sum, *Modern Local Government* concluded that local government had lost touch with local communities and local citizenry.

The recommendations of the White Paper that are the most pertinent for citizens are:

- Giving a bigger say for local people by creating new political structures for councils and improving local democracy.
- Establishing a new ethical framework within which all local government is conducted. This is to include improved means of accountability in finance and decision making.

- Giving new powers and incentives to local authorities to help them to implement the new procedures and structures.

In the vanguard of the reform are to be Beacon Councils, chosen for their innovative approach to local government and expertise in managing the changes to political structures. The White Paper offers three models for political organization from which councils can choose to match local circumstances and needs. There is expected to be some diversity of practice and no standard preferred model. The assumption is that at present councillors spend too much time in too many committees. Decision making is not transparent and participation of local citizens is minimal. The new models aim to reduce committee work by 40 per cent and make distinctions between executive councillors and backbench members. To quote the White Paper:

> Both the executive and backbench roles of councillors are vital to the health of local democracy and to effective community leadership. These roles therefore need to be separated. . . The executive role would be to propose the policy framework and implement policies. . . The role of backbench councillors would be to represent their constituents. . . and scrutinize the executive's policy proposals and their implementation. (DETR, 1998, p26)

The three proposed models allow for:

- a directly elected mayor with a cabinet;
- a cabinet with a leader; and
- a directly elected mayor and council manager.

The local electorate will elect the mayor. The cabinet will either be chosen by the mayor or be elected by the council. The council will elect the leader. The cabinet in this case would be either chosen by the leader or elected by the council from its members. When a directly elected mayor has the assistance of a council manager the recommendations of the White Paper move to a different level. The manager is to be appointed by the council and is to work under the political guidance of the mayor. It is not clear whether the council manager will be an existing council member or a specially appointed professional officer. If the latter is the case then the officer will be similar to the city managers that can be found in US towns. Such a manager will wield considerable power over financial and policy issues. Variants of the cabinet system as advocated by the White Paper can be found, for example, in the City of Liverpool and the Metropolitan Borough of Sefton on Merseyside.

At present 'amateur' politicians run the local government system in the UK. Councillors are paid expenses for the work they do. The White Paper recognizes that changes in roles and responsibilities mean that many councillors will be employed fully in their tasks. Provision is made for payment and pensionable income to cover this service. The introduction of payment, especially for the cabinet members, has the potential of emphasizing the difference between executive and non-executive councillors. The White Paper claims that the new roles will give all councillors a 'more rewarding' (p33) function because all will be nearer to decision making than they are at present. Councillors who have no cabinet position will be encouraged to form local scrutiny committees to monitor cabinet decisions. The aim of this process is to try to keep local citizens in touch with council decisions. It is seen as a form of decentralization, or subsidiarity, that makes all policy issues subject to debate at all levels and will widen public participation in local government affairs. How far this is genuine or pseudo-participation remains to be seen. There is already a concern from the electorate and from councillors themselves that the backbencher role is an inferior and unattractive one.

The central thrust of the White Paper is to improve local democracy. Councils are given the duty to consult local citizens and are promised support and guidance in order to do this. Where necessary councils are encouraged to use referenda to gather public opinion and support for controversial policies. In order to encourage citizens to cast their votes, the system of voting is to be changed, with the possibility of having voting booths in supermarkets and shopping centres. Electronic voting is to be encouraged. Despite the use of a form of proportional representation in the 1999 European and devolution votes, the government preferred to wait for the recommendations of the Jenkins Commission on Voting Systems. Alton (1999), on the other hand, sees the general introduction of proportional representation as a precursor to any initiatives to encourage citizens to use their right to vote.

It has been necessary to cover the happenings of the period from 1997 and particularly the first years of the New Labour Government to convey the near obsession among politicians about what can only be described as the fading of interest by the electorate in the processes of democracy. The aim of the various official documents was to encourage active participation in civic society. The development of the Internet is also seen as a means of providing interested citizens with ways in which they can contribute their voluntary services to local communities. By logging on to the Internet citizens are able to find information on how to become a school governor, how to be considered as a member of a local Heath Trust Board, how to apply to become a magistrate or how to do voluntary work with hospitals, prisons and the RSPCA. The message is clear: there is a great deal of voluntary work in a community that needs to be done and if people know about it and that it is not a closed system then they may volunteer. There was an eroding of the voluntary principle at the end of the 20th century.

As on numerous occasions throughout the century when there is evidence of the falling off of citizens' values and activities in relation to civic and community work the government turned to schools for action. Schools were clearly seen as not imbuing civic values in their students. As indicated earlier in the section, the National Curriculum that emerged from the Education Reform Act of 1988 recognized Citizenship Education as one of the cross-curricular themes that was to permeate the school curriculum. It had become clear even in the early 1990s that Citizenship Education was not making a significant impact on the learning of students. Most of the cross-curricular dimensions and themes were being crowded out of the programmes covered by busy and over-pressed teachers. Areas that are not subject to assessment usually suffer this fate. Citizenship Education also suffers by not being understood, or misunderstood, by many teachers. Many teachers feel that they do not have the competence and specialized knowledge to teach in this area of the curriculum. Some confuse Citizenship Education with Political Education and indeed sometimes with politically biased education. Indoctrination, especially with young students, is the major fear. Both the initial training of teachers and in-service education neglect Citizenship Education. Since the early 1980s it has been difficult for graduates in politics and sociology to train as teachers unless they can offer two National Curriculum subjects at the appropriate level. In England and Wales, the Universities of York and London have remained as centres for training teachers in the area of civics and political education.

The first indication of the New Labour Government's concern over the failure of the school system to deliver a sound education for citizenship came in the White Paper *Excellence in Schools* (DfEE, 1997). The major aim of this White Paper was to spell out the rhetoric that had dominated the General Election of 1997. Labour politicians had repeated the mantra, 'Education, Education, Education', as an emphasis that their education policy was at the core of their policies. The document was about raising standards in the basic subjects and the introduction of such tactics as the daily Literacy Hour in all primary schools, and about accountability, inspection and the proper training of teachers and headteachers. Hidden away in paragraphs 42 to 43 and alongside work-related learning for 14- to 16-year-olds and a need for education in parenting was a statement about citizenship. The White Paper says:

> A modern democratic society depends on the informed and active involve-
> ment of all its citizens. Schools can ensure that young people feel that they
> have a stake in our society and the community in which they live by
> teaching them the nature of democracy and the duties, responsibilities and
> rights of citizens... The volunteering of time and effort by young people
> benefits them and the Community. We shall work closely with national
> and local volunteer organisations and community groups to widen the
> opportunities for the young to volunteer. . . . (DfEE, 1997, p63)

The White Paper then states that the DfEE will set up an advisory group to discuss citizenship and the teaching of democracy in schools.

The Advisory Group was set up in November 1997 and reported to the Secretary of State in September 1998. The report, entitled *Education for Citizenship and the Teaching of Democracy in our Schools* (DfEE, 1998) was chaired by the doyen of political educators in the UK, Professor Bernard Crick, under the patronage of the Speaker of the House of Commons. As can be seen from the quotation from the White Paper, the basic assumption was that the teaching of knowledge about civic society and active experience in voluntary community work **would ensure** active citizenship. The empirical evidence to support this assumption is difficult to find. Crick's committee was given highly directive terms of reference. The group was to provide: 'a statement of the aims and purposes of citizenship education in schools'; and

> a broad framework for what good citizenship in schools might look like,
> and how it can be successfully delivered. . . and the development of personal
> and social skills through projects linking schools and the community,
> volunteering and the involvement of pupils in the development of school
> rules and policies. (DfEE, 1998, p4)

The Crick Report begins with reference to recent research and surveys on the civic values and knowledge and voting patterns of young people. Citing Kerr's survey (Kerr, 1999) the report gives the major barriers to the teaching of citizenship in schools as: pressure on an already cluttered timetable, the lack of funding for resources and an uncertainty about the meaning of citizenship. Significant barriers were also the lack of expertise in the teaching force and the lack of commitment and confidence in teaching citizenship. The lack of suitable teaching and learning materials was also noted.

Despite all these barriers, most of the schools included in Kerr's survey said that they were attempting some teaching of Citizenship Education but that this was often included in other subject areas such as History and Personal, Social and Health Education (PSHE). Most of these schools were presumably meeting their commitment to include citizenship as one of the themes of the National Curriculum. As citizenship as a curricular theme is rarely or never reported on by Ofsted inspections the incentive to include work in the area was not great. In addition, Citizenship Education is not assessed. The low priority and marginal status of Citizenship Education is confirmed from this evidence. Nevertheless, the DfEE in its call for responses to the White Paper *Excellence in Schools* reported that although the comments on citizenship were not extensive, there was a view that the status of the subject should be improved. The responses also reinforced the concern of the teaching profession about lack of time within the existing curriculum.

Taking into account recent work on Citizenship Education and responses from interested parties, the Crick Report (DfEE, 1998) made its recommendations, which are summarized below.

- Citizenship Education is to be a statutory entitlement in the curriculum through all Key Stages.
- Beyond the age of sixteen the place of Citizenship Education will be reviewed.
- For all Key Stages a set of specific outcomes for Citizenship Education will be set.
- The outcomes should be tightly defined in order to make them the subject of Ofsted inspection.
- Citizenship Education should include knowledge, skills and values and involvement in local and wider communities.
- Citizenship Education should take no more than 5% of curriculum time across all Key Stages.
- Citizenship Education can be combined with other subjects.
- The relationship between Citizenship Education and PSHE and Spiritual, Moral, Social and Cultural development (SMSC) should be considered.
- The proposed outcomes curriculum should be implemented over the period 2000 to 2004. Implementation at Key Stage 1 should begin in 2001, Key Stages 2 and 3 in 2002 and Key Stage 4 in 2004.
- All community groups, politicians, education professionals, parents and students should be given a clear definition of Citizenship Education and their central role in it.
- All public bodies should be asked to consider how they might meet their responsibilities in relation to Citizenship Education.
- The Qualifications and Curriculum Authority (QCA) should oversee the fitting of Citizenship Education within the National Curriculum at each Key Stage and how this is managed.
- A Commission on Citizenship Education should be set up to monitor progress and make recommendations about desired changes in outcomes, inspection and teacher training (Crick Report, pp22–25).

The task allotted to the Commission on Citizenship is arduous. Citizenship Education is required by statute to have a space in the curriculum. What is meant by 5 per cent of curriculum? Given the variations in the organizing of the curriculum does this amount to twenty to thirty minutes per week? Does this include spasmodic treatment of the subject by holding a Citizenship Education session half a day per month? There are considerable ways in which schools can meet their statutory obligations and, no doubt, various ways of providing activities will emerge. The Crick Report draws attention to the problem of teacher competence and readiness in the teaching of Citizenship Education. Over the past decade teacher education has had imposed upon it what amounts to a national curriculum supervised by the Teacher Training Agency (TTA). Teacher education programmes are subject to stringent inspection by Ofsted. The demands that this process makes upon both tutors' and students' time is significant. The demands of the TTA also have clear implications for teaching and learning styles employed in teacher education and the amount and quality of school-based training that is provided. A consequence of these imposed innovations has been the increase in the costs of teacher education in a period when there has been little increase in real terms of the money available. Experienced teachers and their schools will have to bear the costs and time needed to provide and to participate in professional development opportunities. There is no doubt that the obligation to provide Citizenship Education will be seen as an unwelcome burden on an already stretched teaching force.

In secondary schools the strain is seen by the Crick Report as likely to be taken by teachers of history, geography and English. In primary schools the problem is a wider one. In the early 1980s the then Secretary of State for Education, Sir Keith Joseph, led an ideological attack against the social sciences and against sociology and political science in particular. From that time it has been difficult for graduates in the social sciences to enter the teaching profession, especially to train to be primary teachers. The Crick Report asks for an easing of this situation. The fact remains that the expertise to be in the vanguard of teaching Citizenship Education is thin on the ground. This is a problem that cannot be solved quickly. The task will need to be taken up in primary schools by teachers with little social science knowledge, education and training. This may also be a problem in some secondary schools. Initial teaching and in-service programmes to support Crick's recommendations need to be up and running at an early date. Teaching and learning materials are urgently needed to support the proposed programme.

Programmes in Citizenship Education include the consideration of controversial issues. These are taken to mean issues on which there is no clear and widely acceptable view and where much depends on the value position of individuals or groups and judgements based on the interpretation of often conflicting evidence. Citizenship Education that does not confront controversial issues becomes anodyne and ineffectual. There is evidence, for example from Kerr's work (1999), that teachers lack the confidence to teach citizenship, fearing that they may be involved in indoctrination. The Crick Report warns that parents and the general public may also be worried about indoctrination and bias. Citizenship Education or Political Education can be interpreted by an uninformed public as party political education. The legal situation over indoctrination in the UK is laid down in the Education Act of 1996. Under Section 406 of this Act school governors, head-teachers and local education authorities (LEAs) are charged with the duty to forbid the teaching of party political views in any subject and to forbid the undertaking of any party political activity in schools for students under the age of twelve. Section 407 of the Act states that in the teaching of controversial issues it is the duty of the teacher to present a balanced argument.

In the UK during the 1970s the teaching of controversial issues was investigated by national curriculum development projects. In the Humanities Curriculum Project (HCP), Stenhouse (1982) advocated the role of the teacher as 'neutral chairman' who was not to put forward a personal point of view but was to produce materials representing different perspectives on a controversial issue and allow students to make up their own minds. This technique is cited in the Crick Report (p59). The HCP was focused on the teaching of adolescents. Work on teaching controversial issues with children of primary school age was undertaken by Derricott and Blyth (1979) and was successful in developing teaching materials that encouraged young children to evaluate information and evidence about controversial issues.

The Crick Report offers advice to teachers about the possibility of indoctrination in the teaching of controversial issues. The report suggests three possible approaches for teachers. First, the neutral role for the teacher as indicated above. Second, the 'balanced' approach, where it is the role of the teacher to make sure that all views on a particular issue are presented. This may mean the teacher playing the role of 'Devil's Advocate' by presenting views that neither the teacher nor the students agree with. The teacher needs to ensure that gesture, tone of voice or any other non-verbal behaviour does not reinforce opinions. Third, the report suggested the use of the 'stated commitment' technique, in which the view of the teacher on the issue is made clear from the outset but is followed by encouraging students to agree or disagree. In using this technique the teacher needs to temper the force and enthusiasm with which a commitment is presented, because tone and attitude may be over-influential. The basis of each of these techniques is sometimes too sophisticated and difficult to use in the teaching of young children and each has to be used with discernment in the teaching of all students. The Crick Report resorts to advising teachers to use their 'common sense'. Presumably what this means is that teachers need to choose a method that they believe to be the most appropriate for their students, their school and the community within which they work. This will prove problematic for teachers who already lack confidence in the range and scope of Citizenship Education. Against this background the implementation of an outcomes curriculum for citizenship will face resistance and will have to take on the challenge of providing an effective staff development programme.

As indicated above, the implementation of the new curriculum will be staged during the period 2000 to 2004. The programme for Key Stage 1, that is, the youngest children, will begin in 2001. It is at this Stage that perhaps the biggest challenge exists. The teachers' tasks will be to interpret the ideas of the specialists and experts in Citizenship so that the children are given a meaningful experience. Taking a closer look at some of the ideas presented by Crick and his committee will illustrate the nature of the challenge that is to be faced.

According to Crick, three strands permeate Citizenship Education: social and moral responsibility, community involvement and political literacy. Social and moral responsibility has to be developed from the beginning of life and essentially fostered in the early primary years. Similarly, students need to learn to become 'helpfully involved in the life and concerns of their communities' (p40). Political literacy is achieved through the acquisition of knowledge, skills and values that enable students to take a positive role in public life. The three strands are linked with the four essential elements within which effective education of citizens takes place. These four elements are: key concepts, values, dispositions and knowledge and understanding. These are summarized in the following table, which is taken directly from the Crick Report (p44). It should be noted that the outcomes expressed in the table are to be achieved after the eleven years of compulsory schooling. The report emphasizes the importance of learning that involves continuity and progression in achieving these outcomes.

The suggested curriculum for Key Stages 1 and 2 (the primary years) contains a number of potentially intimidating phrases both for teachers and primary-school children. For example, at the age of seven children are expected to 'recognize how the concept of fairness can be applied in a reasoned and reflective way to aspects of their personal and social life' (p46). At the end of Key Stage 2 children are expected to 'discuss a range of moral dilemmas or problems, in which choices between alternatives are evaluated, selected and justified, using appropriate language' (p47). There is no doubt that imaginative and creative teachers will be able to contrive situations within the children's own experience that will meet these outcomes. Not all teachers are so gifted.

It is easy to be negative about the suggestions from the Crick committee when considering the primary years, but the outcomes curriculum has a number of characteristics about which it is possible to be positive. At Key Stages 1 and 2 a great deal of emphasis is placed on the importance of developing the language and vocabulary of citizenship. Here many primary school teachers will be more at home. Teachers of children of these ages are used to developing the language of mathematics by encouraging the use and understanding of phrases such as 'more than, less than, greater than, set, average' in order to discuss mathematical problems. Many teachers will take readily to the introduction of the language and vocabulary used in considering civic issues and values. Many examples of basic vocabulary are included in Crick's recommendations. Language useful in describing feelings about relationships with other people includes: happy, sad, disappointed, angry, upset, embarrassed, proud and glad. In helping children to make a judgement about moral aspects of behaviour the words suggested are: kind or unkind, right or wrong and good and bad. All would seem to be easily incorporated into discussions with young children. However, coming to an understanding of terms such as respect or disrespect and point of view represent more of a challenge. Moving to Key Stage 2 the Crick curriculum becomes more related to citizenship, with substantive ideas such as election, Member of Parliament, Member of European Parliament, vote, opposition, Queen, minister, Prime Minister and President. This progression is maintained through Key Stages 3 and 4 where we find, at Key Stage 3, the terms discrimination, equal opportunities, trade unions, prejudice, xenophobia, pressure groups, lobbying and public opinion.

At Key Stage 4 we find: rule of law, civil rights, natural justice, proportional representation, referendum, federalism, devolution, wealth creation and ethical trading. These examples give only a highly selective sample of the outcomes curriculum. The full range of ideas and the structure can be found in the report itself. The strength of the document is in the ways it emphasizes the importance of developing a language, a vocabulary and the understanding of specific terms that can form the basis of understanding citizenship, its responsibilities and the rights that accompany it. Added to the emphasis on participation in affairs both within and in the wider community, the Crick Report has laid down a map of

**Table 2.1** Overview of essential elements to be reached by the end of compulsory schooling

| Key Concepts | Values and Dispositions | Skills and Aptitudes | Knowledge and Understanding |
|---|---|---|---|
| • democracy and autocracy<br>• co-operation and conflict<br>• equality and diversity<br>• fairness, justice, the rule of law, rules, law and human rights<br>• freedom and order<br>• individual and community<br>• power and authority<br>• rights and responsibilities | • concern for the common good<br>• belief in human dignity and equality<br>• concern to resolve conflicts<br>• a disposition to work with and for others with sympathetic understanding<br>• proclivity to act responsibly: that is care for others and oneself; premeditation and calculation about the effect actions are likely to have on others; and acceptance of responsibility for unforeseen or unfortunate consequences<br>• practice of tolerance<br>• judging and acting by a moral code<br>• courage to defend a point of view<br>• willingness to be open to changing one's opinions and attitudes in the light of discussion and evidence<br>• individual initiative and effort<br>• civility and respect for the rule of law<br>• determination to act justly<br>• commitment to equal opportunity and gender equality<br>• commitment to active citizenship<br>• commitment to voluntary service<br>• concern for human rights<br>• concern for the environment | • ability to make reasoned arguments, both verbally and in writing<br>• ability to co-operate and work effectively with others<br>• ability to consider and appreciate the experience and perspective of others<br>• ability to tolerate view points<br>• ability to develop a problem-solving approach<br>• ability to use modern media and technology critically to gather information<br>• a critical approach to evidence put before one and ability to look for fresh evidence<br>• ability to recognize forms of manipulation and persuasion<br>• ability to identify, respond to and influence social, moral and political challenges and situations | • topical or contemporary issues and events at local, national, EU, Commonwealth and international levels<br>• the nature of democratic communities, including how they function and change<br>• the interdependence of individuals and local and voluntary communities<br>• the nature of diversity, dissent and social conflict<br>• legal and moral rights and responsibilities of individual and communities<br>• the nature of social, moral and political challenges faced by individuals and communities<br>• Britain's parliamentary political and legal systems at local, national, European, Commonwealth and international level, including how they function and change<br>• the nature of political and voluntary action in communities<br>• the rights and responsibilities of citizens as consumers, employees, employers and family and community members<br>• the economic system as it relates to individuals and communities<br>• human rights charters and issues<br>• sustainable development and environmental issues |

the area and a welcome blueprint for the guidance of teachers in what for many will be a new experience and a significant challenge.

As indicated in the earlier part of this section, events to the mid 1990s showed the waxing and waning of national efforts to regenerate action through schools in preparing future citizens. The publication *Education for Citizenship* (1990) covered much of the same ground as the Crick committee. It suggested a framework and some examples of how Citizenship Education might be taught. These examples were untried in the test-bed of schools and classrooms. The outcomes curriculum recommended by the Crick committee is also untested, but the text is interspersed with vignettes of teaching from named schools and colleges. The official publications on citizenship produced in 1990 could be said to have ignored earlier work in the area. There was little or no reference to the political literacy movement of which Bernard Crick was a leading figure. The report of 1998 built on to the work of Crick, Porter and colleagues and was much more soundly based. The framework and ideas can now be developed to bring a new beginning to Citizenship Education. Having its own statutory position in the National Curriculum now supports the area. As indicated above, the problems of implementation are considerable but, to date, this is the most solid foundation ever laid down upon which the education of future citizens can be built. The report makes it clear that the education of citizens and the encouragement of community activity are not the sole responsibility of schools and colleges. Local individuals, groups and community organizations are encouraged to consider the contributions they can make to the education of citizens. The voluntary principle is encouraged, which is in line with the government's reform of local government by attempting to bring decision making on civic affairs much closer to the people who are most likely to be affected.

The second half of the 1990s saw the development of electronically available data on citizenship and related matters. Teachers cannot now claim that there is a lack of information about citizenship. In the UK and probably in the countries within the European Union, all governments and individual departments of state have their own Web sites. In the UK the Qualifications and Curriculum Authority (QCA) provides up-to-date information about current educational and curricular initiatives through its Web site. A summary of the Crick Report is available on this site. The point was made above that in England and Wales there is very little curricular coverage of European issues. The last few years of the century have seen the development of transnational projects on citizenship and European democracy. In parallel with this development has been the emerging of European Web sites containing the latest thinking and practice in teaching citizenship in a European context. The homepage addresses of some of these networks are included in the references at the end of this section. Thus, the teachers of citizenship in England and Wales cannot complain about lack of information – it is there in abundance. The challenge for the next few years is not the content of Citizenship Education but the processes that will be employed in putting into practice the high ideals of the Crick Report.

## England references

Alton, D (1999) *Citizen Virtues: A new pattern for living*, HarperCollins, London.
Bell, G H (1995) *Educating European Citizens: Citizenship and the European dimension*, Fulton, London.

Brennan, T (1981) *Education and Democracy*, Cambridge University Press, Cambridge.

Cogan, J J and Derricott, R (1996) 'The Effects of Educational Reform on the Content and Status of the Social Subjects in England and Wales and the USA: A case study', *International Review of Education*, **42**(6), pp 623–46.

Commission on Encouraging Citizenship (1990) HMSO, London.

Crick, B and Lister, I (1975) 'Political Literacy: The centrality of the concept', University of York, York.

Crick, B and Porter, A (eds) (1978) *Political Education and Political Literacy: The report of papers and the evidence submitted to the Working Party of the Hansard Society's 'Programme for Political Education'*, Longman, London.

Department for Education and Employment (DfEE) (1997) *Excellence in Schools*, Cm 3681, HMSO, London.

DfEE (1998) *Education for Citizenship and the Teaching of Democracy in Schools* (The Crick Report), QCA, London.

Department of the Environment, Transport and the Regions (DETR) (1996) *Select Committee on Relations between Central and Local Government: Rebuilding trust*, HMSO, London.

DETR (1997) *Third Report of the Committee on Standards in Public Life: Standards in local government in England, Scotland and Wales*, Cm 3702, HMSO, London.

DETR (1998) *Modern Local Government: In touch with the people*, White Paper, Cm 4014, HMSO, London.

Derricott, R (1979) 'Social Studies in England', in H D Mehlinger and J Tucker (eds), *Teaching Social Studies in Other Nations*, National Council for Social Studies, Washington, DC.

Derricott, R and Blyth, W A L (1979) Cognitive development: the social dimension, in *Cognitive Development in the School Years*, ed A Floyd, Croom Helm and Open University Press, London, pp284–316.

Derricott, R and Parsell, G (1990) 'ESRC 16–19 Initiative: What do they Think about Privatisation, the Poll Tax and Glasnost? – A view from Liverpool', University of Liverpool, ESRC Conference Paper.

DES (Department of Education and Science) (1977) *Curriculum 11–16*, Department of Education and Science, London.

DES (Department of Education and Science) (1986) *Geography, 5 to 16*, HMSO, London.

Dufour, B (ed.) (1990) *The New Social Curriculum: A guide to cross-curricular issues*, Cambridge University Press, Cambridge.

European Commission (1997) Statement from the Dutch Presidency, Brussels.

Fogelman, K (1990), *Citizenship in Schools*, Fulton, London.

Giddens, A (1998) *The Third Way: The renewal of social democracy*, Polity Press, London.

Gleeson, D and Whitty, G (1976) *Developments in Social Studies Teaching*, Open Books, London.

Hahn, C (1993) 'Preparing Citizens: A preliminary report of a cross-national study', Nashville, TN, Conference Paper (NCSS, November, 1993).

Hahn, C L (1998) *Becoming Political: Comparative perspectives on citizenship education*, State University of New York, NY.

Heater, D (1990) *Citizenship: The civic ideal in world history, politics and education*, Longman, London.

HMSO (1949) *Citizens Growing Up*, HMSO, London.

Kerr, D (1999) *Re-examining Citizenship Education: The case of England*, NFER, Slough.

Lister, I (1989) *Research on New Initiatives in the Field of Social Studies and Citizenship in England*, University of York, York.

Marshall, T H (1950) *Citizenship and Social Class*, Cambridge University Press, Cambridge.

NCC (National Curriculum Council) (1990) *Education for Citizenship*, NCC, York.

O'Keeffe, D (ed.) (1986) *The Wayward Curriculum*, Social Affairs Unit, London.

Scruton, R, Ellis-Jones and O'Keeffe, D (1985) *Education and Indoctrination*, Educational Research Centre, London.

Speaker's Commission on Citizenship (1990) *Encouraging Citizenship*, HMSO, London.

Stenhouse, L *et al.* (1982) *Teaching About Race Relations: Problems and effects*, Routledge and Kegan Paul, London.

Stradling, R and Noctor, M (1981) *The Provision of Political Education in Schools: A national survey*, Curriculum Review Unit, London.

Wringe, C (undated) 'The ambiguities of education for active citizenship'.

## Useful Web sites

Government Information Services: *www.open.gov.uk*
Parliament: *www.parliament.uk*
House of Commons: *www.parliament.uk/commons/HSECOM.HTM*
House of Lords: *www.parliament.uk/the-stationery-office.co.uk/pa/Id/Idhome.htm*
The Labour Party: *www.labour.org.uk*
The Conservative Party: *www.conservative-party.org.uk*
Liberal Democrats Party: *www.libdems.org.uk*
Scottish National Party: *www.snp.org.uk*
Politeia Network – a site with information about citizenship, Citizenship Education and active participation in European democracy: *www.politeia.net*
Europe and the Euro: *www.euro.nl*
Homepage for younger Europeans: *www.eurplace.com*
Homepage for teachers of civics and Citizenship Education: *www.academic.com*
Citizens Connection: *www.czc.net*

The Newsletter of Politeia contains information about projects on citizenship and reviews recently published books.

## GERMANY
## RAY DERRICOTT

The reforms which took place after 1989 and began the movement to a unified Germany had and are having a fundamental effect on German schools. To understand the present we need to consider some aspects of the past. Despite its federal system, the schools of the old West Germany were a subordinate part of the bureaucracy or a hierarchical system of public administration. This has made educational change slow to happen and the implementation of change within a school 'not an educational matter that can be left to the professional freedom and competence of teachers, but a political one' (Phillips, 1995). Headteachers and teachers operate under the letter of the law. Students who are training to be teachers are taught and examined in educational law which represents a system far removed from that operating under legislation in the UK. The teacher in Germany is a state servant who will find his or her professional actions answerable in the courts.

Despite this highly bureaucratic system, education in terms of policy and practice is the function of the individual *Länder*. Each *Land* enjoys cultural autonomy and has power over educational provision on a local and regional basis. Each *Land* issues curricular guidelines and schools and teachers are expected to follow these. This means that schools across the federation provide comparable programmes and their systems of assessment and reporting follow the law and are rigorously implemented. This can be seen as a contract to protect the main partners in the educational process, that is, students, their parents and teachers. Parents can obtain a relatively clear view of what they can expect from the school for their children and have procedures which enable them to pursue any dissatisfaction they might have about the ways in which their children's needs are being met. Such a system had great appeal in the 1980s to British politicians who had hopes of establishing a similar system in England and Wales.

The east of Germany after 1989 was to become part of the federal system. This meant that the system had added to it five new *Länder*. These are Brandenburg, Mecklenburg–Western Pomerania, Saxony, Saxony–Anhalt and Thuringia. All began school reform by passing statutes on Education Law in 1991. The structure emerging in the east echoes, to some extent, that of the west. However, the opportunity to reform has produced some diversity. Brandenburg, alone in the five new *Länder*, has introduced a six-year *Grundschule* (elementary) system which extends to a thirteen-year educational programme to all students who stay the course to the upper level of the *Gymnasium*. Across all five *Länder* there are some new labels attached to schools. Brandenburg and Mecklenburg–Western Pomerania have comprehensive schools which operate alongside the three other types of school. All five maintain the distinction between the *Realschule* and the *Gymnasium*. In three other *Länder* we find labels such as *Mittelschule*, *Regelschule* and *Sekundarschule*. All five *Länder* provide for students with special needs. The system will clearly have a period of consolidation and reflection. The opportunity for a new start with a new structure has not been taken. At the most all we see, on the surface, is a process of relabelling. There is some evidence that the transition from an elementary/primary system to a secondary system is treated as sensitive by the provision of orientation classes or observation classes between years 5 and 7. This is an attempt to avoid adjustment problems experienced by some students at this stage and to provide some element of continuity. It is at this stage in the English system that the same issues emerge (Derricott, 1985).

Apart from the relabelling, the period since German reunification can be best viewed as continuity of structure with 'stability, continuity and coherence. . .the hallmarks of its school system'. About one third of any age cohort are now attending the *Gymnasium* with about the same percentage attending *Realschule*. Comprehensive schools (*Gesamtschulen*) take up about 5 per cent of a cohort nationally but in Hesse and Nordrhein-Westfalen the numbers attending comprehensive schools varies between 75 and 95 per cent (Stokes, 1995).

If reunification of Germany has resulted in the maintenance of the well-tried tripartite system in secondary education, there was within the schools a need for fundamental changes in aims, purpose and practice. In the east the schools had been governed by educational policies laid down by the Socialist Unity Party.

The party usually spoke with one voice by following a traditional communistic/ socialistic line which was often described as 'democratic centralism' (Weiler *et al.*, 1996). Under this doctrine Marxism-Leninism permeated the curriculum at all levels as it also did in teacher education courses.

'Marxism-Leninism provided students with a comprehensive concept of the world, a guideline for social development and morality, and a justification for the leading role of the communist party' (Weiler *et al.*, 1996). In this regime the curriculum was seen as transmitting truths about the world from a Marxist-Leninist perspective which was claimed to represent a scientific world view. Teaching in the GDR was seen as teacher-centred and teacher-directed. The curriculum (*Lehrplan*) was closely supervised and followed pre-planned lessons and official textbooks.

The knowledge-based curriculum saw students as passive learners but this often conflicted with the encouragement for youth to be active participants in social and community activities. This challenged students to be absorbers of school knowledge but at the same time needing to be seen as active socialists in other activities. What was true for students also applied to their teachers. In order to develop their careers professionally, teachers needed to demonstrate their ability to transmit school knowledge through rote-learning methods while still being seen to be active in communist party activities and also seen as imbuing their own students with the same kind of attitudes and behaviour. Both teachers and students appeared to be able to cope with this set of double values.

The development of democratic schools in the east is an important aspect of the unification. Future citizens in Germany need to experience a curriculum which develops students' sense of participation in decision-making and political processes. The same kind of culture change is needed in all aspects of socialization; the family and community groups have their role to play. Essential in the changes of the deep structures in the educational system is the part played by teachers. Political change of this nature and on this scale needs initiatives at both the pre-service and the in-service of teachers. Professional autonomy needs nurturing as does a complete rethink of the relationship between parents and teachers. This relationship represents perhaps the widest gap between east and west in Germany. As indicated above, parents in the west of the country know their rights and what they can expect from schools for their children. In the east parents appeared to have had few rights and the word and the assessment of the teacher were dominant. In particular, this situation demands the most significant adjustment from teachers. However, a recent study indicates that teachers remain apolitical in their views about their new role (Weiler *et al.*, 1996). Many teachers remain sceptical about their role as educators of citizens and like many of their counterparts in, for example, the UK have a real fear of being accused of political indoctrination.

How then is a policy of multidimensional citizenship to be implemented in the new Germany? The problem in the whole of Germany is if CE is to be taught and found a regular place within the curriculum, where will that be? As in other countries the place within the curriculum of CE is not uniformly and regularly recognized. In both lower and upper secondary schools CE is subject to a wide range of interpretations. In some schools it might be taught directly and in others it is seen as part of the general socializing influence of the school. In the lower secondary school and in the *Hauptschule* and the *Gesamtschule* there is a subject which is called *Arbeitslehre*. One of the important aims of this subject is to give students a critical point of view on society and problems of inequality in Germany as well as in other western societies. In the upper secondary vocational schools there is a subject called *Staatsbürgerkunde* which can be translated as citizenship education. The assumption here is that students undergoing vocational training need in addition some citizenship education. The curriculum in this area will include topics such as democracy, elections and political participation and some aspects of law and individual rights. However, most schools approach these topics through formal instruction. In the *Gymnasium* some aspects of citizenship might be included in a subject called *Politische Weltkunde* (Merkens, 1994). The situation generally in primary education and lower secondary education has been reasonably stable but recent decades have seen the introduction in some schools of a form of political education comprising studies of social and community matters (Mitter, 1986).

As in other countries included in our case studies, in Germany CE is hard to pin down to one area of the curriculum and the responsibility of teaching the subject varies from *Land* to *Land* and from one type of school to another. The legal controls on the German educational system which have now been adopted by the new *Länder* and the tradition of continuity and tradition make major innovations in the development of multidimensional citizenship a low priority or even only a remote possibility.

## Germany references

Derricott, R (1985) *Curriculum Continuity: Primary to secondary*, NFER-Nelson, Windsor.

Merkens, H (1994) Citizenship Education Policy Study, private communication.

Mitter, W (1986) 'Continuity and Change: a basic question for German education', in D Phillips (ed.) (see below).

Phillips, D (ed.) (1995) *Education in Germany*, Routledge, London.

Stokes, P (1995) 'Education in England and Wales: out of step with Europe?', *Oxford Studies in Comparative Education*, **5**(2), pp 47–62.

Weiler, H N, Mintrop, H A and Futirmann, E (1996) *Educational Change and Social Transformation*, Falmer Press, London.

# GREECE
## ATHAN GOTOVOS

### Introduction

Almost from the foundation of the Modern Greek State in 1830, civic education in various forms was introduced within schools and other educational places, eg, the army. It had a clear aim: to inform the students (future citizens) about their rights and obligations towards the state, the emphasis being on the latter. There is an extensive and repetitive literature in Greece over the last two centuries concerning the alleged lack of loyalty of the Greeks towards the state. This typically negative attitude of the average Greek citizen towards formal authority is usually attributed to historical factors, for example the long period of forced submission to the Ottomans. According to this literature, there is a shift in trust and willingness to accept rules as the individual moves from informal (family) to formal (school, government) (Lee-Demetracopoulou, 1955).

The 'loyalty problem', as it is known, is present not only in the formal relationships between the citizen and the abstract state authority; it can also be seen in relationships where a state agent or an intermediary is involved, for example in the case of the teacher. Fulfilling one's obligations towards the teacher is thought to be some kind of practice for fulfilling one's obligations towards the state in the future. Accordingly, the citizen–state loyalty gap is equivalent to the pupil–teacher respect gap. As some authors observed in the 1950s, one could see the resistance and negation of formal central authority in the attitude of disobedience to the teacher (Lee-Demetracopoulou 1955).

In an empirical investigation from the 1960s Tenezakis and Minturn (1969) found that Greek children rate the rules of informal authority figures (parents) higher than the rules and laws of abstract and formal authority.

The collapse of the military rule (1967–74) in 1974 opened a new era of political and social discourse. The main characteristic of this period seems to be the shift from obligation to protest to one of making demands. Being able to develop initiatives and techniques for demanding qualifies someone as a 'good citizen', whereas the demand is usually a special group demand, not one for the whole society or a big group collectively. The definition of citizenship in this era was clearly affected by the existence of a large variety of pressure groups and their activities towards each other and towards the state. The latest development of this period is another shift appearing in the late 1980s: the art of negotiating. Being a good citizen nowadays means being capable of and good at negotiating with authority.

## Citizenship education as part of the formal curriculum

On the formal level, citizenship education is incorporated in all three levels of general education: elementary, lower secondary, upper secondary. At the elementary school level it is represented by the subject of 'Social and Political Education' that is being taught in both the fifth and the sixth elementary school grades on a year basis for one 45-unit per week. According to the latest Greek curriculum this subject aims at informing the pupils of the merits of human social life, at introducing him/her to basic forms of political systems and at making her/him familiar with the philosophy of the democratic state. It also gives the students some basic information about the formal decision-making procedures, especially about the frames within which decision-making develops (parliament, ministers, head of state, judges, policemen, mayors, unions, etc). In addition, descriptions of the best known roles of the democratic political system of the country are given. The emphasis falls on the benevolent role of the state *vis-à-vis* the citizen (the state as guarantor of the citizen's security, health, education, welfare, employment, etc).

In the lower secondary school (*Gymnasium*, 12–15) citizenship education is represented by the subject 'Elements of the Democratic State' which covers a 45-unit per week on a year basis. Half of the course is devoted to the benefits and problems of social life, with special reference to how citizens fulfil some of their basic needs via the introduction of formal regulations and institutions. The rest of the course refers to the official rights and obligations of the Greek citizen. It gives extensive information about the official limits of these rights and obligations (constitution, laws), emphasizes their similarity to respective regulations in other democratic states and connects them to basic human rights conventions. Special reference is made to the complicated relationship between the citizen and the state, where the state is partly presented in its physical existence. The possibility of even the democratic state transgressing the individual rights of the citizen, for example, is not excluded from the description of the democratic state. The official textbook supporting this course is a rather traditional one, with a strong informative tendency and a clear normative orientation.

In the upper secondary education (*Lyzeum*) explicit citizenship education is embedded within the subject 'Principles of Political Science – Elements of the Democratic State' and covers two 45-units per week on a year basis. This rather advanced citizenship education course aims at both introducing the students to the scientific mode of examining and discussing political phenomena and at making them familiar with the political thought of famous thinkers, from antiquity up to the present. This is done through special selection of texts incorporated in the respective schoolbook. The emphasis in this course, according to the official curriculum, is on discussing the theory rather than on memorizing names, dates, political declarations and articles of constitutions. Special reference is made to the developing nature of the political institutions and of their relativity through time. At least half of the course can be seen as an extension of the *Gymnasium* course in citizenship education.

## Citizenship education and student self-government

Another example of how citizenship education is arranged in Greece can be seen in the regulations (and their enactment) of the so-called 'student communities'. 'Student community' is defined as the group of pupils attending the same school programme, that is a class. Regulations for these communities exist for the whole secondary school.

The basic assumption upon which the practice of student communities is based, is that some form of student self-government at school is considered proper and necessary for them to be educated into good citizens through early experience in the democratic forms of decision making and decision enacting. All types of student representations (at the class and school unit level) and some participation of student representatives in the formal decision-making process of the school aim at the development of democratic citizens through the experience of representation and participation.

Contrary to expectations, the results of this self-government of the last fifteen to twenty years were not very encouraging. In fact, one might say that they sharply contradict the expectations of the education policy makers of the 1970s, who ardently supported this form of student self-government in a wave of 'progressive pedagogy'. The student communities had gradually come to function as extensions of the established political parties at school level, introducing a political–ideological antagonism unfamiliar to the students. Thus student communities degenerated into either mini political parties within the school, or mini 'student unions' fighting their declared 'enemies', that is the teachers and the Ministry of Education. Recent research on this matter shows that there is a very small participation of pupils in the activities of the communities, a 'professionalization' of leadership and very serious deviations between the *de facto* and the institutionalized procedures in the decision-making process. The shift from obligations to demands holds for the student community too: in the last three years the most favoured activity of the student communities at a national level (especially in the *Lyzeum*) is to organize and administer 'sit-ins' as a modern form of protest. It is clear that a sit-in as the arbitrary blocking of a public service (education) is beyond the rights of the students. In that sense, it is interesting to notice that the cradle of citizenship education in the school – the student community – came to foster exactly the type of action it was supposed to prevent: deviation from the rules of the 'democratic game' as the means to obtain a highly respected goal.

## Greece references

Greek Ministry of Education (1987) *Elementary School Curricula*, Athens (in Greek).

Greek Ministry of Education (1989) *Directions for the Contents and Teaching of School Subjects in Gymnasium and Lyzeum, Part A*, Athens.

Lee-Demetracopoulou, D (1955) 'Greece: Cultural Patterns and Technical Change', in M Mead (ed.) (1953), *Cultural Patterns and Technical Change: a manual prepared by the World Federation for Mental Health*, UNESCO, Paris.

Tenezakis, M and Minturn, L (1969) *Authority, Rules and Aggression: A cross-national study of the socialization of children into compliance systems. The Greek Study*. University of Chicago, Chicago, Illinois (unpublished report).

# HUNGARY
## ZSUZSA MATRAI

### Historical background

Citizenship Education (CE) in Hungary has its roots in the late eighteenth century. At that time a conscious effort was made to move Hungary from the periphery of European culture to the centre and CE was seen to have a role in this process. This was not spread to all schools in the country and at the beginning of the nineteenth century academic freedom was granted to the Lutherans and the Calvinists in Protestant schools. The 'official' citizenship education assumed democratic middle-class mentality while the 'oppositionist' position came to be looked upon as provincial and anti-democratic. Throughout the nineteenth century it became clear that citizenship education could not be achieved solely through the teaching of history; teaching social studies would also be required.

After the First World War, CE was characterized by a strong nationalism extending to every type of school subject and was of a normative character. It was started in public elementary and higher elementary schools (the school types for working classes), with the objective of teaching people to understand the notion of nationalism and have respect for the law. Because the country had lost more than two-thirds of its territory as a result of the peace treaty, the nationalistic nature of the CE programme was a natural extension of feelings at the time. CE was still thought to be the business of the teacher of history.

The short period after the Second World War set democratic objectives for citizenship education and temporarily countered the communist ideology. Lessons entitled 'Daily conversations' were introduced in order to discuss political problems.

The communist take-over of power in 1949–1950 created new circumstances in the field of citizenship education. Government, as a subject, was introduced in 1949. In addition to describing the organization of the state and enumerating civic rights and duties, the course contained texts with a clear intention of indoctrination. That subject was eliminated after the 1956 revolution.

## Introduction of civics

In the 1960s, there developed a compromise between the Kádár regime and society in general. The economy started to develop, the standard of living was improving, political prisoners were released and the Hungarian issue was removed from the UN agenda. In other words, the system became stabilized and the dictatorship started to soften: both the economy and politics became liberalized to a certain degree. The idea of introducing civics was raised under such circumstances in the early 1970s.

In the midst of such polemics there started the experimental trial of the first civics curriculum draft in the eighth grade of general school, namely, in the framework of the elaboration of a general curriculum reform. As to its construction, the list of topics in the experimental textbook, annexed to the first draft, adopted the expanding environment approach (family, working place, habitation, Hungary, Hungary in the world), reflecting the curriculum efforts of educators and social scientists. In the course of the trial, the teaching methodology of the subject was refined, the textbook and teaching style of an abstract and descriptive character were replaced by a workbook and a related new teaching style inciting students to participate actively and to express their opinions. The historians, however, still held the view that civics should be integrated into history; this would renew history teaching itself since such a new subject would extend not only to the political but also to the economic, social and cultural spheres. It is characteristic to the polemics that even János Kádár, the leader of the system, expressed support for the general introduction of such a separate and normative subject.

Finally, the lengthy debates concluded with a compromise which resulted in 'integrating' civics into history. The aim of that solution had been that students should be prepared for participation in society not only indirectly by history teaching but also directly by civics. The subject was introduced in every general school in the 1983–1984 school year.

## Citizenship education after the change in the political system

After the change in the political system, with what had been called 'realistic socialism' eliminated, any kind of socialist citizenship education became impossible. In 1990, the new Ministry of Culture and Public Education issued an official list of topics to replace the former 'History and Civics Curriculum': 'History and Social Studies'. The changed name of the subject clearly indicates the strengthened positions of the social science trend against the former civics trend. Though the most important civics topics are still included in the list, the emphasis of the subject matter has been transferred to economic and social knowledge. That changed emphasis is clearly demonstrated by the comparison of the former and the actual lists of topics.

There exists only one approved civics textbook (Balla and Szebenyi, 1993). In its list of topics, economics and history appear integrated; social rights do not play such a key role as they did in the earlier version, in spite of the fact that the social problems have become more serious. The part covering the state has been extended and deals in detail with elections (both at parliamentary and community levels), with citizenship (human rights, civic rights), with the separation of power, the Constitutional Court, as well as with the organization and tasks of the state. Part of the textbook discusses the major international organizations (United Nations, Council of Europe, European Community, NATO) and the concluding section discusses international relations.

An interesting phenomenon is that while the subject is compulsory in general school and there exists no other approved textbook, the textbook has not been ordered by every school. According to the publishing company, 62 per cent of the schools in Budapest did not order the textbook in the 1993–1994 school year. This fact may lead to the conclusion that history is taught instead of civics. Official citizenship education is not popular in Hungary: the state used to be the servant of oppressive regimes (Habsburgs, Russians) and was an embodiment of dictatorship in the 20th century. The 'good citizen' served that state. The years that have passed since the change in the political system have not helped much in removing this opposition. Few people intend to serve the state 'acting in the interest of the people' under the deteriorating economic circumstances.

However, the estrangement from civics is caused not only by that 'repulsion' but also by the 'attraction' of history. In the concluding grade of the secondary school, philosophy or social studies are compulsory subjects, in addition to history. New textbooks are available for both subjects.

As a result of these difficulties, certain experiments performed with Western support may play an important role in changing that situation.

The most significant educational change since political change has been the issue of the National Core Curriculum (NCC) (Ministry of Culture and Education, 1996). The NCC breaks away from a system of central curriculum regulation. The objectives of the curriculum honour basic human rights, children's rights, the rights of minorities and respect freedom of conscience and religion. The NCC is claimed to represent democratic values as it serves common national values and concentrates on 'humanistic European' values in order to strengthen Hungary's place within Europe. Attention is also paid to global values.

The NCC has issued objectives and guidelines in ten cultural domains and suggests the proportion of time available to be devoted to each of these domains. In relation to CE the most important domain is entitled 'Man and Society'. Some objectives are present in almost all the suggested programmes.

- To help students to live in harmony with their natural and social environment they study 'Homeland', a course covering national heritage and the nation's culture. This will 'provide a foundation of national consciousness, and deepen patriotism'.
- 'Integration into Europe and the World' encourages students to adopt a positive approach to common European values and Hungary's role in Europe. Students are also asked to consider the achievements of 'universal human culture' and schools should help their students to participate in international cooperation.
- In 'Environmental Education' students are helped to adopt an 'environment-conscious lifestyle'. There is also a call for students' participation in environmental projects.

- 'Communication Culture' sees the development of communication skills as the 'basis of literacy and condition'. Schools should encourage their students to understand the contemporary audiovisual environment and use it selectively.
- 'Career Orientation' will develop career plans based on self-knowledge, knowledge of the world of work and career possibilities.

This course encourages 'respect for personality, national and civil identity, social responsibility, multicultural tolerance. . .knowledge, attitude and skills in the use of democratic institutions'. The NCC document contains guidelines for grades and includes examples that might be used in schools. Programmes appear under the labels Human Studies, History, Social Studies, Economics and Civics.

The NCC challenges Hungarian teachers to develop their professional autonomy. National guidelines provide a wide range of freedom and choice for individual teachers. Teachers have to learn how to use, and not abuse, this freedom.

## Hungary references

Balla, A and Szebenyi, P (1993) *Civics for the 8th grade of General School*, Korona, Budapest.

Ministry of Culture and Education, Hungary (1996) *National Core Curriculum*, Government of Hungary, Budapest.

## THE NETHERLANDS
## SJOERD KARSTEN

The theme of 'citizenship' has lately received much attention in public debates. The concept is not always defined, but the discussions show that people interpret it from a variety of perspectives. The pedagogical mission of education in The Netherlands has recently received fresh attention. The government stimulates the debate about the tasks of schools in the domain of norms and values. The *Bildungsauftrag*, or pedagogical mission, of education has become a theme, just like the promotion of individual development, citizen participation and responsible citizenship. In social studies, the only compulsory 'general' subject in secondary education, a great deal of attention is given to the *Bildungsauftrag*. Incidentally, this has been happening for nearly a decade – a decade in which educational policy makers showed little interest, until recently, in the pedagogical mission of schools.

Social studies is a compulsory subject for all pupils in the upper years of secondary education, including those who do not take a final examination in social studies. More than any other school subject, social studies should help pupils to prepare themselves for their role in society and to acquire an understanding of the social networks of which they form part, of the social processes that take place within these networks and of the norms and values that are involved. Social studies teaching contributes not only to the cultural education of pupils, for instance by imparting the importance of norms and values; it also aims at the development of pupils' social and political awareness, by providing an insight into important social institutions and cultural and structural aspects that characterize our society, for example the welfare state, the social security system, social inequality, participation in decision-making, equal opportunities, individualization, internationalization, technological development and the environment. These social and political issues are systematically studied from a range of perspectives, using an equal range of concepts taken from the three fundamental sciences related to social studies: sociology, political science and cultural anthropology. As a result, pupils do not only gain practical knowledge about social and political phenomena and problems; they also acquire a frame of reference that enables them to participate in society as responsible citizens. This latter aspect can be seen as a contribution to a democratic society as well as a contribution to pupils' individual development.

Social studies programmes teach pupils to apply knowledge and insights in the study of concrete social problems, to take a position on the basis of sound arguments and to make responsible choices. In this learning process, the aspects of knowledge, attitudes and skills converge:

- knowledge of social problems and their relationship with more general social, cultural and political features of society
- attitudes such as an interest in social phenomena, a willingness to check one's views against relevant information and respect for fundamental rights and the views of other people
- skills such as the ability to distinguish facts from opinions, to compare different interpretations of the same event and to formulate a personal opinion.

Social studies lessons are usually thematically organized. The teacher collects and presents subject matter material on the basis of recognizable social themes. These themes can be taken from six domains: 'education', 'work and leisure', 'state and society', 'international relations', 'the living environment' and 'technology and society'. Although the teacher can in principle select any theme from any domain, some themes are more important than others for a compulsory core programme which aims to provide pupils with a basis for the study of social problems from a social, cultural and political angle. This programme also forms the basis for the optional social studies course at the upper secondary level. The core programme for senior general secondary schools (HAVO) and pre-university schools (VWO) covers three so-called 'basic themes':

- 'culture and the transfer of culture', including the core concepts of culture, values, norms, cultural pluralism, prejudice and discrimination
- 'social differences and social structures', including the core concepts of the social position, interests, interest groups, social classes, social inequality and social stratification
- 'political views and political decision-making', including the core concepts of political movements and parties, pressure groups, social movements, government, democracy, statutory rights, international relations and supra-national organizations.

To encourage pupils to form their own opinions, special attention is given to the application of knowledge about basic themes to concrete social problems. Social studies teaching is not only concerned with knowledge and insights. Pupils are constantly encouraged to form an opinion and to develop certain attitudes. In the debate about the relative importance of 'head, heart and hands' in social studies teaching, it is frequently assumed that the emphasis on the development of attitudes means that cognitive aspects automatically receive less attention. However, cognitive aspects are a condition for the development of an attitude. An attitude towards a particular topic presupposes knowledge about that topic, as well as a personal opinion and a willingness to act. Given the stage of moral development in which most adolescents find themselves, schools need to give attention to the formation of values and opinions in their pupils. This is done in various ways.

As part of the basic theme of 'culture and the transfer of culture', pupils are made aware of the influence of the views, norms and values of different groups in society on their own perceptions. The aims of the other two basic themes include helping pupils recognize different political and social views, interests, norms and values in concrete viewpoints with respect to social problems. Pupils are also made aware of the existence of different general value systems, which are included in the Human Rights and in the Constitution.

At the end of the one-year social studies programme pupils are able to distinguish different political perceptions of concrete social problems and they are encouraged to form an opinion of their own, drawing on the knowledge they have acquired as part of the basic programme. Besides the transfer of the norms and values, the basic themes also address the conflicting interests of individuals (moral conflicts) and institutions (political conflicts), inviting pupils to engage in moral argumentation and to take a personal stand. Research shows that pupils regard thinking about conflicting interests as a challenge. This type of reflection and argumentation can lead to different levels of moral judgement. Where some are capable only of considering possible consequences for themselves, in terms of punishment or reward (pre-conventional level), others approach a moral conflict from a predominantly 'legalistic' perspective: what is tolerable within the group or the community to which a person belongs. Yet other pupils are capable of ignoring these conventions, adopting a 'social contract' perspective to determine what ethnic principles underlie social relationships and how these principles lead to a decision in cases of moral conflict.

By giving systematic attention to pupils' considerations when they are comparing and judging different perspectives, social studies instruction is able to contribute to the development of values and norms in pupils. A major objective of social studies programmes is to enable pupils to make well-founded choices with regard to social problems and to form an individual opinion. This objective refers to a combination of knowledge, attitudes and skills. In the American debate on the place of 'critical thinking' in the school curriculum, the view that critical thinking skills should be developed in relation to concrete social problems seems to be gaining ground. This approach would enable an optimum transfer of these skills, both within and outside school. The comparative perspective plays a central role in the thematic domain of 'international relations'. A comparative view can help pupils place the values of their own culture in a broader perspective and can thus help to prevent ethnocentric thinking.

If schools are to achieve their pedagogical mission and if they are to contribute to the fostering of citizen participation and responsible citizenship, it is necessary that social and political education is given a place in its own right in the secondary school curriculum. Fortunately, the relative neglect of norms and values in educational science and policy in the 1980s has not led to the disappearance of general education from the secondary school curriculum. There are many reasons why the *Bildung* (the education of the whole person through academic study) component of education must be maintained. Social studies education is one of the cornerstones that provide a basis for the realization of *Bildung* in practice.

So how are schools coping? A major difficulty which they face is the fact that the majority of courses require a cross-curricular approach. This is not so much a problem for primary schools, where cross-curricular teaching is a relatively familiar phenomenon, but in secondary schools, where the curriculum is more clearly divided into distinct subjects. That is why the schools themselves will have to come up with solutions if issues such as the European dimension and development education are to be given the place they deserve. Familiar in this context are 'project weeks', which are organized around one central theme. These weeks require a great deal of preparation; they are generally of an incidental nature and they disturb the regular school routine, so that when they are over most teachers return to the order of the day with a sigh of relief. Obviously, more structural arrangements are needed, for example subject combinations or specific lesson periods for the integrated presentation of subjects as part of the regular time-table.

## The Netherlands references

van Riessen, M and Broekhof, K (eds) (1993) *A Key to the World: Education in Flanders and The Netherlands*, GEU, Utrecht.

# CANADA
# ROLAND CASE, KENNETH OSBORNE, KATHRYN SKAU

## Historical context

Historically, there has been a close link between schooling and citizenship in Canada. Indeed, it can be reasonably argued that compulsory school attendance in Canada was first mandated in order to nurture Canadian citizenship (Henley and Pampallis, 1981). The modern state of Canada had been created in 1867, and by 1900 or so there was widespread recognition of the fact the schools could play an important part in producing a sense of Canadian citizenship, which was seen early on as a compound of patriotism, national identity, British heritage and basic political literacy. Early calls for Canadian nationalism arose partly in response to the large numbers of non-British immigrants who came to Canada in the late nineteenth and early twentieth centuries and who somehow had to be 'Canadianized' in order to assimilate them to the host society (Joshee, 1996). The school, more than any other social agency, was seen as the prime promoter of Canadian traditions and sentiments. Education leaders also emphasized the citizenship role of education in meeting the demands of a new urban, industrial order which was reshaping Canadian society in those years. It was thought that schools must take on more than an academic mandate. They had to become centres of social training by including within the mandate 'the development of a sense of social and civic duty, the stimulation of national and patriotic spirit, the promotion of public health and direct preparation for the occupations of life' (Winnipeg School Board, 1913, p23). Although definitions of what constitutes good citizenship have been and are contested, the role of the Canadian school in producing good citizens is almost universally accepted (Chaiton and McDonald, 1977; Osborne, 1996; Sears, 1994, 1996). As one prominent Canadian put it in the late 1980s, 'It is to the schools we must look for the good Canadian' (Osborne, 1987). The difficulty then and now is, of course, to decide just what are the characteristics of the good Canadian, as well as to decide who is to define them. Citizenship, after all, was and is a concept that can be given a wide range of interpretations.

## Definitions

Early visions of Canadian citizenship were intensely Anglocentric. Many national-ists believed that a truly independent Canada needed its British connection if it was to maintain its difference and independence from the United States (Berger, 1970). For the most part, however, they ignored the experience of indigenous people, French-speaking Canadians, minority cultures and women, in their determination to produce a distinctively Canadian citizen. The federal govern-ment's most significant efforts to redress this Anglocentric view emerged from a 1971 parliamentary declaration that Canada was henceforth officially bilingual and multicultural. This development has had far-reaching consequences for Canadian education. It provided a new pluralistic definition of Canadian identity, based upon the two principles of bilingualism and multiculturalism. Multi-culturalism quickly became an important component of Canadian education, a development which was also prompted by Canada's turning to new sources for immigrants, including the West Indies, Asia and Central and South America. This led to a rapid development of second language immersion programmes, especially in French and English but also in other languages, and though these were above all language programmes, they affected existing definitions of what was meant by 'Canadian'. This shift to multiculturalism occurred with remarkable speed and ease considering Canada's long-standing use of education as an Anglicizing and assimilative force (Troper, 1978). National identity has been a long-standing and especially troublesome component of citizenship education in Canada. As indicated above, the early thrust was to use education as an assimilating, socializing force that would mould the young into an essentially Anglocentric vision of Canada. For obvious reasons, such a vision of Canada was unacceptable in the French-speaking province of Quebec, which largely saw itself not so much as one province among others, but as the embodiment of one of the two founding peoples of Canada and a nation in its own right. Nor, for equally obvious reasons, did it much appeal to indigenous Canadians, who did not welcome a future of cultural assimilation. Subsequent attempts to define a pluralistic vision of Canadian identity have left many looking for the distinctively 'Canadian' elements in this profile.

National sentiments or patriotic affiliation is another unresolved aspect of Canadian citizenship (Hughes, 1997). As with schools around the world, Canadian schools teach a version of Canadian identity though rituals and ceremonies and observances such as flags, anthems, national holidays and special occasions. For the most part, though, these reinforce the message to students that they live in a country called Canada and are Canadian. They are informative rather than self-glorifying. There is little if any celebration or enthusiasm. Within the curriculum, history, social studies, literature, and to a certain extent music and art, carry the main responsibility of conveying Canadian content to students, but again overwhelmingly in a detached, 'academic', even questioning, fashion, rather than in any celebratory, chest-beating sense. It is a standard Canadian complaint that Canadians, and especially Canadian students, do not know enough about their own country, and that what they do know they often do not value (Hughes, 1997). The absence of a strong sense of national cohesion has become even more noticeable over the last forty years, as the provinces exerted their strength against the federal government, thus adding to the regional forces that, in some people's eyes, threatened both the political unity of Canada and even its territorial integrity. The most obvious example of the phenomenon is the growing national and nationalist assertiveness of Quebec, especially with the onset of the so-called Quiet Revolution of the 1960s and more recently with the narrowly defeated referenda on the separation of Quebec from the rest of Canada.

## Policy decisions

Any description of Canadian citizenship education must be read in the awareness that there is no national system of education in Canada. Historically and constitutionally, education is a responsibility of the country's ten provinces and three territories. There is no federal ministry of education, though the federal government exercises some educational responsibilities through its jurisdiction over job training, prisons, indigenous peoples, external affairs and some other areas. In addition, the federal government provides the bulk of the funding for post-secondary education. Despite such federal responsibilities, however, it remains true that school education is a fiercely guarded responsibility of the provincial and territorial governments.

As a result, Canadian education resembles a patchwork about which it is not easy to generalize. The situation is made even more complex by the fact that the provinces and territories exercise their educational responsibilities somewhat lightly, at least by international standards, with the result that local school boards have a fair amount of autonomy, especially in large metropolitan areas.

## Curricular issues

Citizenship education is carried on in a wide variety of ways in Canadian schools, the most important of which are summarized below. It must be remembered that these approaches are not always the norm in schools, though there are signs that they are beginning to make some headway. In Canada, as elsewhere, there is often a substantial gap between the ideals and the realities of citizenship education (Hodgetts, 1968; Pammett and Pepin, 1988; Trottier, 1982).

## History, the social sciences and the social studies

The main burden of formal citizenship education has traditionally fallen on history and various social science disciplines, but especially on history. Since the 1930s, the integrated, interdisciplinary social studies approach that had become popular in the United States has become a central aspect of Canadian citizenship education (Tomkins, 1983). Since that time, all provinces have adopted interdisciplinary social studies in the elementary school (up to Grade 6), but the high school picture is more mixed, with some areas using the social studies and others retaining the more traditional disciplines of history and geography. Where social studies is used as the organizing base of the curriculum, courses are usually built around themes or concepts, with subject-matter being drawn from a range of social science disciplines, including sociology, economics, political science, anthropology and so on. The advantages and disadvantages of single disciplines, and especially history, as opposed to integrated social studies, continue to be a subject of some debate (Bennett, 1978; Egan, 1983; Osborne, 1993; Parsons *et al.*, 1983).

### Political education

Until relatively recently, what Canadian students learned about politics could best be described as civics, rather than as a genuinely political education. The courses of study were heavily factual, emphasizing the structure and institutions of government while avoiding the processes of politics, concentrating on historical background at the expense of current issues and controversies, and generally lacking connection with students' concerns and experiences. The implicit, and sometimes quite explicit, view of citizenship in this traditional approach saw the main task of the citizen as consisting of voting in elections. More active forms of political involvement were largely ignored. In essence, the key citizenship values were seen to be trust, acceptance, duty and loyalty (Osborne, 1984, 1988).

Recent years have seen the beginning of a turning away from the idealized, but passive, world of traditional civics towards a more genuinely political education whose focus is the real world of politics and political action. In Canada, as elsewhere, one sees a turn towards a political education which focuses on problems and issues, on participation, on critical inquiry, on linking the classroom with the world of politics outside it, and which often takes the local community as its locus of inquiry and action (Heater, 1990; Ichilov, 1990; Osborne, 1991; Pammett and Pepin, 1988). Increasingly, elementary and secondary students in all provinces are involved in social and political issues, such as taking part in election campaigns, in environmental and other political action movements, in community action groups, human rights campaigns, anti-racist and other anti-discriminatory activities.

### Law-related education

It has long been recognized that a basic knowledge of the law and, perhaps more important, an appreciation of the role of law in democratic society, are fundamental to effective citizenship (Case, 1985; Case and Ross, 1996; Coombs *et al.*, 1990). Most provinces have some sort of public legal education branch designed to help people of all ages understand something about the law. These organizations work in the community at large and in the school system, and they have all produced programmes which usually include some school-related work, be it in the development of units of study, the production of classroom materials, the in-service training of teachers or other relevant work. Many Canadian schools offer either discrete courses, or at least separate units of study, on the law. Law-related education has become increasingly important since 1982, the year in which Canada adopted a new constitution which included a constitutionally entrenched charter of rights. The result is that one now finds in all provinces some opportunity for students to study law and the role of law, albeit usually at the high school level (Case, 1985; Couse and Gianelli, 1988; Crawford, 1989; Daniels and Case, 1992).

*Human rights education*

Respect for human rights is an obvious component of citizenship in any society that claims to be democratic, and especially in a country such as Canada which is officially both bilingual and multicultural. Recent years have seen a greater concern for human rights education in Canada for various reasons including the greater salience of human rights on the international political agenda and causes internal to Canada such as adoption of multiculturalism as official policy and constitutional entrenchment of the Charter of Rights (Bala *et al.*, 1988). Instances of racism have also drawn attention to the importance of human rights education in Canada. The result has been a good deal of activity across Canada in the area of human rights education (Conley, 1984; Ray and D'Oyley, 1983). Most social studies curricula, for example, have included some discussion of human rights, though often in a somewhat schematic manner. In addition, various organizations promote human rights education in schools, and indeed in the community at large (eg, Canadian Human Rights Foundation, Amnesty International, United Nations Association, Red Cross).

*Global and international education*

These are two related but separate strands in the education of Canadian youth about the world at large. International education has an emphasis on international affairs and on promoting knowledge. The overriding goal is typically to improve Canadians' ability to succeed on the world stage. Global education, on the other hand, is more concerned with the state of the planet as a whole, and especially upon the relationships between the developed and developing worlds. Its over-riding aim is typically to improve conditions for all the world's inhabitants through increased student knowledge but also by encouraging them to live and act in ways that alleviate the world's problems not exacerbate them (Werner and Case, 1997).

Recent years have seen an increasing interest in global education in Canadian schools. There is a growing number of exchange arrangements between Canadian students and students in other countries. Many schools have international affairs clubs, United Nations societies or other voluntary activities that introduce students to the world. Some years ago peace education was fairly widespread, though it seems to have declined considerably with the apparent end of the Cold War.

Although there is a wealth of activity, by its very nature, it touches only a minority of students. What is missing in most provinces is a sustained and organized attempt through the authorized curriculum to teach students about the world as a whole. It is probably fair to say that the global, and even the international, aspect of citizenship education remains unduly undeveloped in Canada.

*Environmental education*

It has become increasingly obvious in recent years that any discussion of effective citizenship must encompass environmental concerns. Whether one thinks of citizenship in local, national or global terms, or in some combination of all three, the concept inevitably has an environmental context of some sort. Thus, one has to think in terms of environmental citizenship, and this spills over into more conventional conceptions of social and political citizenship, since protection of the environment increasingly involves political action.

Canadian schools have within the last twenty or so years increasingly turned to environmental education, at all grade levels, and in the last few years have taken a particular interest in sustainable development (Drewe, 1993). Most often, environmental education has been included within science programmes and has set out to achieve these goals:

- to give students the knowledge they need to understand the environment
- to inform them about the threats facing the environment
- to interest them in ways of solving environmental problems; and
- to arouse in them a commitment to living in ways that do not harm the environment.

Besides formal studies within the curriculum, many schools have some kind of environmental club or project which involves students directly in some sort of environmental activity. Examples include neighbourhood clean-ups, recycling projects, political action campaigns, often involving students even in the elementary grades.

*Multicultural education*

As noted above, in 1971 the Canadian parliament declared multiculturalism to be a defining characteristic of Canada and since then school systems across the country have made multicultural education an integral part of their programmes. In one sense, multiculturalism can be seen as a continuation of that long tradition in Canada which sees the country as a 'mosaic', in contrast to the 'melting-pot' tradition of the United States. In another sense, the 1971 declaration was also intertwined with a new assertiveness on the part of Quebec, which in turn aroused a response from Canadians who were of neither Anglophone nor Francophone background and who demanded recognition of their cultural traditions. Understandably, the acceptance of multiculturalism led to the development of explicitly multicultural education, which quickly became established in all parts of Canada. Broadly speaking, multicultural education has four main goals.

- In some versions it is intended to make children from a wide variety of cultural backgrounds feel at home in Canada and thus serves an essentially assimilative function. This is seen as especially important in view of the changing nature of Canadian immigration patterns, with most immigrants now coming from areas other than Europe.
- It is also intended to teach all children to accept and respect each other's cultures, through a combination of knowledge and information and of attitude and values development. In other words, it is intended to foster interpersonal harmony and respect.

- It is intended to teach students to welcome the concept of multiculturalism as an organizing principle of Canadian society.
- It acts as part of a wider social programme which aims to give people from all backgrounds, and especially those of other than French or British descent, an equal chance to participate in Canadian society.

Most multicultural education is concentrated in history, social studies, language and literature, music and art, with a major effort also being mounted through extracurricular activities, such as social occasions, exchange visits, cultural festivals and ceremonies. Despite the commitment to multicultural education in Canadian schools, there remain many practical problems. There are difficulties in ensuring cooperation between schools and parents, especially where parents come from backgrounds where authority was to be distrusted. Inter-cultural and inter-ethnic tensions persist. There is still systemic discrimination. All this said, however, it remains true that Canadian schools have taken multicultural education extremely seriously and no discussion of citizenship education in Canada would be complete were it to ignore the important place now assigned to multiculturalism (Bagley, 1988; Burnet, 1981; Henley and Young, 1981; McLeod, 1981; Orlikow and Young, 1993).

## Community service

As noted above, recent years have seen a small but growing trend in political education, environmental education and global education, to involve students in real-world issues so that they learn by direct experience. Thus, for example, students operate recycling programmes, engage in action projects to do with the environment and with global issues, involving in some cases actual experience in developing countries.

Closer to home, students work in community action projects such as food banks, help senior citizens and work with community action groups (Ashford, 1995; Clark, 1997).

Beyond this is an emerging interest in making community service a required part of the school curriculum. The International Baccalaureate is offered in many Canadian school systems and it mandates some form of community service as a condition of graduation. In addition, some Canadian schools have seen in community service a way of injecting 'relevance' into their programmes and of reducing the gap between schools and the world around them, while at the same time appealing to the idealism of adolescents. Community service includes a host of possibilities: working with children or senior citizens, volunteering in hospitals or other such institutions, taking part in community action groups, working with social service agencies, and so on. At their best, these programmes can develop in students a sense of caring and of concern for others. At the same time, however, they often do not go beyond the spirit of 'volunteerism' so that they lack the critical edge needed for democratic citizenship. In this sense, they can be profoundly conservative, seeking to remedy or alleviate social problems but not to inquire into their causes and solutions. To date, only a minority of high schools offer such programmes but there are signs of a growing interest.

## Conclusions

Schools at all levels are under increasing pressure. They find themselves driven to act as social service agencies in order to respond to pressing needs that are not being met elsewhere in society. Thus, they offer breakfast and other nutrition programmes; they are making increasing use of conflict-resolution and peer-counselling techniques; and in general they are more and more performing functions that once would have been performed within the family. Teachers report their frustration that much of their time has to be devoted to non-teaching tasks. In such circumstances, where schools have no choice but to respond to problems that originate outside their bounds, to be reactive rather than proactive, it is obviously difficult for them to devote themselves to citizenship education in any major way. Despite these demands, as this survey makes clear, there is a considerable activity in Canadian schools in citizenship education. For the most part, these efforts consist of specific responses to specific concerns, largely undertaken in isolation from one another. There is no cohesive coordinating policy that would bring all the various activities into one coherent endeavour. Moreover, citizenship education seems largely to comprise a series of curricular add-ons or innovations rather than being fully integrated into the curriculum as a whole. And, except for the activities of a handful of people across Canada, citizenship education has not yet entered into the mainstream of teacher education. What would be especially useful now would be some concerted effort to call national attention to the question of citizenship and what it means for education. To date there have been isolated activities (Pammett and Pepin, 1988; Senate of Canada, 1993) but no national, sustained and collective effort.

## Canada references

Ashford, M-W (1995) 'Youth Actions for the Planet', in R Fowler and I Wright (eds), *Thinking Globally about Social Studies Education*, Research and Development in Global Studies, University of British Columbia, Vancouver, pp 75–90.

Bagley, C (1988) 'Education for All: A Canadian Dimension', in G K Verma (ed.), *Education For All: A landmark in pluralism,* Falmer Press, Lewes, pp 98–117.

Bala, N, Fantain, S and Perron, F (1988) *Youth and the Charter of Rights*, Canadian Youth Federation, Ottawa.

Bennett, P (1978) *Rediscovering Canadian History*, OISE Press, Toronto.

Berger, C (1970) *The Sense of Power: Studies in the ideas of Canadian imperialism, 1867–1914*, University of Toronto Press, Toronto.

Burnet, J (1981) 'Multiculturalism Ten Years Later', *History and Social Science Teacher*, **17**(1), pp 1–6.

Case, R (1985) *On the Threshhold: Canadian law-related education*. University of British Columbia Centre for the Study of Curriculum and Instruction, Vancouver.

Case, R and Ross, M (1996) 'On the Need to Dispel Popular Myths about Law', *Canadian and International Education*, **25**(2), pp 146–66.

Chaiton, A and McDonald, N (eds) (1977) *Canadian Schools and Canadian Identity*, Gage, Toronto.

Clark, P (1997) 'All Talk and No Action? The Place of Social Action in Social Studies', in R Case and P Clark (eds), *The Canadian Anthology of Social Studies*, Field Relations, Simon Fraser University, Burnaby, BC, pp 265–74.

Conley, M (ed.) (1984) *Teaching Human Rights*, Acadia University Institute, Wolf-ville, NS.

Coombs, J R, Parkinson, S and Case, R (eds) (1990) *Ends in View: An analysis of the goals of law-related education*, Centre for the Study of Curriculum and Instruction, University of British Columbia, Vancouver.

Couse, K and Gianelli, M (1988) *Legal Education for Saskatchewan Youth: A research report on the impact of a law-related curriculum on the legal literacy and attitudes of grade eight students*, University of Regina Prairie Justice Research Institute, Regina, SK.

Crawford, W (ed.) (1989) *Law vs. Learning: Examination for discovery*, Canadian Legal Information Centre, Ottawa.

Daniels, L and Case, R (1992) *Charter Literacy and the Administration of Justice in Canada*, Department of Justice, Government of Canada, Ottawa.

Drewe, F (1993) 'From Environmental Education to Education for Sustainable Development', *Manitoba Social Science Teacher*, **19**(3), pp 16–24.

Egan, K (1983) 'Social Studies and the Erosion of Education', *Curriculum Inquiry*, **13**(2), pp 195–214.

Heater, D B (1990) *Citizenship: The civic ideal in world politics, history and education*, Longman, London.

Henley, R and Pampallis, J (1981) 'The Campaign for Compulsory Education in Manitoba', *Canadian Journal of Education*, **7**(1), pp 59–83.

Henley, R and Young, J (1981) 'Multicultural Education: Contemporary Variations on a Historical Theme', *History and Social Science Teacher*, **17**(1), pp 7–16.

Hodgetts, A B (1968) *What Culture? What Heritage? A Study of Civic Education in Canada*, OISE Press, Toronto.

Hughes, G (1997) *Manufacturing Identity: Some educational insights into English Canada's national self-image*, Unpublished Masters thesis, Faculty of Education, Simon Fraser University, Burnaby, British Columbia.

Ichilov, O (ed.) (1990) *Political Socialization, Citizenship Education and Democracy*, Teachers' College Press, New York.

Joshee, R (1996) 'The Federal Government and Citizenship Education for New-comers', *Canadian and International Education*, **25**(2), pp 108–27.

McLeod, K A (1981) 'Multicultural Education: A Decade of Development', (Canadian Society for the Study of Education), *Education and Canadian Multiculturalism: Some problems and some solutions*, CSSE, Saskatoon, SK, pp 12–26.

Orlikow, L and Young, J (1993) 'The Struggle for Change: Teacher Education in Canada', in G K Verma (ed.), *Inequality and Teacher Education*, Falmer Press, Lewes, pp 70–88.

Osborne, K W (1984) *Working Papers in Political Education* (Monographs in Educa-tion XII), University of Manitoba, Winnipeg.

Osborne, K W (1987) 'To the Schools We Must Look for the Good Canadian: Developments in the Teaching of History since 1960', *Journal of Canadian Studies*, **23**(3), pp 104–26.

Osborne, K W (1988) 'A Canadian Approach to Political Education', *Teaching Politics*, **17**(3), pp 275–93.

Osborne, K W (1991) *Teaching for Democratic Citizenship*, Our Schools Ourselves, Toronto.

Osborne, K W (1993) 'Democratic Citizenship and the Teaching of History', *Synthesis/Regeneration*, Winter, pp 19–21.

Osborne, K W (1996) 'Education is the Best National Insurance: Citizenship Education in Canadian Schools, Past and Present', *Canadian and International Education*, **25**(2), pp 31–58.

Osborne, K W and Seymour, J W (1988) 'Political Education in the Upper Elementary School', *International Journal of Social Education*, **3**, pp 63–77.

Pammett, J H and Pepin, J-L (eds) (1988) *Political Education in Canada*, The Institute for Research on Public Policy, Halifax, NS.

Parsons, J, Milburn, G and van Manen, M (eds) (1983) *A Canadian Social Studies*, Faculty of Education, University of Alberta, Edmonton, AB.

Ray, D and D'Oyley, V (eds) (1983) *Human Rights in Canadian Education*, Kendall Hunt, Dubuque.

Sears, A (1994) 'Social Studies as Citizenship Education in English Canada: A Review of Research', *Theory of Research in Social Education*, **22**(1), pp 6–43.

Sears, A (1996) '"Something Different to Everyone", Conceptions of Citizenship and Citizenship Education', *Canadian and International Education*, **25**(2), pp 1–16.

Senate of Canada (1993) *Canadian Citizenship: Sharing the responsibility*, Standing Senate Committee on Social Affairs, Science and Technology, Ottawa.

Tomkins, G S (1983) 'The Social Studies in Canada', in J Parsons, G Milburn and M van Manen (eds), *A Canadian Social Studies*, Faculty of Education, University of Alberta, Edmonton, AB, pp 12–30.

Troper, H (1978) 'Nationalism and the History Curriculum in Canada', *History Teacher*, **12**, pp 11–28.

Trottier, C (1982) 'Les enseignants comme agents de socialisation politique au Québec', *Canadian Journal of Education*, **7**(1), pp 15–43.

Werner, W and Case, R (1997) 'Themes of Global Education', in I Wright and A Sears (eds), *Trends and Issues in Canadian Social Studies*, Pacific Educational Press, Vancouver, pp 176–94.

Winnipeg School Board (1913) *Annual Report, 1913*, Winnipeg School Board, Winnipeg.

# JAPAN
## KAZUKO OTSU

### Historical Context

The rate of turn-out in the Japanese general election in 1996 was 59.7 per cent, and as for the population aged between 20 and 29, it was less than 50 per cent. According to research, the students answered 'indifferent', 'troublesome', 'busy with part-time job', 'busy in dating', 'nothing to expect from politicians', and so on, as the reasons of abstention from voting. Voting is just an action as a citizen, of course. Generally speaking, the youth in Japan seem to be apathetic to politics. One of the reasons for this might be found in the education they receive.

Modern citizenship education has been mainly implemented as Civics in high schools and as Social Studies in junior high schools. What problems are there in citizenship education? This section begins with a historical overview associated with the concepts of citizen and citizenship, and then analyses policy decisions and curricular issues. The section ends with more discussion of what should be done to promote citizenship education.

## Historical background

Japanese education has been centrally planned since the Meiji era (19th century). After Japan's defeat in the Second World War, the principle of education drastically changed from militarism to democracy. In this context the subject of Civics was added to the school curriculum. It emphasized fostering the ability to make a positive contribution to society and to change society actively in order to exclude militarism and build a democratic society. However, this subject was absorbed into a new subject, called Social Studies which consists of General Society and Current Topics begun as the core of new education in 1947. Problem-solving methods including research and discussion were adopted in those subjects. Soon, a criticism of the empirical approach in Social Studies occurred. That is to say, Social Studies should focus on teaching the structure and method of each of the social science disciplines. In 1955, the Ministry of Education changed the Courses of Study strikingly. In junior high schools, General Society was changed into sectional Social Studies which consists of three subjects, Geography, History, and Politics/Economy/Society. In high schools, General Society and Current Topics were changed into Society. In 1960, Society was changed into two subjects, Ethics/Society and Politics/Economy.

In 1960, the revision of the Japan–US Security Treaty, which was approved without voting in the Diet (Parliament), brought about antagonism and polarized the public. The Government then tried to promote economic growth and national conformity by national events such as the Olympic Games. The Government also implemented educational policies corresponding to political and economic needs. In 1968, the name of Politics/Economy/Society in junior high schools was renamed Civics, and was fixed in the third grade. At that time, the emphasis was put on building national consciousness.

In the mid-1970s the high growth of the economy slowed down. Quality of life became a higher priority than economic growth. Thus educational policies needed to change. In 1977/78, the Courses of Study by the Ministry of Education emphasized 'to foster human qualities', and 'to learn in a comfortable school environment'. As for Social Studies, a new subject, Contemporary Society, was set up in high schools. It did not necessarily correspond to each of the social sciences disciplines, such as politics, economics and sociology, but took a comprehensive approach to develop learners' thinking and decision-making skills.

As internationalization has increased in Japan since the middle of the 1980s, the Courses of Study issued in 1989 have stressed the national identity of the Japanese. At that time, Social Studies in high schools was changed into two subject areas, Geography/History and Civics which consisted of three subjects: Contemporary Society, Ethics and Politics/Economy. World History become a required course instead of Contemporary Society by reason of corresponding to internationalization. Although citizenship education was begun as the basis of a democratic society, it has not been developed successfully. Social Studies including Civics have been regarded as rote learning. This might be one reason why democracy has not taken deep roots yet in Japan.

## Definitions

*Citizen*

In Japan, the term *komin* (citizen) is hardly used in daily life. It is difficult to define 'citizen' because the meanings of 'citizen' differ in different historical periods. In the Nara period (the 8th century), 'citizen' meant a tax payer who received the divided land from the government. In modern times, the eligible voters within the residents were called 'citizens' after local self-government had begun. In 1925, when universal suffrage became a reality, the necessity of citizenship education for voters became recognized as important. Civics was set up as a required subject in secondary schools in 1935. When militarism grew before the Second World War, the government stressed 'loyalty and nationalism' and fostered 'fellowship' with the emperor. At that time, 'citizen' meant 'fellow'.

After the war, a new education system was begun under the new constitution, and the same term 'citizen' was used in a different way. The Ministry of Education explained that 'citizen' had two meanings: a member of civil society and a member of the state. In addition, the difficulty of definition comes from the distinction between 'citizen' and 'nation'. While 'nation' has historically been taken to mean all residents who live in the area under a unified government, 'citizen' has meant some classes who had considerable property after the civil revolution in Europe. It was possible to distinguish 'citizen' from 'non-citizen' at that time. The range of meanings attributed to 'citizen' has become wider, extending beyond the restriction of property and gender influenced by movements to widen suffrage. Now 'nation' and 'citizen' are almost synonymous and overlap each other functionally. This is the reason why it is difficult to define 'citizen'.

*Citizenship*

Related to the definition of 'citizen', 'citizenship' has a much wider meaning and can be used differently in different contexts. When Social Studies was begun as the core subject in 1948, the Ministry of Education explained that 'Social Studies fosters not people who follow the Government policy blindfold but people who intend to learn about their own society and to develop their attitudes and skills to participate positively in their society in order to build a democratic society.' When Civics as a subject was set up in junior high school in 1970, the Ministry of Education described the basic purposes of citizenship education as follows:

- to develop an awareness and understanding of Japan as a nation and the principle of sovereignty
- to develop a concept of local community and the state and ways in which the individual can contribute to the work of the community and the state
- to appreciate the rich culture of the nation, its place in economic and international relations
- to appreciate rights and responsibilities and duties of the individual in the community and wider society
- to develop an ability to act positively in relation to rights and duties.

This definition of citizenship is still in use.

## Policy decisions

### The Courses of Study

National educational activities are under the authority of the Ministry of Education. The minister decides the educational policies on the basis of recommendations from the Central Council for Education which is composed of university professors, school principals, leaders of educational organizations and other persons appointed by the Minister of Education. Curriculum standards for elementary, junior high and high schools are prescribed in the Courses of Study issued by the Ministry of Education. The minister decides the Courses of Study on the basis of recommendations from the Curriculum Council. The Courses of Study provide the basic framework for curricula: the aim of each subject and the aims and content of teaching at each grade. It is possible for each school to organize its own curriculum on the basis of the Courses of Study, taking into consideration the actual conditions of the school and the developmental level of pupils. However, schools in a community tend to organize the same curriculum.

### Authorized textbooks

All textbooks used in elementary, junior high and high schools are authorized by the Ministry of Education. To maintain and improve the national standard of school education, the Courses of Study and authorization are effective to some extent. However, they have been strongly influenced by conservative trends because the government has been controlled by the Liberal Democratic Party for more than four decades. For example, concerning the history of the Second World War, some writers of textbooks were asked by the Ministry of Education to replace the term 'invasion' with 'entering' into other Asian countries in wartime. One prominent professor had instituted a lawsuit against the textbook authorization system and thirty years later the Supreme Court ruled that authorization was constitutional. Writers tend to voluntarily censor what they write in the textbooks so as to gain acceptability in the authorization process.

## Curricular issues

### Citizenship education in the curriculum

Citizenship education in elementary school is implemented in Life and Environment Studies at grades 1–2, and Social Studies at grades 3–6 for three hours (1 hour = 45 minutes) a week. In junior high schools, Social Studies consists of three subjects, Geography (4 hours a week at grade 1 or 2, 1 hour = 50 minutes), History (the same), Civics (2–3 hours a week at grade 3). The content of Civics is as follows:

- contemporary social life
- improvement of national life and economy
- democratic government and international community.

In junior high schools, students study Civics in the final year, grade 3. Civics lessons tend to be knowledge-centred and emphasize memorization because many students and teachers are solely concerned about the entrance examination to high school.

The curricula of high schools consists of subject areas and specific subjects under them. Students should take four credits from the Civics subject area which consists of Contemporary Society (4 hours, 1 hour = 50 minutes), or Ethics (2 hours) and Politics/Economy (2 hours). The contents of Contemporary Society are as follows:

- the individual and culture in contemporary society
- environment and human life
- contemporary politics and economy and the individual
- international community and global issues.

In Contemporary Society many innovative lessons have been produced. In order to develop learners' skills and attitudes as well as knowledge, some teachers created innovative lessons taking up contemporary issues using a comprehensive approach with various activities, such as discussions, games and simulations. Although Social Studies in high schools had been regarded as a memory subject for a long time, Contemporary Society changed the image of Social Studies to some extent. Creative lessons in Contemporary Society were publicized and had a favourable influence upon other teachers across the nation. Of course, Ethics and Politics/ Economy are also essential subjects for citizenship education. But these subjects have tended to focus on teaching the structure and methods of each of the social science disciplines. Since Contemporary Society was changed from a required subject to an elective, citizenship education in general has suffered some loss of status. This is happening at the same time that citizenship education in junior high and high schools should be getting more important as these students will become voters and work in the society soon after graduation.

### The status of citizenship education

As mentioned before, citizenship education is implemented in Social Studies in junior high schools, and in Civics in high schools. In junior high schools, the main subjects are Japanese, English and Mathematics, followed by Science and Social Studies. While Japanese, English and Mathematics tend to be regarded as the basic subjects, Social Studies and Science are considered as rote learning subjects.

Within Social Studies, History is the most popular to students, and Civics the least popular. Many students have been interested in historical figures from TV programmes and lessons in elementary schools. In Civics students have to memorize a great deal of knowledge about political, economic and social systems. Moreover, as the subject of Civics is placed in the final year in junior high schools, teachers and students at that time are concerned about entrance examinations to high schools. It is difficult to successfully teach lessons which aim at developing skills and attitudes as well as focusing on the acquisition of knowledge.

In high schools, students have the freedom to choose some subjects according to their preferences or they can follow the requirements of a chosen course of study. Those who want to go to public university have to take the common written tests administrated by the Ministry of Education. The common tests usually are in Japanese, English, Mathematics, Science, and one in History, Geography or Civics. Approximately three-quarters of students take History and Geography, while only a quarter take Civics. Those who want to enter the departments such as Medical Science or Technology at universities mainly focus on Mathematics, Science and English. Those who want to go on to Social Sciences or Liberal Arts mainly take Japanese, English and History. Thus, Civics is marginalized in entrance examinations and given little status and attention in school education.

## National vs global perspective

Recently there has been considerable discussion over citizenship. Some emphasize the national perspective in citizenship education. They recognize that many Japanese lack consciousness and pride of being Japanese and are indifferent to and ignorant of Japanese culture. Japanese now should be proud of their unique culture though many people have adopted and idolized Western culture for a long time. Therefore, citizenship education should emphasize national identity which is the basis of citizenship. In this context, the Ministry of Education has required all schools to sing the Imperial national anthem and raise the national flag at school ceremonies, which some people have regarded as a symbol of aggression carried over from the Second World War. Others emphasize that a global perspective is needed as well as a national view in citizenship education. They recognize that the Japanese already have a strong national identity. As Japanese society is relatively homogeneous and centralized, the Japanese have been educated to some extent to appreciate Japanese culture explicitly and implicitly. It is quite different from being a heterogeneous society, such as in the USA. Therefore it is no longer necessary to emphasize national identity in Japan.

Today, we live in an interdependent world, 'a global village', where we are confronted with global issues, such as environmental and development issues. We will not be able to survive if we think and act only based on a nation-centric view of the world. However, it is difficult to have a global perspective compared to a national perspective. Therefore, I would contend, it is also necessary to emphasize global perspectives in school education, particularly in citizenship education.

## The future

*Towards a complete citizenship education*

As described above, citizenship education is given low priority in Japan. This might be one of the causes for political apathy and low levels of social participation of youth in community and societal activities. To promote citizenship education, I would suggest the following. First, much more time should be allocated to citizenship education. Only 2.2–3.3 per cent of lessons in junior high schools and 4.2 per cent in high schools are used for Civics at the moment. However, it might be difficult to increase Civics lessons because the total number of lessons available will decrease due to the introduction of a five-day school week, eliminating Saturday classes.

Second, teaching methods should be more effective. Various activities, such as discussion, research, interviews, simulations and games, as well as lecture-based lessons can be used to develop the skills and attitudes required of a citizen.

Moreover, Civics might be implemented not only in the classrooms but also in the community where students can gain a lot of practical experience.

Third, the assessment methods, particularly in entrance examinations, should be improved. If Civics remains a subject of written entrance examinations, Civics lessons will tend to continue to be knowledge-centred. If Civics is excluded from the entrance examinations, few pupils may be motivated to study hard. This is a dilemma. Apart from entrance examinations, Civics should be implemented as a core subject of education because citizenship education is essential for the development of a democratic society and responsible citizens.

*Citizenship education in the 21st century*

Citizenship education can be expected to become wider and richer as it is associated with new curricula which are concerned with the concept of citizenship. Human rights education which has been developed mainly by the Education for Buraku (a minority group in Japan) Liberation involves civil, political and social rights. Multicultural Education was begun with ethnic education for Korean-Japanese children in 1970s and is now moving to one for the children from other Asian countries and Japanese-Brazilian children. This education is concerned with civic identity and human rights of minority people. Environmental Education provides ecological perspectives which are more and more essential in the 21st century. Peace Education in Japan had focused for a long time on the study of war history including the atomic bombing of Hiroshima. Now some teachers are attempting to teach conflicts in the contemporary world. Global Education and Development Education have developed slowly in Japan since the 1980s. These kinds of education provide awareness of human rights and global issues to citizenship education.

If teachers learn and introduce these programmes into Civics and Social Studies, citizenship education will fully develop. Teachers and citizens must show the younger generation that they are the driving force of Japan and the global community in the 21st century.

## Japan references

Association for Social Recognitive Education (1996) *Civic Education*, Gakujutu-tosyosyuppansya, Tokyo.

Japanese Association for Civic Education (1992) *Theories and Practices in Civic Education*, Daiichigakusyusya, Tokyo.

Japanese Association for the Social Studies (1984) *Citizenship Education in Social Studies*, Toyokansyuppansya, Tokyo.

Ministry of Education (1989) *The Courses of Study*, Tokyo.

## THAILAND
## SOMWUNG PITIYANUWAT AND CHANITA RUKSPOLLMUANG

The trend towards globalization together with the era of the development of an information-based society have had significant effects on Thai society with both desirable and undesirable impacts. The quality of life of Thai people is thus the key factor to enable the society to develop in the right direction. For this reason, civics education is recognized as a principal goal of schooling. Civics education in Thailand is based on Buddhism, the Thai culture, the institution of the monarchy, family values and the Thai way of life. In the recent past we realized that economic development without human development leads to disaster. It leads to prodigal use of natural resources, environmental deterioration and the breaking-up of rural communities which all lead to a reduction in the quality of life. Civics education is one programme which has a chance to save the country from the risks outlined above.

In this section we present a description and analysis of the condition of civics education in Thailand and analyse selective innovative practices and policies in civics education.

## Description and analysis of the condition of civics education in Thailand

The history of civics education in Thailand can be divided into four major periods; the period before the development of a formal curriculum (before 1870), the beginning of the formal curriculum to the end of absolute monarchy (1870–1932), the period of constitutional monarchy with a formal curriculum in place (1932–1977), and from 1978 up to the present.

Before 1870 there was no formal curriculum. Education or schooling took place mainly in the Buddhist temples. Boys were formally educated by the monks and instructed in how to read, write and do simple arithmetic. This was accompanied by some teaching of Buddhism. Girls were kept at home and were taught by their mothers to read and write and practised the tasks of house-keeping and cooking to prepare for their married life. There was no stated official policy concerning civics education at that time. However, education was very much related to religious teaching.

The second period (1870–1932) was marked by the establishment of the secular curriculum with schools seen as separate organizations from the temple. This first nationwide scheme of education was proclaimed by King Chulalongkorn (Rama V). Guidance for schools management stated that the aim of schooling was for children to become morally good citizens. In 1895, a national framework for an official school curriculum was developed. However, it was not until the National Education Scheme of 1902 that the teaching of moral principles and values (ie, honesty, truthfulness and gratitude) was advocated. Monks still helped in teaching Buddhism to stimulate children's devotion to religion. During this period there were significant developments in education such as the establishment of the first university, Chulalongkorn University in 1916, with the mission indicated by King Chulalongkorn.

> This university was established not only for elites but also for all Thai citizens from any social background to study equally. (Suthinirunkul *et al.*, 1987, p3)

In 1910, there emerged a new generation of educated youth with overseas training. There was strong influence from Western civilization, propaganda of Chinese political ideology (nationalism) and also the British ideology of 'God, King and Country'. King Vajirawudth (Rama VI) advocated patriotism and introduced the Boy Scouts into the education system to instil and emphasize moral and civic responsibilities. At the end of this period, civics education, namely moral education, was well specified as the practising of 'palace manners', civic responsibilities and a religious way of life.

The third period (1932–1977) saw the change from the absolute to a constitutional monarchy. The government proposed universalization of education and included in the curriculum an emphasis on responsibilities towards the country, society, family and to oneself. The first National Education Scheme of 1951 represents an important stage of development of the education system of Thailand. It was the first real attempt to identify National Educational objectives with some clarity. The system was changed from the 4-6-2 (four years of elementary, six years of lower secondary and two years of upper secondary) to a 7-5 (seven years of elementary and five years of secondary). Based on this framework, the curriculum was developed to reflect the four principles of Thai education: intellectual, moral, physical and practical education, or the 4Hs principle (Heart, Health, Head and Hand). These were given to all children with the objective that 'they would be moral and cultured citizens with discipline and responsibility, with good mental and physical health and with a democratic outlook'. The intellectual aspect leads children to be curious and inquiring as well as teaches them how to seek information and knowledge. The moral aspect makes children realize their role, function and responsibilities as a good citizen. The physical aspect teaches children how to take care of their health, both mind and body. Finally, the practical education leads children to develop skills and a positive attitude towards working, as well as training them to be creative and imaginative in working. The philosophy of the 4Hs principles is very wise and was a very strong element behind the concept of the new education system.

From 1954 to 1977, the curriculum emphasized the importance of content. There was no time for learners to digest the explosion of knowledge. This type of curriculum had harmful effects as learners concentrated on and mastered only the cognitive aspects of morality. They could cite the rules, the principles, the responsibilities of the citizen, the rights and the wrongs according to the moral reasoning, but these were separated from affective learning and the development of social attitudes. Students often behaved with an awareness of the moral dimension of an artificial environment but would not always behave consistently in other situations. The failure of this type of curriculum led to the development and transition to the present Thai education system.

The present period began in 1978. The National Assembly passed the new National Scheme of Education Act in 1977 which required a new curriculum in both elementary and secondary education. The system was changed to the 6-3-3 scheme (six years of elementary, three years of lower secondary and three years of upper secondary). In elementary education the training covered four areas of learning experiences: skill training, life experiences, personal development and work education.

Specifically, the skill training includes mathematics and the Thai language. The life experiences are the integration of the natural sciences, social sciences and social studies. Physical education, arts, music, moral and civics education are combined into personal development. All practical education, including handicrafts and basic educational skills, is called work education.

In the Secondary Education Curriculum, the same main principles were utilized with the exception that students had more freedom to choose among various courses. In the previous period, there were separate civics courses in the area of social study, the functions of the citizen, moral study, geography and history. Previously separate courses of civics education had not attained these objectives.

Civics education is integrated into all courses in the curriculum. For example, in learning science children were taught to be scientific-minded, to reason, to be broad-minded and objective. The scientific method was compared to the four noble truths of Buddhism which can be used for solving any problems in life. Civics education in the new curriculum is similar to citizenship education. Civics education aims to make children good national citizens while citizenship education aims to make them good world citizens. This was seen in social studies courses in secondary level which brought together the area of Our Country, Our Neighbouring Countries, Our Continent, and Our World.

The new curriculum defined civics education as fostering desirable aspects of the human mind, such as honesty, responsibility, kindness, good reason, diligence and fairness. Responsibility for elementary children was of a different level from responsibility for secondary children. The specific desirable behaviours of each aspect guide the teaching methods and assessment.

Innovative practices in civics education in Thailand were shown in the policies, curriculum, teaching and learning as well as the research.

## The Eighth National Socio-Economics Development Plan (1997–2001)

The National Socio-Economic Development Plan in the past concentrated on economic development and was successful in encouraging continuous expansion. However, behind the admirable high economic growth rate is the negative effect on natural resources, the environment, the collapse of rural communities, social organization and morals as well as the family and the general quality of life.

The Eighth National Socio-Economics Development Plan was developed by experts from all occupations and socio-economic levels from farmers to high level business administrators, to reform the concept of sustainable development to accompany the modernization of Thai society. Humans are at the centre of development. The desirable Thai Society was defined under the Plan as

the society of learning, of competitiveness and cooperation; having capacity, discipline, morality, freedom, justice, happy people, happy families, strengthened communities, peaceful society, a balanced and steady economy, sustainable environment, recognition of human rights; being prosperous and at peace with neighbouring countries and the global community; coexistence and in harmony with nature (NEC, 1997, p87).

The present National Socio-Economic Development Plan defined the vision of Educational Development as 'having a high quality and efficient education process aiming at a balanced physical, intellectual, spiritual and social development, and relevant to the needs of individuals, communities, society and the nation' (NEC, 1997, pp 87–8).

According to this concept, education is seen as the most powerful instrument for development, and will be based on a learner-centred system. Learners will be the centre of development, being able to gather information and knowledge by themselves through life-long learning with the help of the various education services provided by all sectors of society.

## The Eighth National Educational Development Plan (1997–2001)

The Eighth National Educational Development Plan was constructed to serve the mission of the Eighth National Socio-Economic Development Plan which emphasized human development. The objectives of the Plan are as follows:

- to expand and extend an equal provision of basic education for all people; and to extend basic education to secondary education level
- to improve the quality of education and its relevance to the needs of individuals, communities and the nation, and to enable learners to achieve their full potential for self-development
- to enhance Thai education in strengthening the national potential for self-reliance, and to contribute to national economic stabilization and the role of Thailand in the global economy (NEC, 1997, p92).

In order to achieve these objectives, the following policies are recommended:

- to accelerate and extend an equal expansion, and further extension of high quality basic education services, for all
- to reform the teaching and learning system in order to enable learners at all levels to achieve their full potential
- to reform teacher education in order to enable teachers to improve teaching and learning to help learners to live a happy life in a changing society, and to improve the teaching profession and enhance the status of teachers
- to accelerate the production and development of middle level skilled and higher level skilled manpower in order to enhance national economic potential, progress and stability within the global community, in the context of the Thai tradition and in the spirit of self-reliance
- to reform education administration and management so that it becomes more flexible; to decentralize educational management so that all sectors of society are appropriately involved in decision-making, so as to provide equitable, high quality and diversified models of education (NEC, 1997, pp92 and 95).

## The draft National Constitution

There is for the first time in Thai history a National Constitution which has been developed by all Thai citizens for all Thai citizens. In the section on education in the first draft of this constitution there is an indication that the government has to provide twelve-year compulsory quality education for all children. There should be no disadvantage for the children whether they live in rural or urban environments. The educational administration must be decentralized gradually while the community should be involved in school management in an appropriate way.

*Curriculum in civics education*

The new Primary Education Curriculum organizes all subject matter into four groups:

- learning skills composed of language and mathematics
- life experience, combining science and social studies
- personal development education consisting of moral education, civics education, arts and physical education, and
- work education to include all basic working skills.

For this concept, the integrated approach should be used. For each of the six years of primary education, about 106 twenty-minute periods of civics education teaching are integrated into social studies and other subjects and 44 periods are provided solely for topics in civics education.

The Secondary Education Curriculum organizes all learning experiences according to courses for various credits. Civics education is provided under social studies which is a compulsory core course and Buddhism studies which is a compulsory selective course. The students have to take two periods per week in social studies and one period per week in Buddhism studies. Buddhism studies will become a compulsory core course in the same way as social studies.

### Teaching and learning

At both primary and secondary levels, the teachers present specific instructional behavioural objectives to learners before the actual learning task. Systematic approaches to teaching are advocated. The method of the Four Noble Truths is strongly recommended for moral and civics teaching.

The Four Noble Truths are the truths enlightened by the Buddha. These are the basis of how humans come to understanding in a search for truth by enquiring, searching and studying. The Four Noble Truths are the tool for dealing with problems in life. They are composed of four procedures:

1. *Tokh* is the process of identifying and defining the limits of a problem.
2. *Samutai* involves recognizing the causes of problems that have to be eliminated. This procedure involves the investigation, analysis and diagnosis of the causes of problems.
3. *Niroth* means realizing how a problem might be eliminated. This procedure means recognizing solutions to problems and the possibility· of solving the problems.
4. *Makh* refers to the process of eliminating or solving a problem. This involves developing detailed stages in eliminating or solving a problem (Payutto, 1995, p902).

Other instructional strategies, apart from lectures and story-telling with class discussion, are linear programming with self-instructional materials. Techniques of value clarification, enquiry approaches and group dynamics are also recommended. Role-playing is usually to be used for classroom simulations. But it seems that real-life experiences are more effective in teaching than teachers' classroom instructions. The classroom teaching is often distanced from real-life situations. On the other hand, schools are trying to teach students to be honest and fair, while the newspapers and television present and admire those who are rich and ignore the fact that they are rich because they cheat, corrupt or abuse their governmental authority. Thus Real Situation Learning (RSL) is popularly used by teachers.

In Buddhism, mind and body are inseparable. Both must be cultivated together through the control and elimination of three root causes of conflicts namely: selfish desire for pleasure and acquisitions; anger and hatred; and delusion or ignorance. To be good citizens, these causes of conflicts can be eliminated by training the minds of people, in order to help them to conquer their own selfish desire, anger and delusion. Human beings may liberate themselves from the obsessive power of the three unwholesome motives, and at the same time develop the wholesome qualities known as the four Divine Abiding principles as follows:

1.  loving-kindness towards all beings
2.  compassion towards those in distress who need our help
3.  ability to rejoice with those who are justly happy
4.  impartiality towards all beings.

This approach and the training of the mind are seen as the way to cultivate values and ethics in students who are to become good citizens.

## Research in civics education

Secondary school students' views concerning the characteristics of good citizens in Bangkok Metropolitan were studied by Wanpen Khummuang (1979). A questionnaire consisting of a Likert-type scale was administered to a group of ninety students randomly selected from the lower and upper secondary school students. It was found that boys and girls did not differ significantly in views concerning the characteristics of good citizens but significantly correlated with the mothers' educational background and the fathers' and mothers' occupations.

In terms of the characteristics of world citizenship, it was found that secondary school students in Metropolitan Bangkok strongly agreed with ten characteristics of world citizenship:

*   good citizenship responsibility
*   respect for one's rights and freedom
*   acceptance of different cultures
*   understanding the use of natural resources
*   the acceptance of different religions
*   understanding and acceptance of different political ideologies
*   understanding of world economics
*   interest in world affairs
*   developing an awareness of world problems and solutions, and
*   participating in the promotion of world peace (Buranasiri, 1989).

## Conclusion

Civics education emerges as a crucial aspect of the Thai education system according to the goals of the Eighth National Educational Development Plan and the Eighth National Socio-Economics Development Plan with the emphasis on human development, not only the cognitive aspects but equally also the affective. Thai civics education is developed on the basis of Buddhism, the institution of monarchy, Thai culture, family and life. The awareness of the significance of civics education is reflected in the essentials of the Eighth National Socio-Economics Development Plan. The Ministry of Education is in the process of reforming the system. In 'New Aspiration for Education in Thailand Towards Educational Excellence by the Year 2007', the Minister of Education indicated that education is the instrument for human development, creating peace for mankind and national security. Civics education will play an important role in this process.

## Thailand references

Buranasiri, S (1989) 'Opinions Concerning Characteristics of World Citizenship of Secondary School Students in Bangkok Metropolis', Master's Thesis, Graduate School, Chulalongkorn University.

Department of Curriculum and Instruction Development (1991) *Overview of Primary and Lower Secondary School Curricula* (1978) (revised version 1990) and *Upper Secondary School Curricula* (1981) (revised version 1990), Karusapha, Bangkok.

Department of Curriculum and Instruction Development (1995) *An Evaluation of Lower Secondary School Curricula* (1978) (revised version 1990) and *Upper Secondary School Curricula* (1981) (revised version 1990) Karusapha, Bangkok.

Khummuang, W (1979) 'Secondary School Students' Viewpoints Concerning Characteristics of Good Citizens in Bangkok Metropolis', Master's Thesis, Graduate School, Chulalongkorn University.

NEC (National Education Commission) (1997) *State of the Practice Study no. 4: Value education in Thailand*, SouthEast Asian Research Review and Advisory Group, Bangkok.

Office of the National Education Commission (1997) *Synopsis of the Eighth National Educational Development Plan*, Karusapha, Bangkok.

Payutto, PA (1995) *Buddhamma*, Maha Chulalongkornrajvitayall Printing, Bangkok.

Sukavich, Rangsitpol (1996) 'New Aspiration for Education in Thailand towards Educational Excellence by the Year 2007'. Paper presented at Second UNESCO-ACEID International Conference on 'Re-Engineering Education for Change: Educational Innovation for Development', Bangkok.

Suthinirunkul, C et al. (1987) *Seventieth Anniversary of Chulalongkorn University: Chulalongkorn University in the Decade of 1977–86*, Danuth Printing, Bangkok.

## THE UNITED STATES
## WALTER PARKER

### Historical context and definitions

Democratic citizenship education has been a central rationale for public schooling in the United States since the founding of the public school system in the latter half of the 19th century. Attempting in 1845 to persuade the people of Boston to pay for free public schooling out of tax revenue, Horrace Mann argued that a nation of immigrants, many of whom were bred in other nations under dictators, could not survive without citizenship education:

> The great moral attribute of self-government (popular sovereignty) cannot be born and matured in a day; and if children are not trained to it, we only prepare ourselves for disappointment if we expect it from grown men. . .As the fitting apprenticeship for self-government consists in being trained to self-government.

At one level, of course, citizens need not be created through the school system because they were already created by birth or naturalization. The 14th Amendment to the US Constitution reads: 'All persons born or naturalized in the United States and subject to jurisdiction thereof, are citizens of the United States and of the State wherein they reside'. For those who are citizens by these means, then, no preparation for citizenship is required or imposed. Consequently, citizenship education programmes are not geared to preparing future citizens because most school children already are citizens. Instead, such programmes attempt to develop a particular kind of citizen. This citizen typically is called a 'democratic' citizen or simply a 'good' citizen and has been described as a citizen who is informed through liberal studies and experience, is skilled in the arts and procedures of public policy making, is committed to democratic values (eg, justice, equality, liberty, limited government), and is disposed to participate in democratic public life.

Many analyses of citizenship have argued that this kind of citizen is anything but 'natural'. In fact, democratic citizenship seems more or less unnatural, requiring considerable preparation. Consider the following statement by political scientist Benjamin Barber. Barber harbours no romantic notions of what 'government by the people' would do if, uneducated for it, the people were to participate in more than the ritual, biennial voting act.

Give the uneducated the right to participate in making collective decisions, and what results is not democracy but, at best, mob rule: the government of private prejudice once known as the tyranny of opinion. For Jefferson, the difference between the democratic temperance he admired in agrarian America and the rule of the rabble he condemned when viewing the social unrest of Europe's teeming cities was quite simply education. Madison had hoped to 'filter' out popular passion through the device of representation. Jefferson saw in education a filter that could be installed within each individual, giving to each the capacity to rule prudently. Education creates a ruling aristocracy constrained by temperance and wisdom; when that education is public and universal, it is an aristocracy to which all can belong (Barber, 1993, p44).

## Goal and means

The goal of the citizenship education in the United States typically is taken to be 'participatory citizenship'. To define this, we can look to Barber's analysis, favouring as it does the stronger, Jeffersonian view of popular sovereignty, that the people themselves can rule *if* they are educated for the task. They will, it follows, need to participate in more than the nominal act of voting. They also will need to engage frequently in discussions of public issues with an eye towards formulating public policy. They may also become involved in campaigning for political office or in 'direct action', such as organizing and marching for particular causes, boycotting products, and perhaps participating in protests and acts of civil disobedience. This amalgam is what Barber calls strong democracy: 'a self-governing community of citizens who are united less by homogeneous interests than by civic education and who are made capable of common purpose and mutual action by virtue of their civic attitudes and participatory institutions rather than their altruism or good nature' (Barber, 1984, 117).

There is not much disagreement among educators in the United States over the stronger, participatory aim. But there is a long-standing disagreement over the best means to that end. Two distinctly different approaches to citizenship education have competed with one another throughout the 20th century: academic rationalism and pragmatism. Each has had numerous expressions across the decades and, to simplify, we concentrate here on only one of each: the 'structure of the disciplines' movement (SOD) and the 'problems of democracy' approach (POD).

### Structure of the Disciplines (SOD)

SOD was promoted most notably by psychologist Jerome Bruner and educator Joseph Schwab. It typifies a recurring phenomenon in US education: the occasional ascendancy of university academic departments to a commanding position over the K-12 school curriculum. SOD resonated to mid-century North American thought: two world wars had been won, but the Soviet Union had launched Sputnik and the era of the Cold War was upon the schools. School critics were claiming that Sputnik represented Soviet education's victory over American education, and they blamed this situation on John Dewey, the reconstructionists (eg, Rugg, 1939), and the Progressive education movement (eg, Aikin, 1942). Before Congressional committees, these critics argued for what they considered to be higher curriculum standards in American schools and the abandonment of what they considered to be 'soft-headed' schooling created by professors of education.

The kinds of reforms they had in mind reflected the age: reason had been reconceptualized as scientific rationality, which in turn was thoroughly established in the universities where teachers and administrators were trained. With scientific rationality came 'experts', and with the experts came the elevated status of university academic departments. Within this traditional Western paradigm, it made perfect sense to look to university disciplines (and no further) for subject matter. The content selected for SOD curricula, therefore, were the facts, concepts, generalizations, theories and modes of enquiry used by scholars as they practised their distinct academic disciplines.

The most recent instance in the 'new' history lobby was led by historians Diane Ravitch (1985) and Paul Gagnon (1987). The members of this group enjoyed extraordinary influence throughout the 1980s and early 1990s. They claimed that the school subject called social studies, with its mission of citizenship education, had distracted educators from pure history and geography instruction. These subjects, in this group's judgement, would do a much better job of preparing democratic citizens than social studies.

### Problems of Democracy (POD)

Advocates of the problems of democracy approach (POD) have a different analysis altogether. Citizenship education is paramount in the discourse of this group, and the means they advocate is an apprenticeship in public problem-solving and decision-making. The rationale has three aspects. First, since the daily labour of strong democracy is public problem-finding and public policy formulation/ decision-making, the fitting apprenticeship is actually to do it. Second, such deliberation, done well, requires a store of knowledge and competence along with the wherewithal to access and apply it. Again, the fitting apprenticeship is to do it – grapple with problems and, in the course of doing that, work to construct and access a storehouse of pertinent knowledge. These two notions add up to a third, the interdisciplinary nature of democratic deliberation. Disciplinary knowledge is integrated as public problems are deliberated. As the authors of the original Problems of Democracy (POD) course wrote in 1916,

> In actual life, whether as high school pupils or as adults, we face problems or conditions and not sciences. We use sciences, however, to interpret our problems and conditions. Furthermore, every problem or condition has many sides and may involve the use of various sciences. (Commission on the Reorganization of Secondary Education, 1916, p54)

The original POD course was designed for high school seniors by a commission of the National Education Association called to attempt a sensible articulation of college and high school curricula. Its work soon broadened to a reformulation of the entire secondary curriculum for grades seven through twelve ending in a culminating course which had 'the purpose of giving more definite, comprehensive, and deeper knowledge of some of the vital problems of social life, and thus of securing a more intelligent and active citizenship' (p52). This became the original POD course. It would rely heavily on what students had learnt in a course of study called Community Civics in grades seven through twelve.

Careful to mollify the social sciences competing for dominance over the secondary school curriculum, the planners clarified that POD would not 'discard one social science in favour of another, nor attempt to crowd the several social sciences into [POD] in abridged forms'. Rather, it would have students 'study actual problems, or issues, or conditions, as they occur in life, and in their several aspects, political, economic, and sociological'. In this way, students might 'acquire the habit of forming social judgements' (deliberation) which would necessitate 'drafting into service the materials of all the social sciences as occasion demands for a thorough understanding of the situations in question' (p56). Accordingly, the problems recommended for the POD course required for their proper deliberation knowledge gleaned from history and the social sciences but, beyond this, the students' own judgement. Furthermore, problems had to meet the committee's twin criteria for problem selection: immediate interest to the class and vital importance to society. A handful of illustrative problems were given: fluctuation in the cost of living, the impulsive action of crowds, power and effects of tradition, the church as a socializing agent, and immigration.

Later versions of the problems approach were developed by Oliver and Shaver (1966), Hunt and Metcalf (1968), and Newmann (1975). True to the problems approach, none looked to academic disciplines as the starting points of the school curriculum; instead, each examined democratic aims and, from them, derived necessary citizen behaviours and attitudes. Academic disciplines were incorporated as resources or lenses. Referring to the SOD movement occurring at the same time, Oliver and Shaver wrote:

[S]tructure can be provided for the social studies by a careful consideration of the role of the citizen in the community, rather than resorting to arbitrarily selected, and still fragmented, university disciplines. Consequently, we shall first consider the nature of democracy and democratic commitments, then present a conceptual framework for a curriculum based on such considerations. (1966, p6)

More recently, Engle and Ochoa's *Education for Democratic Citizenship: Decision making in the social studies* (1988) analysed the inherent tension in democratic citizenship education, which is its dual and somewhat contradictory purpose: creating persons loyal to the nation-state while at the same time developing persons capable of critically examining and, if needed, reforming their society. 'This tension, between the competing goals of political freedom and diversity on the one hand and social conformity on the other, creates the context for debate and controversy about how citizens in a democracy should be educated' (1988, p28). And in 1996, a wide-ranging collection of examples and analyses of the problems approach was published by the National Council for the Social Studies. Entitled *Handbook on Teaching Social Issues* (Evans and Saxe), it has made an important contribution to the literature on the problems approach.

In summary, citizenship education in the United States has always been central to the mission of the public schools, and it has been seen as the particular responsibility of the social studies curriculum. It has been approached by two quite different routes, however. One concentrates on the problems; the other concentrates on disciplinary knowledge itself. This is an old and popular debate in citizenship education in the United States. Both have been criticized for resting on faulty positivist assumptions about the nature of knowledge, values, and science, but this line of criticism (eg, Cherryholmes, 1980), like much of post-structural analysis in education, has not been widely embraced in the United States.

## The policy context

The system of schooling in the United States is radically decentralized. Because there is no federal constitutional provision for it, education is left to each of the fifty states which, in turn, delegate much of the responsibility to over 15,000 local school districts. This arrangement has far-reaching policy implications for the finance and governance of schools, curriculum and instruction, textbooks and other curriculum materials, the licensing of teachers, reform efforts and setting graduation requirements.

To be sure, there is a federal department of education in Washington, DC, but it has little impact upon the schools in the nation. Schooling has from the very earliest days of the republic been a state and local responsibility, and this 'local control' is jealously guarded. It was therefore a major test and clarification of the federal system when, for example, the national government, acting on the famous Supreme Court case, Brown versus the Board of Education, forced the racial integration of segregated schools in the 1950s. A contemporary test involves the current effort to identify and assess national curriculum standards in each of the major curricular areas, including citizenship education. More than a few educators worry that this effort will lead to a 'national curriculum' at the expense of local inventiveness and initiative.

This current debate began in April 1983, when the federal Department of Education during the Reagan administration issued a report on the condition of the nation's education and schooling entitled, *A Nation at Risk*. The report stimulated an intense, decade-long discussion on the need to reform US schools. Much of it focused on the schools' role in helping the nation regain a competitive edge in the international marketplace. The culmination of this discussion can be traced to September 1989, when President George Bush and the nation's governors convened an 'education summit' in Charlottesville, Virginia. At the close of this meeting, a set of six national goals were put forward to guide educational reform in the United States towards the year 2000. Two of these goals specify responsible citizenship as necessary to the attainment of the reform agenda. One states that 'every school in America will ensure that all students learn to use their minds well, so they may be prepared for responsible citizenship, further learning, and productive employment in our modern economy'. Another states that 'every adult American will be literate and possess the knowledge and skills necessary to compete in a global economy and exercise the rights and responsibilities of citizenship'.

As indicated above, overt citizenship education in the school curriculum in the United States is situated mostly within the social studies curriculum. In the primary grades, for example, law-making typically is introduced along with local government studies in the third grade. In the better curricula, this involves the comparative study of local government in several communities in both the US and abroad. In a middle track curriculum, students may study only the local community government without the conceptual advantage of comparison. In a lower track curriculum, students may be deprived of community study in favour of intensive skills instruction in reading the mathematics. In the upper grades, an introduction to constitutional democracy in the US typically is part of the 5th grade US history curriculum. A law and government course called 'civics' may be offered in the junior high school years. A contemporary world problems of democracy course may be required or elected in the high school. As well, school district curriculum guides typically list democratic citizenship education as a key school social studies curriculum goal.

## Curriculum initiatives

### Voluntary national curriculum standards

Since 1994, state and local social studies curriculum planning committees have had for their consideration three new sets of (voluntary) curriculum standards that bear on citizenship education – one each for History, Social Studies, and Civics and Government. These standards projects were the most significant curriculum initiatives in US education in the 1990s and are relevant to citizenship education in several ways, but in one way particularly: each standards projects claims citizenship education as its mission. The history standards document states:

[K]nowledge of history is the precondition of political intelligence. Without history, a society shares no common memory of where it has been, of what its core values are, or of what decisions of the past account for present circumstances. Without history, one cannot undertake any sensible inquiry into the political, social, or moral issues in society. . .or achieve to the informed, discriminating citizenship essential to effective participation in the democratic processes of governance and the fulfilment for all our citizens of the nation's democratic ideals. (National Center for History in the Schools, 1993, p1)

The social studies standards document states:

Social studies is the integrated study of the social sciences and humanities to promote civic competence. . .The primary purpose of social studies is to help young people develop the ability to make informed and reasoned decisions for the public good as citizens of a culturally diverse, democratic society in an interdependent world. (National Council for the Social Studies, 1994, vii)

The civics standards project document states:

The goal of education in civics and government is informed, responsible participation in political life by competent citizens committed to the funda- mental values and principles of American constitutional democracy. (Center for Civic Education, 1994, p1)

Twenty-two exit standards for the twelfth grade are identified in the civics standards, and they are grouped under the five 'organizing questions' below. These same questions (with slight modification) have guided the development of a national survey of students' knowledge and skills related to civics and government that was administered in 1998 by the National Assessment of Educational Progress.

1. What is government and what should it do?
2. What are the foundations of the American political system?
3. How does the government established by the US Constitution embody the principles and purposes of American democracy?
4. What is the relationship of American politics and government to world affairs?
5. What are the roles of the citizen in the American political system?

We turn now to alternatives to mainstream citizenship education in the United States. Each is to some degree now a trend, and each has been practised for some time among a small number of innovative teachers and curriculum directors.

*Law-related education*

The American Bar Association has for several decades established committees to promote education on constitutional law and principles. It is joined by several other organizations with a similar purpose, including the Constitutional Rights Foundation, Center for Civic Education, and Street Law. This movement, called law-related education (LRE), is concerned with providing 'education for citizenship in a constitutional democracy, not specialized legal education' (Patrick and Hoge, 1991, p428; see also Miller and Singleton, 1997).

LRE is a small but palpable force in the social studies curriculum. Since 1975, LRE has been added to the social studies curriculum in over half of the fifty states. Reliable data is difficult to come by, however, because LRE overlaps the study of government and civics, which is mandated in nearly 75 per cent of the fifty states and offered as an elective in the rest.

*Community service*

There is growing interest in the United States in what is called 'community service' or 'service learning' at the precollegiate level as a component of democratic citizenship education. In part, this interest is in response to the perception that North American society is increasingly fragmented and that young people are increasingly alienated from their communities (Bellah *et al.*, 1985). According to a national survey, 27 per cent of secondary schools offered some form of community service (Rutter and Newmann, 1989).

Proponents suggest that the experience may heighten young people's sense of civic responsibility and belonging, their personal development and intellectual growth (Kahne and Westheimer, 1996; Pratte, 1988). It can promote both charity and social change. In an influential study of secondary schools, Boyer (1983) recommended that students be required to perform some service to their school or community. As part of a course for which students would receive academic credit, Boyer saw the service requirement as a way to help students see that they are not only autonomous individuals but also members of a larger community to which they are accountable.

The term service learning is used to indicate the second generation of community service projects. Service learning's distinguishing attributes are its connection to the academic curriculum and the importance it places on reflection. 'In contrast to community service, service learning is a teaching method that combines academic content with direct service experiences in which students provide genuine service to their school or community. . . This new context gives what students have learned in the classroom new and deeper meaning' (Schukar *et al.*, 1996, p9). Service learning includes a wide range of service experiences; volunteer service (eg, in a nursing home or food centre), school service (eg, tutoring), community study (eg, recording oral histories), community projects (taking on tasks not addressed by existing agencies), internships (eg, with a county attorney or local business person), and social action, in which the goal is to influence public policy (Conrad, 1991).

Research on the advantages of service learning indicates that most students do benefit in terms of personal development. However, increases in political efficacy or later civic participation are much less likely. Rutter and Newmann (1989) offer three suggestions for increasing the likelihood that involvement in service programmes will result in a higher sense of civic responsibility. First, service should be in direct response to a public need. Internships to explore career options are not appropriate for service learning. Second, students should meet regularly throughout the service project to reflect on the experience. During these 'reflective seminars', teachers should help students explore issues of social responsibility. Third, students need to be involved in the project long enough to reflect on the complexity of social issues.

*Multicultural education*

Multicultural education and democratic citizenship education are seen by many US educators as altogether different initiatives. Indeed, they have developed as distinct topics, literatures and professional communities. While multicultural educators have concentrated generally on problems of inclusion, citizenship educators have concentrated on the question: inclusion in what? Clearly, the two are related, and uniting them in a single framework is arguably the most important issue in US education as the 21st century arrives.

But there are serious obstacles. Citizenship education in the US has ignored social heterogeneity for most of this century. One reason can be found in the concept 'democratic citizenship' itself, which by definition excludes culture. Democratic citizen is intended to be a culturally neutral social identity: in one's citizen role, one is a cypher, an 'individual' with rights. Another reason is a combination of ethnocentrism and power politics. The larger civic realm in the United States has not in fact been neutral but to a significant extent the province of the male members of a particular ethnic group. To wit: John Jay wrote in *The Federalist No. 2* in 1787, trying to win public approval of the new constitution, that 'Providence' gave this land 'to one united people – a people descended from the same ancestors, speaking the same language, professing the same religion. . .' They were, he asserted, a 'band of brethren'. In order to assert this social cohesion, Jay had to ignore native peoples, blacks, women, and others who were not figured into 'we the people'. Years later, along the same lines, Arthur Schlesinger (1991) feared the 'disuniting' of the brethen. He regarded *e pluribus unum* (from the many have come the one) as a more-or-less established fact which now would be undone if multiculturalism wasn't constrained. Both men perceived a neutrality in the public realm that did not actually exist, the effect of which was to conceal existing power imbalances. Citizenship education in the US has not yet come to grips with this legacy.

Multicultural educators and democratic citizenship educators in the US may continue to ignore the big picture – democratic living in a diverse society – attending only to one piece of it. Contemporary theorizing, however, suggests ways by which multicultural education and citizenship education can be joined (Avery *et al.*, 1992; Banks, 1997; Hahn, 1994; Mosher *et al.*, 1994; Parker, 1997). If democratic citizens (as defined earlier) are liberally informed, skilled in the arts and procedures of public policy-making, committed to democratic values, and disposed to participate in public life, then multicultural education is the movement that hopes to make this learning available to all students rather than only to some.

## Conclusion

Many educators in the United States, probably most in the social studies community, uphold the citizenship mission of the schools, but many criticize its implementation as being too weak to amount to anything. Free public schooling for all children has, in fact, been the primary citizenship education achievement in the United States. While this is an enormous achievement, stronger forms of citizenship education have been developed but not widely implemented. In other words, as a curriculum innovation, democratic citizenship education is an idea that really has not been tried vigorously on a wide scale.

## USA references

Aikin, W M (1942) *The Story of the Eight-Year Study*, Harper & Brothers, New York.
Avery, P G, Bird, K, Johnstone, S, Sullivan, J L and Thalhammer, K (1992), 'Exploring Political Tolerance with Adolescents', *Theory and Research in Social Education*, **20**(4), pp 386–420.

Banks, J A (1997) *Educating Citizens in a Multicultural Society*, Teachers College Press, New York.

Barber, B R (1984) *Strong Democracy*, University of California Press, Berkeley.

Barber, B R (November 1993) 'America Skips School', *Harper's Magazine*, **287**(1722), pp 39–46.

Bellah, R N *et al.* (1985) *Habits of the Heart*, University of California Press, Berkeley.

Boyer, E L (1983) *High School: A report on secondary education in America*, Harper & Row, New York.

Center for Civic Education (1994) *National Standards for Civics and Government*, Center for Civic Education, Calabasas, CA.

Cherryholmes, C H (1980) 'Social Knowledge and Citizenship Education: Two views of truth and criticism', *Curriculum Inquiry*, **10**(2), pp 115–51.

Commission on the Reorganization of Secondary Education of the National Education Association, Committee on Social Studies (1916) *The Social Studies in Secondary Education*, Bureau of Education Bulletin No. 28, US Government Printing Office, Washington, DC.

Conrad, D (1991) 'School-community Participation for Social Studies', in J P Shaver (ed.), *Handbook of Research on Social Studies Teaching and Learning*, Macmillan, New York, pp 540–8.

Engle, S H and Ochoa, A S (1988). *Education for Democratic Citizenship: Decision making in the social studies*, Teacher's College Press, New York.

Evans, R W and Saxe, D W (eds) (1996) *Handbook on Teaching Social Issues*, National Council for the Social Studies, Washington, DC.

Gagnon, P (1987) *Democracy's Untold Story*, American Federation of Teachers, Washington, DC.

Hahn, C L (1994) 'Controversial Issues in History Instruction', in M Carretero and J F Voss (eds), *Cognitive and Instructional Processes in History and the Social Sciences*, Lawrence Erlbaum Associates, Hillsdale, NJ, pp 201–19.

Hunt, M P and Metcalf, L E (1968) *Teaching High School Social Studies: Problems in reflective thinking and social understanding* (2nd edn), Harper Collins, New York.

Kahne, J and Westheimer, J (1996) 'In the Service of What? The politics of service learning', *Phi Delta Kappan*, **77**(9), pp 593–9.

Mann, H (1846) *Ninth Annual Report of the Secretary of the Board of Education*, Dutton and Wentworth, Boston.

Miller, B and Singleton, L (1997) *Preparing Citizens: Linking authentic assessment and instruction in civic/law-related education*, Social Science Education Consortium, Boulder, Col.

Mosher, R, Kenny, R A, Jr and Garrod, A (1994) *Preparing for Citizenship: Teaching youth to live democratically*, Praeger, Westport, Vir.

National Center for History in the Schools, University of California at Los Angeles (1993) *National History Standards for United States History*, University of California Press, Los Angeles.

National Commission on Excellence in Education (1983), *A Nation at Risk*, US Department of Education, Washington DC.

National Council for the Social Studies (1994) *Curriculum Standards for the Social Studies*, National Council for the Social Studies, Washington, DC.

Newmann, F M (1975) *Education for Citizen Action: Challenge for the secondary curriculum*, McCutchan, Berkeley.

Oliver, D W and Shaver, J P (1966) *Teaching Public Issues in the High School*, Utah State University Press, Logan, UT (republished in 1974).

Parker, W C (1996) 'Curriculum for Democracy', in R Soder (ed.), *Democracy, Education, and the Schools*, Jossey-Bass, San Francisco, pp 182–210.

Parker, W C (1997) 'Democracy and Difference', *Theory and Research in Social Education*, **25**(2), pp 220–34.

Patrick, J J and Hoge, J D (1991) 'Teaching Government, Civics, and Law', in J P Shaver (ed.), *Handbook of Research on Social Studies Teaching and Learning*, Macmillan, New York, pp 427–36.

Pratte, R (1988) *The Civic Imperative*, Teachers College Press, New York.

Ravitch, D (1985) *The Schools We Deserve*, Basic Books, New York.

Rugg, H O (ed.) (1939) *Democracy and the Curriculum: The Life and Program of the American School*, Appleton-Century, New York.

Rutter, R A and Newmann, F M (1989) 'The Potential of Community Service to Enhance Civic Responsibility', *Social Education*, **53**(6), pp 371–4.

Schlesinger, A M, Jr (1991) *The Disuniting of America: Reflections on a multicultural society*, Whittle, Knoxville.

Schukar, R, Johnson, J and Singleton, L R (1996) *Service Learning in the Middle School Curriculum: A resource book*, Social Science Education Consortium, Boulder, Col.

## SUMMARY

What emerges from the case studies presented in this chapter is that some of the issues are universal and some regional but all offer significant challenges if the notion of multidimensional citizenship is to become both policy and practice. In taking a global perspective, one would expect most need for development in relation to citizenship education (CE) would be not in the Old World as represented by Europe or even in the New World as represented by North America but in the nations of the Pacific Rim – in the case of Thailand and Japan. In our sample of nine nations this does not seem to be the case. At this time, at the beginning of the 21st century, it is changes in the Old World which offer a significant challenge. Traditional ideas of what constitutes sovereignty or what constitutes a nation-state in Europe are in a state of turbulence.

The five European countries sampled in this chapter face many common problems and some distinct and unique national problems. In terms of curriculum in three of the countries – England (and Wales), Hungary and the Netherlands – there has taken place since 1985 in the Netherlands, in 1988 in England and in 1996 in Hungary the development of national curriculum guidelines for primary and secondary education. All three of these recent curricular reforms have laid down clear signposts for how CE in those countries should develop. Germany has been preoccupied with the aftermath of reunification and Greece shows little signs of joining the curricular reform movement. Common in the three recent reforms is the need to develop a European perspective through the curriculum.

Recent literature from within European countries, from the European Commission and from the Council of Europe have been generous in their efforts and suggestions for developing a European vision in the continent's young people through appropriate curricular initiatives. The development of this vision cannot rest with a European heritage and Europe's traditional place in global affairs. At the end of the 20th century things were changing. Therborn sums this up succinctly in his scholarly analysis of modern Europe.

On the eve of the twentieth-first Century, Europe is no longer the centre or vanguard of modernity, and whether it constitutes a major alternative for the future is at least open to doubt. . . To the Europeans themselves, the legacy of a specific history remains and will remain important. Its sediments, from Antiquity to the industrial class struggle, are built into the European House. To the rest of the modern world, however, the lights of Europe are growing dim. (Therborn, 1995, p363)

This is perhaps too dismal a picture. The European movement towards monetary and political union is still providing a model for other parts of the world – in, for example, the Americas, through NAFTA, in the Asian Pacific and in the new Central Asia. Unity and integration are the watchwords of the development of international markets, the globalization of environmental problems, all of which demand legal and political interventions which transcend the borders of the nation-state.

For those educationalists who strive to develop a concept of Europe and the European citizen there is some evidence that curriculum development tends to look to the past rather than to the future. McLean (1995) and Starkey (1995) both see the idea of a European curriculum as a distant prospect. However, they also see the aim of establishing a European vision and understanding worth attempting.

Despite CE being difficult to find on the ground, Jones and Jones (1992) and Bell (1995) have all published descriptions and analysis of vignettes of classroom practices in CE in England. All provide examples of what is possible. The Council of Europe (1996a, 1996b) provides reports of European-wide conferences on education for citizenship, and the European Commission (1997) produced a report on accomplishing a European perspective through education and training. In England and Wales much of the development on the study of contemporary Europe is led by the universities. Both the 'old' and the 'new' (post-1992) universities provide us with many examples of undergraduate and graduate studies on European themes in their degree courses. Students and faculty in higher education institutions are also provided with opportunities to visit and study in other European countries through the enigmatically named Erasmus, Socrates, Tempus and Leonardo projects. University courses are usually interdisciplinary and involve contributions from history, the social sciences, law, economics and business. Unfortunately few of the graduates from such courses will find their way into schools. The National Curriculum in England and Wales is defined in terms of traditional school subjects – and a European dimension is often omitted from courses. Despite the restructuring of the curriculum in at least three of the countries from which case studies have been written for this chapter, much work still has to be done to incorporate a vision and understanding of Europe and what it means to be European for our future citizens.

It has been necessary to dwell on the European situation because if multi-dimensional citizenship is to be developed across the continent then it has to be established within Europe as well as globally. European teachers therefore face an additional burden when compared with some of their colleagues in, for example, Thailand and Japan. Looking across the nine nations included in the CEPS project there is considerable agreement about what constitutes an approach to a programme for multidimensional citizenship.

Certainly, across Europe and in North America, it is possible to discern a different emphasis coming from, on the one hand, politicians and on the other hand, educationalists. The former still hang on to the notion that CE raises and maintains loyalty, national consciousness and loyalty to the nation. Educationalists seem to see CE as encouraging tolerance, understanding, systemic and constructively sceptical thinking and producing individuals who are encouraged to question the status quo. There may be some East–West differences here. Educationalists from both East and West may agree on the desirability of characteristics to be developed in students but the case studies from Japan and Thailand show that in these two countries much more is expected of CE programmes in terms of loyalty and national consciousness.

What experiences should students be given through programmes of CE? There is a general agreement that basic knowledge of social and political systems is necessary for all students and there is a consensus that participation and involvement of students, preferably in real issues, should be the basis of teaching and learning strategies. There is some preference in the studies for cross-curricular approaches to CE using the resources of history, the humanities, social sciences and in some cases, moral education. CE is taught under several labels but this seems to be an unimportant issue. What seems to be more crucial is whether or not CE is assessed and makes a contribution to a student's assessed portfolio of activities. Subjects that are not assessed carry low priority. In most of the cases, importance was attached to understanding and using modern technology as ways of learning and communicating. There is little evidence from the cases that IT is used extensively in CE. This reflects the differing resource bases from which systems operate and a shortage of appropriate and challenging technology-based teaching materials for use by teachers of citizenship education.

There is considerable agreement about the themes which should be included in a CE programme. These are unsurprising. All countries include work on Human Rights, Environmental Education and Multi-cultural Education. These issues are either included in CE programmes or are part of associated cross-curricular themes as they are in England. There is also evidence of an increasing focus on the development of courses on the world of work and career choice. Globalization and Global Education figure as desirable approaches. With the demise of the Cold War, Peace Education seems to have disappeared and with few expectations Political Education is not used as a course label.

From all this it can be seen that much is demanded from CE. Can this be delivered? Much depends on how the politics of the curriculum are handled. The school curriculum is heavily guarded territory. In most countries traditional subjects have marked out their discrete estates and they fight hard to hold on to what they have. How many history teachers will give up coverage of a traditional piece of history content for a theme on economic understanding and the world of work? What remains is that if the multifaceted elements of multidimensional citizenship education are to be successfully implemented then the territory of the traditional curriculum needs replotting and a different map needs to be drawn. This is the battle that has to start in the perceptions of committed teachers but (unfortunately) finally rests in the hands of the politicians and policy makers.

## References

Bell, G H (1995) *Educating European Citizens: Citizenship values and the European dimension*, Fulton, London.

Council of Europe (1996a), *Education for Democratic Citizenship*, Consultation meeting report, Strasbourg, France.

Council of Europe (1996b), *Citizenship Education*, European Teachers' Seminar, Uppsala, Sweden.

European Commission (1997) *Accomplishing Europe through Education and Training*, European Commission, Brussels.

Jones, B and Jones, N (eds) (1992) *Education for Citizenship*, Kogan Page, London.

McLean, M (1995) 'The European Union and the Curriculum', *Oxford Studies in Comparative Education*, **5**(2), pp 29–45.

Starkey, H (1995) 'Re-inventing Citizenship Education in a New Europe', *Oxford Studies in Comparative Education*, **5**(1), pp 213–26.

Therborn, G (1995), *European Modernity and Beyond*, London, Sage Publications.

# 3

# USING THE DELPHI CROSS-CULTURALLY: TOWARDS THE DEVELOPMENT OF POLICY

*Ruthanne Kurth-Schai, Chumpol Poolpatarachewin and Somwung Pitiyanuwat*

The Citizenship Education Policy Study (CEPS) represents an unprecedented attempt to design and implement a cross-cultural variation of the Delphi technique. It engaged a distinctively large team of researchers with diverse national, cultural, linguistic, conceptual, and professional resources in a collaborative effort to solicit, integrate and interpret the collective wisdom generated by a prestigious, multinational panel of experts. The expert opinion was then used to develop educational policy relevant both within the participating nations and beyond any particular policy system. In attempting this, the present study joins the tradition of its methodological predecessors in grappling with the risk, rigour and creativity required to address questions of significance to present and future social and educational systems.

## ORIGIN AND EVOLUTION OF THE DELPHI METHOD

### Development and description of the conventional Delphi

The Delphi was originally conceived as an intuitive, exploratory method to solicit and synthesize the forecasts of groups of experts regarding problems that did not lend themselves to precise analytical techniques but that could benefit from the application of carefully derived collective judgement. It originated in the United States as a spin-off of national defence research in the early 1950s. The US Air Force commissioned the Rand Corporation to conduct a study entitled Project Delphi, the goal of which was to 'obtain the most reliable consensus of opinion of a group of experts', by means of 'a series of intensive questionnaires interspersed with controlled opinion feedback' (Linstone and Turoff, 1975, p10).

Iteration with controlled feedback, as developed by Norman Dalkey and Olaf Helmer, was the principal methodological innovation in the original project. In 1959, with a third Rand researcher, Nicholas Rescher, they published *The Epistemology of the Inexact Sciences* to begin the process of establishing a theoretical justification for use of the Delphi in various forms of anticipatory research. The authors contended that the judgement of experts is permissible as scientific evidence in fields which have not yet developed to the point of establishing formal scientific laws. The validity and applicability of the Delphi were supported by a series of forecasting experiments conducted by Rand in 1968. Regarding estimates generated by groups, Rand researchers concluded that assessments formulated on the basis of anonymous controlled feedback tended to be more accurate than estimates emerging from face-to-face discussions (Linstone and Turoff, 1975).

These initial studies provided evidence in support of three central assumptions which have served as a philosophic basis for the development of Delphi research since its inception:

1. Human judgements represent legitimate and useful inputs in addressing research problems that are long-range, ill-defined, highly complex, and/or lack a well-developed theoretical foundation.
2. The judgement of a group is likely to be superior to that of any individual, especially if judgements are arrived at in an interactive manner involving carefully structured sharing of information.
3. Responses shared anonymously are likely to be superior (more numerous, detailed, creative and candid) to those publicly identified with their source because participants who respond anonymously are not subjected to the biasing effects of dominant individuals, group pressures towards conformity, irrelevant communication, and fear of public disapproval.

Based upon these assumptions, conventional Delphi studies are generally conducted in the following manner:

The researcher uses explicit criteria to select a panel of experts and designs a well-structured questionnaire concerning the issue(s) under consideration. Panellists are then asked to respond to the questionnaire during a series of rounds (iterations). All responses are provided individually and anonymously. Question-naires are usually administered through the mail, and in most cases panellists are unaware of each other's identity and interact only with the researcher or small research team (two to four members) conducting the process.

Between rounds, panellists are provided with descriptions of previous individual and group responses (controlled feedback). Group opinion is generally expressed in the form of statistical indices, a measure of central tendency (usually the median response) and a measure of dispersion (usually the interquartile range). Panellists are frequently asked to submit comments and/or justification of their personal views for review by the researchers which are often summarized and reported in subsequent iterations.

The Delphi process is concluded either when a predetermined level of agreement among panellists is achieved (group consensus), or when the responses of individual panellists have stabilized from round to round making it apparent that further repetitions will not produce the predetermined level of agreement (stabilization of disparate opinion). Between two and four rounds are usually sufficient to complete the process.

## Cultural futures variations of the conventional Delphi

Although conceived as a quantitative method for acquiring expert opinion regarding technological forecasts, expanded conceptualizations acknowledging the potential of the Delphi as a method for enhancing group communication and judgement concerning complex issues soon emerged (Linstone and Turoff, 1975). Many of the most significant problems confronting the emerging discipline of futures research were broadly cultural rather than narrowly technical in scope. For researchers compelled to respond to such concerns, the primary purpose of futures research began to shift from an emphasis on social forecasting to an emphasis on social systems design. More specifically, the purpose of cultural futures research is to engage a 'community' in developing both a shared *vision* of ways of life that are possible, desirable and sustainable, and feasible *strategies* necessary to enact that vision. The Delphi appeared particularly promising as a tool for social systems design due to its demonstrated capacity to build consensus and to enhance understanding of complex issues.

The educational impact of participation in Delphi exercises has been repeatedly demonstrated (eg, Hill and Fowles (1975), Kurth-Schai (1984, 1988, 1991), Linstone and Turoff (1975), Palkert (1986), Poolpatarachewin (1980), Scheele (1975), Weaver (1971), Weingand (1980). In addition to broadening and deepening understanding of the topic under consideration, past studies suggest that participation catalyses and supports clarification of facts and values, exploration of alternative perspectives and possibilities, and development of critical, creative and systemic thought. These effects are accomplished while emphasizing the importance of collaboration across diverse opinions and experiences in processes of social problem-solving and design. Of particular significance to the prospect of conducting cross-cultural Delphi research are the thoughts of Sam Scheele (1975) who has suggested that the educational impact of the Delphi, more specifically the opportunity to experience others' conceptions of reality, represents perhaps a greater contribution to society than the sharing of final results. He contends that focusing attention on differences in reality constructs usually yields a more refined and widely accepted definition of the appropriate construct or at least a clearer and more precise distinction between competing constructs. The redefinition of contextual realities facilitates the generation of new options and may create impetus for change whereby, 'both the dominant reality and the required change technology are invented as well as inherited, and culture is transformed as well as transmitted' (Scheele, 1975, p43).

## Adaptation of the Delphi to support cross-culturally relevant policy

Once a cultural systems design variation of the Delphi was selected, the process of adapting the technique to meet the goals, needs, constraints and challenges specific to this study could begin. A review of the literature suggested that although 'traditional professional strategies for building consensus, such as policy statements, publication and conferences, often have failed to chart a clear and uncontested sense of group agreement . . . in education the Delphi has been used effectively for applications such as curriculum planning and development and goal setting' (Martorella, 1991, pp 83–4). The Delphi has further been described as particularly well suited to the task of generating educational policy due to its ability to accommodate multiple competing insights and interests (Cookson, 1986), its ability to accommodate multiple interpretations and to expand educators' aware-ness of alternative future options (Palkert, 1986), and its future orientation deemed essential due to the time lag between the imposition of policy and its educational impact and the rapid pace of social change with which educational policy must keep pace (Weaver, 1971).

A review of past studies also revealed an important adaptation, that of using data obtained by interviewing expert panellists as the primary source of items to be incorporated in Delphi questionnaires, rather than relying solely on the judgement of researchers in completing this crucial task. Perhaps the most comprehensive efforts at integrating interviews in the Delphi are represented in the work of Chumpol Poolpatarachewin (1980) who pioneered the development of Ethnographic Delphi Futures Research (EDFR). The procedural steps of EDFR are quite similar to those of the Delphi, the primary distinguishing feature being the inclusion of a future-oriented approach to ethnographic interviewing during the first round. Drawing from past experience with EDFR, round one interviews were utilized in the CEPS study so that expert opinion could be used to guide questionnaire development, thereby assuring that central themes would be addressed from multiple, diverse and knowledgeable perspectives.

## OVERVIEW OF THE RESEARCH PROCESS

In September 1993, members of the steering committee met in Hiroshima, Japan, to clarify the project's purpose and identify focal research questions. As described in Chapter 1, working definitions of key terms and concepts were negotiated, and criteria were established for the selection of research team members and policy shapers and scholars from the participating nations. The committee also began the process of developing the analytic framework and specific research strategies necessary to identify a wide range of possible future global trends, characteristics and strategies relevant to the topic of citizenship education. These results would then used be to shape policy decisions – either directly (results would be used to develop new educational policy and practice) or indirectly (results and the experience of the Delphi would serve to educate all who participate regarding the scope and complexity of the issue, and change their personal and professional attitudes and behaviour).

The project was to be completed over a period of forty-five months ending in March 1997. During the first year, twenty-six researchers (with areas of expertise that included social studies education, comparative and international education, science education and a variety of research methodologies), representing nine nations were organized into four research teams: Japan, Thailand, Europe (England, Germany, Greece, Hungary, the Netherlands) and North America (Canada, United States).

## Selection of research panellists

The Delphi method is designed to collect and synthesize the opinions of panels of experts. Unlike more conventional survey methods the goal in selecting Delphi panels is not to develop a random sample representative of the general public. Instead, a purposive sampling approach is adopted. The intent is to select persons who have special knowledge or expertise in the domain(s) being examined. Predetermined selection criteria are strictly adhered to to ensure both validity and reliability.

| July '93–May '94 | Organization of research teams<br>Background reading<br>Identification of expert panel pool |
|---|---|
| June '94 | First international research meeting, Bangkok<br>Final selection of experts |
| Aug '94–Jan '95 | Round One interviews (n=110) |
| Feb–May '95 | Analysis of interview data and development of draft Delphi survey items |
| May '95 | Second international research meeting, Minneapolis<br>Finalization of Delphi survey instrument |
| Aug–Oct '95 | Round Two Delphi survey of panellists (n=182) |
| Nov–Dec '95 | Analysis of Round Two survey data |
| Jan–Feb '96 | Round Three Delphi survey of panellists (n=182) |
| Mar–Jun '96 | Third international research meeting, Hiroshima<br>Analysis of final (third) round survey data |
| Jul '96–Mar '97 | Development of final and executive summary project reports |

**Figure 3.1** Project Schedule

Attention was also devoted to balancing and diversifying the membership of each panel (by gender, race/ethnicity, geographic region and area of expertise, eg, environment, economics) to ensure that a wide variety of perspectives on the topic would be carefully considered.

## Delphi Round One: the interview process

During the months of August 1994–January 1995, members of the four research teams conducted interviews with carefully selected members of each expert panel. In all, 110 interviews were conducted producing a rich body of thoughtful social analysis. Three broad, open-ended questions were posed to each interviewee:

- What are the major global trends likely to have a significant impact on the lives of people during the next twenty-five years?
- What will be the characteristics required of individuals in order to cope with and/or manage these trends?
- How might these characteristics be developed, ie, what educational approaches, strategies or innovations might best implement these citizen characteristics?

*97*

The questions were sent to the interviewees for their consideration prior to the interview. Most interviews were conducted in person, and in a few cases by telephone, and tape-recorded if agreed upon. Interviews lasted 45 to 120 minutes with many respondents showing willingness to continue well beyond the time allotted and indicating enthusiasm for their involvement in what they found to be an important, thought-provoking and enjoyable process.

Upon the completion of each interview, the researcher produced a written summary identifying each concept raised by the expert. As the interview data were to be used *only* to generate Delphi statements, it was not necessary to translate the summary transcripts into English. Researchers then aggregated their interview data, grouping similar concepts together into statement categories such as environment, economic development, politics and government, etc, and developed draft Delphi statements.

Nearly 900 draft Delphi statements were generated across the four research teams, organized as trends, characteristics and educational strategies/approaches/ innovations in relation to the three focal interview questions. In May 1995, researchers met in Minneapolis to face the task of condensing the draft statements into a workable Delphi instrument of 106 items. The researchers were divided into five multinational working groups who used the following criteria to guide their discussions and decisions in arriving at the final listing of Round Two Delphi survey instrument statements:

- State items at the appropriate level of specificity (statements should allow for discrimination in responses and should challenge respondents' thinking).
- Synthesize related statements to avoid redundancy.
- Work towards clarity in meaning.
- Determine whether the issue provides valuable insight for developing educational policy related to citizenship.
- Ensure that the statement is relevant across cultures.
- Ensure that statements cover the range of issues raised by interviewees.

From the collection of items proposed by each working group, one shared multinational Delphi questionnaire was developed and divided into three sections, each with a specific pattern of response requested as follows:

*Section I: Trends*

This section of the survey consisted of sixty global trends identified by experts participating in the interview round as likely to have a significant impact upon the lives of people during the next twenty-five years. Policy experts responding to the questionnaire were asked to assess both the *probability* and *desirability* of each trend using a six-point scale ranging from Highly Likely or Highly Desirable to Not Likely or Not Desirable. For example:

| Desirability | | | | | |
|---|---|---|---|---|---|
| Highly desirable | | | | | Not desirable |
| 6 | 5 | 4 | 3 | 2 | 1 |

| Probability | | | | | |
|---|---|---|---|---|---|
| Highly likely | | | | | Not likely |
| 6 | 5 | 4 | 3 | 2 | 1 |

**Figure 3.2** People will continue to support economic expansion even though it may increase the stress on the environment

*Section II: Characteristics*

This section of the survey consisted of twenty characteristics of future citizens identified as necessary by experts participating in the interview round. Policy experts responding to the questionnaire were asked to select the five characteristics that will be most urgent for policy makers to consider and act upon during the next twenty-five years. For example:

Willingness to change one's lifestyle and consumption habits to protect the environment

*Section III: Strategies/Approaches/Innovations*

This section of the survey consisted of twenty-six feasible strategies, approaches or innovations identified by experts participating in the interview round as useful in preparing effective citizenry for the 21st century. Policy experts responding to the questionnaire were asked to indicate which statements they would recommend for consideration and action by policy makers during the next twenty-five years by assessing each in relation to a six-point scale ranging from Highly Recommended to Not Recommended. For example:

| Recommend | | | | | |
|---|---|---|---|---|---|
| Highly recommended | | | Not recommended | | |
| 6 | 5 | 4 | 3 | 2 | 1 |

**Figure 3.3** Promote schools as active centres of community life and as agents for community development

An invitation to comment on statements, to add additional statements, and/or to respond to open-ended questions describing the respondent's rationale for a particular response was also included. The original multinational questionnaire was developed in English and then translated into the native languages spoken by expert panellists (Japanese, Thai, German, Greek, Hungarian, Dutch). Back-translation was then carried out to ensure validity.

## Delphi Round Two: first response to questionnaire

Questionnaires for Round Two were distributed and responded to from August through October 1995. Of the 264 policy experts who were identified and approached, 182 completed and returned questionnaires.[1]

As in other Delphi studies, analysis of initial responses to the research instrument focused on determining the level of consensus reached on each item and on reporting this information back to the respondents in a manner that would be useful to them in reconsidering their initial judgements during later rounds.

### Criteria for analysis of consensus data

For section I, Trends, the mode, median and interquartile range scores were calculated for responses to each item. Items meeting *each* of the following criteria were accepted as having reached consensus:

- the mode minus the median is less than or equal to 1.0, *and*
- the interquartile range score is less than or equal to 1.5.[2]

For section II, Characteristics, items meeting *each* of the following criteria were accepted as having reached consensus:

- the characteristic appears in the top ten list for three of the four research teams, and
- the characteristic is selected in the top five by 25 per cent or more of all respondents.[3]

For section III, Strategies/Approaches/Innovations, the mode, median and inter-quartile range scores were calculated for responses to each item. Items meeting *each* of the following criteria were accepted as having reached consensus:

- the mode minus the median is less than or equal to 1.0, *and*
- the interquartile range score is less than or equal to 1.5.

Additional comments made by the respondents for all items were coded and recorded. Because the questionnaire was designed to solicit a multinational (rather than nation or region specific) response, it was determined that only information describing the aggregate responses of all the policy experts would be reported during the Third and final Round.

## Delphi Round Three: final response to the questionnaire

Questionnaires for Round Three were distributed and responded to by policy experts from January through February 1996. Respondents received questionnaires personalized by research team members to reflect (1) the expert's Round Two response to each item, and (2) the median and interquartile range scores for trend and strategy statements and (3) the percentage of respondents selecting each characteristic as one of their five most important for the characteristics section.

For Sections I and III (Trends and Strategies/Approaches/Innovations), respondents were informed that consensus had not been reached for 43 of the 60 trends and 17 of the 26 strategies. These were circled on the questionnaire. Respondents were informed that although they were encouraged to review and reflect again on their judgements for every item, the researchers were most interested in responses to the circled items where there appeared to be more diversity of opinion.

For Section II (Characteristics), percentages of trait selection were reported along with indication of the expert's initial choices for feedback purposes only. No further response was requested. Experts were again invited to provide comments for all items.

In follow-up communications, respondents were encouraged to return their Round Three responses. They were also informed that should they choose not to return this final Round questionnaire by a specified date, the study would assume that their Round Two responses were to be accepted as final and would include these responses in the analysis of Round Three data. Upon conclusion of Round Three, of the 182 questionnaires distributed, 141 were returned.

## Analysis and interpretation of Delphi results

The fourth and final year of the study was devoted to the analysis, interpretation and preliminary reporting of Round Three results. Early stages of these processes were completed during the Third International Meeting in Hiroshima, Japan, in June 1996. Although a range of secondary analyses focusing on comparative issues was possible, analytic activities at the Hiroshima meeting focused on interpretation of the aggregate data and development of multinational reports.

In preparation for this meeting, consensus items were organized into a prioritization scheme to assist research team members in focusing on the trends, characteristics and the educational strategies/approaches/innovations judged to be most important for shaping educational policy to prepare citizens for the 21st century. Trends reaching consensus with respect to both probability and desirability were grouped into three categories numbered in descending order of importance. The eight characteristics identified by the experts as most urgent for policy makers to consider were then listed, followed by very highly and highly recommended strategies/approaches/innovations.

Responsibilities for developing educational policy recommendations based upon key Delphi findings were then divided into categories reflecting the broad trends identified by participating experts as likely to provide the most significant challenges facing future citizens. These were: Growing Environmental and Resource Concerns, Crisis in Social Ethics, Explosion of Media and Information Technologies, and Changing Political and Demographic Patterns. Research team members were assigned to one of four multinational working groups and asked to develop draft educational policy recommendations relevant to their group's focal trend (see above) to be implemented through: Curriculum, Pedagogy/Instructional Methods/Assessment, School Organization and Administration, Teacher Education and School and Societal Interactions (ie, relationships between local, national and international organizations/communities).

After moving through several iterations of drafting and redrafting potential policy recommendations, researchers were reorganized into writing groups, with each group assigned to synthesize policy recommendations reflecting the organizational framework of the final report. As the Delphi process invites multiple interpretive paths, researchers as members of both multinational and national writing groups still continue to pursue the complex analytic and creative tasks of translating Delphi results into varied forms of educational policy relevant to the preparation of future citizens.


## THE PROMISE AND PERIL OF CROSS-CULTURAL DELPHI RESEARCH

### Challenges and opportunities of methodological innovation

Though intellectually exciting, significant challenges are posed by adopting a research technique that is not widely utilized or well understood in educational policy circles. First, the cultural futures Delphi has both variant and invariant aspects thereby inviting multiple interpretations. Second, it emerges from a distinctive philosophic framework on the basis of which methodological adaptations and innovations must be judged. And third, it provides limited opportunity for guidance or justification based on precedent. Thus, throughout the study, the demands of high levels of uncertainty, ambiguity and risk were met with a healthy sense of scepticism by research team members. In a large research team there were some for whom the Delphi was totally new. Some approached it from a psychometric stance while others were more used to dealing with qualitative data. Along this continuum the researchers worked hard to arrive at a constructive way of proceeding.

For those experienced with ethnographic techniques and skilled in eliciting rich, finely detailed and context-referenced descriptions of informants' conceptual lives, the process of 'reducing' and decontextualizing material derived from interviews into Delphi statements was highly problematic. Similar discomfort was experienced by researchers committed to forms of inferential psychological analysis for whom an expert's response to any particular Delphi statement could only be accurately understood in the context of the respondent's dispositional state and conceptual rationale for each choice.

Other methodological concerns were raised consistently by those grounded in statistically based comparative survey and scaling techniques. Pressures to employ methodological procedures ensuring construction of representative samples and comparison among essentially similar objects of study, as necessary for the appropriate use of inferential statistics, were deeply challenged by Delphic commitments to *purposive sampling*, as in the case of selecting experts on the basis of accepted criteria and then working to diversify and balance panels in relation to variables deemed important by the researchers' gender, ethnicity, area of expertise, etc. Project statisticians were also challenged by the wide range of obstacles to direct comparison inherent within the design of this study, eg, variation in composition of research teams, with Japan and Thailand as teams representing one nation and cultural heritage in sharp contrast to the North American and European teams. Similarly, the cultural/conceptual/linguistic diversity among researchers and expert panels resulted in varied interpretations of such key terms and concepts as 'citizenship' and 'expert'.

In response to these challenges, the researchers were faced with the need continually and collectively to work to articulate, clarify, question, reconsider, revise and newly develop both philosophic foundations and research strategies in order to achieve the study's broad-based goals. Working together, across diverse cultural and methodological experiences, the project researchers found themselves moving into largely uncharted methodological territory, catalysed by intense, engaging reflection and debate, while seeking to deepen and extend their under-standing of educational research and policy design in general, and of the Delphi method in particular.

## Challenges and opportunities of cross-cultural collaboration

Complex challenges are also raised by attempting to adapt a research technique centred on developing consensus, and relying traditionally on expertise emerging from shared conceptual contexts, to accommodate the varied judgements generated across multinational, cross-cultural teams of researchers and panels of experts. Throughout the course of the study, significant thought, time and energy were devoted to attempts to accommodate and constructively utilize the diversity in language, cultural heritage and patterns of social organization represented among researchers and experts. The strongly held objectives were to develop shared conceptual understandings, to reach consensus on significant policy recommenda-tions, and to ensure full, egalitarian participation of all research participants across multiple dimensions of difference.

### Developing shared conceptual understandings

Examples of the challenges posed by the struggle to arrive at shared understandings of key concepts across nine distinct social/political/cultural contexts and seven languages abound (Derricott, 1996; Ninomiya, 1996). Three are presented here, the first centred on the concept of expertise. In spite of agreements reached on criteria for expert selection, attempts at standardization in composing expert panels were challenged by definitions of 'expert' ranging from one who has achieved a high level of specialization in a specific field of study (eg, a nuclear physicist or social historian), to one who holds high-level administrative or political position and power (eg, a minister of foreign affairs or corporate CEO), to one intensely engaged in a particular experiential context (eg, a musician as expert on trends in popular music or a child as expert on the quality of life in contemporary classrooms).

A second example concerns the nature and purpose of citizenship. Philosophical and political discussions concerning its definitive and desirable characteristics were both enlightening and highly problematic in producing Delphi statements that would be relevant within and beyond the participating nations. Contrasting images of the ideal citizen as loyal and disciplined subject willing to sacrifice personal gain to enhance the common good versus the citizen as insightful social critic and active participant in formulating and enacting social policy appeared to correspond to differences between Asian and European/North American political traditions and values. Perhaps the most difficult component of doing cross-cultural research is finding ways to cope and to collaborate across diverse and deeply held values such as these.

The third example describes the struggle for shared meaning within one research team. Euro-team meetings and written communications were conducted in English. Because four of the team members had to use their second, third, or fourth language, considerable time and effort was required to arrive at precise meanings. For example, the phrase 'Non-governmental organization' (NGO) was problematic. Early in their deliberations team members learnt that there appears to be no direct translation into German or Greek. Further consideration revealed that in the United Kingdom, NGOs are appointed and largely controlled by the government, so the concept of a 'non-governmental' organization made little sense.

### Reaching consensus on policy recommendations

The struggles noted above raised interesting dilemmas upon completion of data collection, when processes of interpreting results and developing recommendations were again complicated by cross-cultural, multinational variations in the philosophy and practice of formulating and implementing social policy. Again returning to an example from the Euro-team, early in the process of developing draft policy recommendations it became clear that the five countries embraced very different practices and perspectives on educational policy. In the UK in recent years the power base for educational administration had moved from the periphery to the centre. Under the Educational Reform Act of 1988 the Secretary of State for Education assumed more than 400 new powers. The Netherlands had also developed a National Curriculum, thereby moving the balance of power in the same direction. In Germany the Federal States remained powerful, while in post-Communist Hungary the movement has been toward increasing local and professional autonomy. Variations within the Euro-team were further extended in comparison to the nations represented in the three other research teams, encompassing approaches to educational governance ranging from the highly centralized systems of Japan and Thailand to the distinctively decentralized systems of Canada and the United States.

### Ensuring full participation

The task of encouraging full, egalitarian participation across an unusually large and diverse group of researchers generated its share of challenges. In addition to conventional research skills and dispositions, the need to establish and sustain trust, and to remain sensitive to the concerns of others, became essential to successful completion of all research tasks. Such qualities as patience, persistence, open-mindedness, curiosity and humour were also necessary. Because research meetings were conducted in English, careful scheduling was required to help ease the demands on non-native English speakers. Intensive two to three hours multinational working sessions were interspersed with national/regional team meetings providing opportunities to strategize, converse, relax and commiserate with colleagues sharing more similar linguistic and cultural backgrounds. Attempts were made to diversify and balance all multinational working groups taking into consideration factors including gender, English proficiency, area of interest and expertise, degree of comfort with and style of presenting personal opinions, and preferred approach to dealing with conflicting opinions. Native English speakers in multinational groups assumed responsibilities for writing and recording, and continually reminded each other to be careful not to rush or dominate discussions. Perhaps most importantly, the structure of the study allowing for face-to-face interaction, over a three and one half year period, was crucial in building trusting working relationships and significant skills in cross-cultural collaboration.

## Addressing concerns for methodological credibility

All research methods, but particularly those that are exploratory, must undergo careful scrutiny to assess their credibility. For all of the reasons cited throughout this chapter, and more importantly due to the social significance of the project's goals, ensuring the reliability and validity of findings generated through this unprecedented attempt at cross-cultural Delphi research was an on-going concern.

In a well-known analysis of the conventional Delphi technique, Hill and Fowles (1975) note that reliability is usually defined in terms of the precision of measurement instruments, often demonstrated by the dependability of measurement across different replications, and usually addressed through standardization of research procedures. Although complete standardization across the complex data gathering and interpretive procedures employed here is neither necessary nor possible, the need to develop data collection and analytic techniques that could be comparable across diverse linguistic/cultural/political contexts was keenly felt. A primary rationale for actively engaging such a large, diverse and potentially unwieldy group of researchers in the design and implementation of all aspects of the research was the need to develop Delphi statements capable of soliciting comparable judgements concerning issues of shared significance across the participating nations. Intensive efforts to conscientiously translate and backtranslate questionnaires and responses between English and the native languages of respondents were also employed for the purpose of achieving this goal. Rather than relying only on the large and diverse research team to generate the Delphi questionnaire, interviews were conducted with an extensive sample of expert panellists to ensure added breadth and depth of consideration. Further, although it would have been possible in analysing Delphi results to defend the acceptance of less stringent consensus rules in light of the complexities introduced in accommodating linguistically and culturally diverse expert panels, the research team consistently chose to use the most conservative indices employed in prior studies.

Hill and Fowles (1975) further address two types of validity in their critique of the Delphi. They suggest that the first type, *data validity*, demonstrated by the accuracy of future projections, raises limited concern in relation to studies of this type because with respect to planning and policy-making, forecast utility is of greater importance than forecast accuracy. The second type, *method validity*, defined as whether the design of the method makes it possible to produce the results intended, is, however, of crucial importance here. Has participation in this Delphi process supported the generation of insights that will assist us in envisioning and enacting positive social change through education? Will the results of this study enhance our understanding, expose us to new perceptions and possibilities, expand our options, and deepen our resolve to work collaboratively and cross-culturally to prepare citizens to meet the challenges of the coming century? The chapters that follow provide evidence to answer these questions and to judge the methodological validity of this project.

## IMPLICATIONS FOR THE FUTURE OF CROSS-CULTURAL DELPHI RESEARCH

In addition to providing a basis for assessing the validity and reliability of the Delphi as a tool for cross-cultural research and policy development, this study demonstrates:

- the feasibility of using a cross-cultural variation of the Delphi to enhance understanding and imagination concerning the complex topic of citizenship education
- the value of exploring specific domains of agreement and disagreement to sharpen perspectives on the status and prospects for citizenship at the dawn of the next century
- the possibility of generating significant understandings, prioritizations and projections that transcend nations, cultures and policy systems
- the opportunities and challenges posed by engaging a large, multinational team of researchers in a complex and collaborative effort
- the complexities of establishing consensus, and the generative tensions revealed in measurement and interpretation debates
- the possibility of soliciting and synthesizing the collective judgement of a prestigious panel of experts representing diverse nations and areas of specialization, and
- the possibility of affecting social and educational policy by engaging policy shapers in the Delphi process, thereby providing them with opportunities to consider a wide range of reflective and imaginative perspectives, and to develop a broader and deeper understanding of the problem under consideration and possible solution paths.

This study neither exhausts the Delphi method's exciting potentials, nor overcomes its persistent limitations. Similarly, the project represents both the promise of engaging multinational research teams and participants, and the many areas of difficulty imposed by such an endeavour. Apart from all considerations of the validity of the methodology, the quality of analyses and interpretations, or the utility of the findings and recommendations, this is the story of a complex accomplishment. A justifiable consensus is expressed by a distinguished international panel. A rigorous and innovative research design is executed with prodigious effort by an international research team. And a defensible body of challenging ideas and interpretations is generated to provide a basis for the development of educational policy.

## ENDNOTES

1. Based upon his research, Thomas Macmillan (1971) noted that a panel size of at least 17 is necessary to ensure the lowest rate of error in Delphi studies, thus requiring at least 68 experts distributed across the four panels used in this study, a number well exceeded by the total number of 182 expert respondents. Further, it is the question of the quality of the panel experts that is most important in the Delphi, ie, that each of them met the selection criteria.
2. Following Dalkey and Helmer's (1963) and then Helmer's (1966) lead, Delphi studies have traditionally used two indices to determine consensus and to report

findings back to Delphi panellists: the median and interquartile range. The median is used instead of the mean as a measure of central tendency because expert panels are not comprised of a random sample. Interquartile range is used to provide a sense of each statement's degree of clarity, ie, statements for which the interquartile range falls beyond a prescribed range are considered ambiguous and therefore not indicative of consensus. The smaller the acceptable interquartile range, the more likely it is that the results reflect authentic consensus of expert judgement.

3. The concept of consensus is a complex one. Although an item may have reached consensus in reference to the aggregate data determined in the manner described here, it may not have reached consensus among experts responding from a particular nation or region. Because experts were selected based in part on their ability to think globally from within their particular cultural context (to balance culturally specific and global perspectives), it was determined that formulation of multinational policy recommendations would focus on items reflecting aggregate consensus, whether or not consensus is also achieved on a team by team basis.

## REFERENCES

Cogan, J J (1994) Notes from February CEPS Steering Committee Meeting, Bangkok, Thailand.

Cookson, P (1986) 'Charting the Unknown: Delphi and Policy Delphi Strategies for International Cooperation', *International Journal of Lifelong Education*, **5**, pp 3–13.

Derricott, R (1996) 'The Citizenship Education Policy Study: A European Perspective on Methodological Issues in Conducting Cross-Cultural Research', Paper presented at the Annual Western Regional Conference of the Comparative and International Education Society, University of Hawaii, January 3–5.

Helmer, O (1966) *The Delphi Method for Systematizing Judgments about the Future*, Institute of Government and Public Affairs, UCLA.

Hill, K Q and Fowles, J (1975) 'The Methodological Worth of the Delphi Forecasting Technique', *Technological Forecasting and Social Change*, **7**, pp 179–92.

Kurth-Schai, R (1984) *Reflections from the Hearts and Minds of Children*, doctoral thesis, University of Minnesota, Minneapolis.

Kurth-Schai, R (1988) 'Collecting the thoughts of children', *Journal of Research and Development in Education*, **21**, pp 53–9.

Kurth-Schai, R (1991) 'Educational Systems Design by Children for Children', *Educational Foundations*, **5**, pp 19–39.

Linstone, H and Simmons, W H C (eds) (1977) *Futures Research: New directions*, Addison-Wesley, Reading, MA.

Linstone, H and Turoff, M (eds) (1975) *The Delphi Method: Techniques and applications*, Addison-Wesley, Reading, MA.

Macmillan, Thomas T (1971) 'The Delphi Technique', paper presented at the annual meeting of the California Junior Colleges Association Commission on Research and Development (3 May 1971), Monterey, California.

Martorella, P (1991) 'Consensus Building among Social Educators: A Delphi Study', *Theory and Research in Social Education*, **19**, pp 83–94.

Ninomiya, A (1996) 'A Methodological Reflection and Comparative Education from a Japanese Perspective', Paper presented at the Annual Western Regional Conference of the Comparative and International Education Society, University of Hawaii, January 3–5.

Palkert, L (1986) 'A Delphic Perspective on the Reactions of Teachers to Prospective Future Occurrences', doctoral thesis, University of Minnesota.

Poolpatarachewin, C (1980) 'Ethnographic Delphi Futures Research: Thai University Pilot Project' *Journal of Cultural and Educational Futures*, **2**, pp 11–19.

Scheele, S (1975) 'Reality Construction as a Product of Delphi Interaction', in H A Linstone and M Turoff (eds), *The Delphi Method: Techniques and applications*, Addison-Wesley, Reading, MA.

Weaver, T (1971) 'The Delphi Forecasting Method', *Phi Delta Kappan*, **52**, pp 267–71.

Weingand, D (1980) 'A Delphic Perspective on Lifelong Learning in Minnesota: Focus on the Public Library as Provider', doctoral thesis, University of Minnesota.

4

# CHALLENGES FACING THE 21ST CENTURY CITIZEN: VIEWS OF POLICY MAKERS

*Sjoerd Karsten, Patricia Kubow, Zsuzsa Matrai and Somwung Pitiyanuwat*

This chapter describes the points on which the experts reached consensus, and those that were not, in their response to the Delphi survey instrument over the course of its iterations. In both cases, the data are divided into the three categories described in the previous chapter, ie, trends, characteristics and educational strategies.

In the first section, the initial discussion is about the convergence of group opinion regarding the probability of certain future global trends occurring and their desirability. Thus, we can envision how the future will look if policy remains unchanged, according to the expert panellists consulted, as well as in what direction future policy should develop. Next, the panel's opinions regarding the desirable characteristics of future citizens are examined and rated for their importance by the panellists, and finally, educational strategies which the panellists have recommended to implement these characteristics are explored. Given the unique composition of the panel of experts, opinions are not only analysed at the whole group (multinational) level, but differences of opinion between East (Thailand and Japan) and West (North America and Europe) are also examined.

## CONSENSUS OPINIONS

The cross-cultural Delphi methodology was utilized in this study to ascertain if a certain measure of consensus amongst the panellists in the three areas could be reached as a precursor to policy development. This process was outlined in the previous chapter. The panellists received two iterations of the survey, the second being revised to reflect both their own individual ratings as well as the aggregate ratings of their anonymous peers across the nine nations. They were then encouraged to reconsider their previous responses based upon this aggregate feedback.

## GLOBAL TRENDS

The 19 global trends on which the 182 expert respondents reached consensus have been grouped into three categories: 'increasingly significant challenges', 'areas to monitor', and 'areas to encourage'. Each category indicates the particular level of consideration and attention required on the part of policy makers, as well as of citizens, to ensure that educational policies are developed to encourage desirable trends and counter the negative direction of undesirable ones.

### Increasingly significant challenges

The first category, termed 'increasingly significant challenges', is composed of seven trends identified by the experts as undesirable but highly probable. These trends should be given the highest priority and require the greatest attention by policy makers during the next twenty-five years:

- The economic gap among countries and between people within countries will widen significantly.
- Information technologies will dramatically reduce the privacy of individuals.
- The inequalities between those who have access to information technologies and those who do not will increase dramatically.
- Conflict of interest between developing and developed nations will increase due to environmental deterioration.
- The cost of obtaining adequate water will rise dramatically due to population growth and environmental deterioration.
- Deforestation will dramatically affect diversity of life, air, soil and water quality.
- In developing countries population growth will result in a dramatic increase in the percentage of people, especially children, living in poverty.

A dominant theme arising from these seven trends is that of increased inequalities, as seen in the likelihood of a widening economic gap, unequal access to informational technologies, environmental resource depletion and an increased number of people in developing nations, especially children, living in poverty. Inequality, as depicted in these trends, is not limited to one sphere of influence impacting on citizens' lives but operates in a variety of contexts which are not mutually exclusive but rather interrelated.

### Areas to monitor

The second category, termed 'areas to monitor', is composed of seven trends identified by the experts as either undesirable but only moderately probable, or very probable but only moderately desirable. These trends listed below, along with those just described above, must be priorities for policy makers during the next twenty-five years.

*Undesirable but only moderately probable:*

- Individuals, families and communities will lose political influence due to the increased level of regulation and control by governments.
- It will be increasingly difficult to develop a shared belief of the common good.
- Drug-related crime will increasingly dominate social life in urban areas.
- People's sense of community and social responsibility will decline significantly.
- Consumerism will increasingly dominate social life.

*Highly probable but only moderately desirable:*

- Migration flows from poor to rich areas, both within countries and between countries, will have a major impact on the internal and external order of nations.
- The increased use of genetic engineering will create more complex ethical questions.

These seven trends are also negative in direction and are most directly related to some of the most important areas of citizens' daily lives, ie, values and ethical behaviour and political and economic choices. They also represent critical issues which cut across national borders. If these trends are not carefully monitored, the data suggest that increases in drug-related urban crime, consumerism, and regulation and control by governments will be accompanied by declines in citizens' political influence, social responsibility, community bonds and ability to develop a shared belief of the common good. The data raise the prospect of a declining sense of efficacy among citizens and this, once lost, is very difficult to restore. Moreover, migration patterns are highly likely to have an impact, internally and externally, on the stability of nations, while the increased use of genetic engineering will raise ethical questions for citizens living in the 21st century.

The dominant theme that emerges from these trends is an increasing citizen disempowerment, as evidenced by a lack of unity and community among people and an inability on the part of citizens to change the forces (governmental, social and economic) that affect their lives. To safeguard personal autonomy, assuming that this is an important value, and to increase citizen participation and involvement in public affairs, these trends must be monitored carefully and attended to by policy makers. Education must be a key part of any attempt to address these trends but significant involvement of the community and government agencies will also be required.

## Areas to encourage

The third category, termed 'areas to encourage', is composed of five trends identified by the experts as highly or very highly desirable and highly to moderately probable. These trends provide some grounds for optimism and should be nurtured and developed by policy makers.

*Highly desirable and highly probable:*

- Economic growth will be fuelled by knowledge (ideas, innovations and inventions) more than by natural resources.

*Very highly desirable but only moderately probable:*

- Corporations will increasingly adopt measures of environmental conservation in order to remain competitive.
- Systematic inequalities (eg, racism, ethnocentrism, sexism) will decrease significantly.

*Highly desirable and moderately probable:*

- Previously marginalized groups of individuals (eg, women, ethnic minorities) will occupy more positions of power.
- More regional alliances will be developed as a way of achieving peace and security.

The trend identified as both highly desirable and probable by the experts, that knowledge and ideas as opposed to natural resources will generate economic growth, is an encouraging trend in the economic sphere. This, coupled with the moderate probability that corporations will increasingly adopt environmentally conscious measures to remain competitive, may be potentially helpful in protecting the environment and in addressing some increasingly significant challenges, such as deforestation and increasing costs of obtaining adequate water.

In the social sphere, the experts concur that it is desirable for societies to strive towards greater equality with more positions of power being occupied by individuals who have previously been denied access to positions of leadership and promotion, such as women, ethnic minorities and other marginalized groups. In the governmental or political sphere, the experts highly desire a future characterized by peace and security and view the development of regional alliances as a possible approach to realizing this goal.

Peace and security, equity and fairness, and environmental conservation are the themes emerging from these trends that are identified by the panellists as areas to encourage. These themes may serve as indicators by which policy makers can measure the degree to which citizens are experiencing an acceptable quality of life during the next twenty-five years.

## EAST–WEST DIFFERENCES 1

A number of interesting differences can be found between the views of the experts from the East and West, ie, Japan and Thailand, and Europe and North America. First, judgements differed considerably as to the desirability of some of the trends. Only the statement, 'the majority of the world population will achieve basic literacy' was seen as very desirable by both the Eastern and Western panellists. Western experts regarded trends in the area of the environment and technological innovation especially as very desirable, while those from the East consider it very important that governments become more effective in preventing wars.

Second, there is only one trend which both groups identify as very probable, ie, 'the growth of the communications industry will increase the influence of the English language in the daily lives of the world's people'. The Western experts designated only one other trend as very probable, ie, 'the ageing of the populations in developed countries will dramatically increase the stress on social services, especially health care and pensions'. Eastern experts, in contrast, judged a large number of trends as very probable.

Third, when comparing the opinions of the East and West panellists, the division into three categories ('increasingly significant challenges', 'areas to monitor' and 'areas to encourage') loses its force. The opinions of the Eastern experts still fit into all three categories, but those of their Western counterparts do not as there is little consensus among Western experts.

## CITIZEN CHARACTERISTICS

The panellists reached consensus on eight characteristics which constitute the traits, skills and specific competencies with which citizens living in the 21st century will need to cope and to manage the undesirable trends and cultivate and nurture the desirable ones. The eight characteristics identified by the panellists are presented below in descending order of importance, and include:

- the ability to look at and approach problems as a member of a global society
- the ability to work with others in a cooperative way and to take responsibility for one's roles/duties within society
- the ability to understand, accept, appreciate and tolerate cultural differences
- the capacity to think in a critical and systemic way
- the willingness to resolve conflict in a non-violent manner
- the willingness to change one's lifestyle and consumption habits to protect the environment
- the ability to be sensitive towards and to defend human rights (eg, rights of women, ethnic minorities)
- the willingness and ability to participate in politics at local, national and international levels.

These characteristics of 21st century citizens can best be understood in terms of participatory competencies. This means that people living during the next twenty-five years will need to be actively engaged, both personally and socially, in their local, regional, national and global environments. The data suggest that the way citizens can fully participate in and contribute to their environments is by possessing abilities to think critically and systemically, to understand cultural differences, and to approach problems or challenges as members of a global society.

However, the findings suggest that merely having the abilities to think, problem-solve and understand cultural diversity are inadequate by themselves. Citizens must also be inclined, willing and able to cooperate with others and take responsibility for their roles and duties within society, to resolve conflict in non-violent ways, to be sensitive towards and to defend human rights, to change their lifestyles and consumption habits to protect the environment, and to participate in politics at local, national and international levels.

When seen in the context of the emerging global trends, the development of these eight characteristics or participatory competencies requires urgent attention and action by policy makers during the early part of the 21st century.

## EAST–WEST DIFFERENCES 2

The differences of opinion between the Eastern and Western experts on what characteristics will be important for citizens of the future will be discussed in more detail later in this chapter. Here we merely list the five most selected characteristics in order of importance for both the East and West. There was agreement in both East and West regarding four of the five most important characteristics:

- ability to look at and approach problems as a member of a global society
- ability to understand, accept and tolerate cultural differences
- ability to work with others in a cooperative way and to take responsibility for one's roles/duties within society
- willingness to resolve conflict in a non-violent manner.

We believe it is noteworthy that four of the five characteristics appear on both lists. The experts differ on the 'willingness to change one's lifestyle and consumption habits to protect the environment' (East) and the 'capacity to think in a critical and systemic way' (West).

## EDUCATIONAL STRATEGIES

There was consensus among the expert respondents that sixteen strategies, approaches or innovations should be very highly or highly recommended for urgent consideration and action by policy makers during the next twenty-five years (see Table 4.1).

With respect to the fourteen educational strategies highly recommended for consideration, these can be divided into four major areas of reform:

- making an international component an integral part of teaching and learning
- embracing a community-oriented concept within educational institutions
- creating education–social institutional collaborations
- requiring that other spheres of influence (those existing outside educational systems) recognize and share in the responsibility of citizen development.

First, these data on strategies suggest that an international component be made an integral part of formal education. To illustrate, the experts agree that extensive international linkages between educational institutions at all levels should be established to support a more multidimensional perspective on citizenship. In addition to creating international networks, the panellists highly recommend that a teaching population with international experience and cross-cultural sensitivity be cultivated, as well as international student exchange programmes to promote mutual understandings among different cultures. The experts also highly recommend that increased curricular attention be given to both global issues and international studies and that a curriculum which uses the potential of information-based technologies be established.

**Table 4.1** Consensus strategies

| Very highly recommended | Highly recommended |
|---|---|
| • Support the teaching of subject matter in a manner that encourages children to think critically.<br>• Emphasize students' ability to critically assess information in an increasingly media-based society. | • Establish a curriculum which uses the potential of information-based technologies.<br>• Establish extensive international links among educational institutions at all levels to support international studies, and research and curriculum development focusing on citizenship education.<br>• Cultivate a teaching population with international experience and cross-cultural sensitivity.<br>• Implement programmes of international student exchange in order to promote mutual understandings among different cultures.<br>• Increase attention to global issues and international studies in the curriculum.<br>• Establish extensive liaisons and joint projects among schools and other social institutions (eg, industry, NGOs, churches, community groups) to support education.<br>• Require that opportunities for community action and involvement be an important feature of the school curriculum.<br>• Promote schools as active centres of community life and as agents for community development.<br>• Decentralize decision-making so that local communities and individual schools have considerable control of curriculum and educational administration.<br>• Increase opportunities for students to be involved in cooperative learning activities.<br>• Require that the mass media act in a socially responsible, educative manner.<br>• Implement programmes that effectively use the talents and skills of an ageing population.<br>• Demand that all major social institutions and their officials set high standards of civic responsibility.<br>• Ensure that all social institutions (including the family, and educational and religious institutions) have an abiding respect for the basic rights of children and contribute to their well-being. |

These strategies serve as specific ways to foster the development of the desirable citizen characteristics identified in the previous section, eg, the ability of individuals to understand, accept and tolerate cultural differences; to see the interconnectedness of global issues; and to foster a willingness to approach problems as members of a global community. Using the potential of information-based technologies within schools may help facilitate the study of global issues and international events, while also fostering students' critical assessment of the information obtained.

Second, the strategies' findings suggest that schools embrace a community-oriented concept that emphasizes action and involvement, as is demonstrated by the consensus reached by the experts that opportunities for community action and involvement become an important feature of the school curriculum. However, the experts do not view a community-oriented concept as limited to the school curriculum. Rather, they highly recommend that schools serve as active centres of community life and as agents for community development. A possible first step in instituting a community-oriented concept may be to involve students in cooperative learning activities, another strategy highly recommended by the experts and also a characteristic viewed as urgent for policy makers to cultivate during the next twenty-five years.

While the first two areas of reform, ie, making an international component an integral part of teaching and learning and embracing a community-oriented concept of action and involvement, focus on strategies geared towards schools themselves, the third and fourth areas require the support of social institutions outside the schools. The data suggest that if the negative global trends are to be reversed and the desirable citizen competencies developed, then collaborations between education and other social institutions are necessary. Thus, education and social institutional collaborations constitute the third area of reform emerging from the strategies' findings. To illustrate, the experts agree that extensive liaisons and joint projects among schools and other social institutions (eg, industry, NGOs, churches, community groups) be established to support education. The respondents also highly recommend decentralizing decision-making so that local communities and individual schools have considerable control of curriculum and educational administration. A need to draw upon the human resources available within communities can also be inferred from the findings, for the experts favour the implementation of programmes that effectively use the talents and skills of an ageing population.

The fourth area of reform concerns the involvement of other agencies and institutions outside the education system in the development of policies and practices that are intended to foster the desired citizen characteristics noted earlier in this chapter. Specifically, the experts reached consensus that the mass media be required to act in a socially responsible, educative manner and that all major social institutions and their officials set high standards of civic responsibility.

Finally, the experts highly recommend that all social institutions, including the family, and educational and religious institutions, respect the basic rights of children and contribute to their well-being. The data strongly suggest that educating the 21st century citizen is everyone's responsibility. Therefore, it is recommended that all social institutions and spheres of influence, including mass media, recognize and share this responsibility in contributing to citizens' well-being.

## EAST–WEST DIFFERENCES 3

When the views of Eastern and Western experts on the educational strategies necessary to develop the citizen characteristics are compared, a kind of mirror image emerges. The experts from the East reached consensus on no less than twenty-five out of twenty-six strategies, whereas panellists from the West agreed on only four. The strategy which Western experts recommended most highly was to:

- support the teaching of subject matter in a way that encourages children to think critically.

## NON-CONSENSUS OPINIONS

The second section of this chapter is intended to bring some contrast into the consensus by examining those points on which consensus was not reached by our panellists. This section also follows the division into trends, characteristics and educational strategies. The data are also analysed at whole group (multinational) level and for differences between East and West.

Although reaching a certain measure of consensus was a goal of this study, this does not mean that the items on which there was no consensus become irrelevant. It is important that policy makers and others are informed about differences of opinion, as well as where consensus was achieved. In this context, Turoff (1970) pointed out the danger of paying insufficient attention to the diversity of viewpoints within a group of experts, as this can lead to an artificial consensus which does not reflect the real proportions of different viewpoints. Accordingly, we shall now look more closely at those items on which consensus was not reached.

### Non-consensus criteria

As in the case of items that achieved consensus among our panellists, we also developed statistical criteria for those items which did not reach consensus:

- $|Q2 - MO| > 1.00$, or
- $|Q3 - Q1| > 1.50$.

Just as with the items on which consensus was reached, each category (trends, characteristics and strategies) will first be examined for the opinions of the whole group of 182 experts (multinational level) and then for differences between East and West.

### GLOBAL TRENDS

While the nineteen consensus trends examined earlier were done so with the consideration of both desirability and probability together, in looking at the non-consensus items, the picture becomes clearer if we examine the two aspects of evaluation separately. The distribution of the non-consensus trends can be grouped as follows:

- non-consensus trends from the aspect of desirability only (16)
- non-consensus trends from the aspect of probability only (21)
- non-consensus trends from the aspect of desirability and probability together (2).

The non-consensus trends will now be examined within these groups. Based on the rate of lack of consensus they will first be separated into three possible categories: (1) 'very far from consensus', (2) 'far from consensus' and (3) 'near consensus'. We shall then examine the data in terms of explanations for the differences between the experts' opinions.

## Non-consensus trends from the aspect of desirability only

The interquartile range scores were used to calculate the size of lack of consensus and three categories were formed accordingly: 'very far from consensus', 'far from consensus' and 'close to consensus' (see Table 4.2).

The evaluation of the desirability of a trend is primarily value dependent and is thus strongly determined by the value system of the individual panellist. Some of the non-consensus trends, mostly those belonging to the first two categories, seem to cover topics that differentiate the ratings of the experts to a greater degree. This latter viewpoint is supported by the fact that each of the three trends in the first category (very far from consensus) can be associated with topics focusing upon social rights that are rather provocative (eg, privatization of social services, capitalism as a global system, political importance of social services).

In the second category ('far from consensus') we can also find at least two topic groups that trigger value judgements. The first is globalization versus cultural diversification with which the first six trends are associated (standardization, English as a common language, cultural diversification, national identity–decentralization of power, transnational companies – nation-states, racial/ethnic mixed marriages). The second is economic development versus environmentalism, which is associated with three out of the five remaining trends.

The fact that most of the non-consensus trends are associated with value-differentiating topics (social rights, globalization versus cultural diversification, economic development versus environmentalism) is the major reason for the opinions being far from consensus. This is also confirmed by the comments of the experts regarding these trends. Several of the experts explained, specified or gave some condition to their judgements, and sometimes even rewrote items or provided additions to them in accordance with their own value systems.

## Non-consensus trends from the aspect of probability only

Considering the interquartile range scores, only two categories of non-consensus trends can be identified: (1) 'far from consensus' and (2) 'near consensus'. The distribution of the trends in these two categories is as follows (see Table 4.3).

**Table 4.2** Non-consensus trends from the aspect of desirability

| Very far from consensus (>1.99) | Far from consensus (>1.59 but <1.99) | Close to consensus (<1.59 but >1.5) |
|---|---|---|
| • Privatization of public social systems (eg, health care, education, social services) will decrease dramatically. | • The globalization of markets will lead to more standardization in terms of economic, social, political and cultural relations among societies. | • The United States' sphere of influence will decline while that of Asian nations increases. |
| • Capitalism will become the dominant political and economic system. | • The growth of the global communications industry will increase the influence of the English language in the daily lives of the world's people. | • Control and regulation of formal educational systems will become increasingly decentralized. |
| • The ageing of the populations in developed countries will dramatically increase the stress on social services, especially health care and pensions. | • Cultural diversity will increasingly become a focal point for world and national politics. | |
| | • Regional and ethnic identities will increase dramatically, thereby encouraging decentralization of authority around the world. | |
| | • In an increasingly borderless world, powerful transnational corporations will play a larger role and take over functions of nation-states. | |
| | • The level of tension between economic development and competition for finite resources, on the one hand, and ethical and environmental responsibilities on the other, will increase dramatically. | |
| | • The influence of mass media on human behaviour will increase dramatically. | |
| | • People will continue to support economic expansion even though it may increase the stress on the environment. | |
| | • The ageing of the populations in developed countries will change the conditions and length of employment. | |
| | • The development of nuclear power will increase as an important energy source, in spite of its ecological risk. | |

**Table 4.3** Non-consensus trends from the aspect of probability

| Far from consensus (>1.59 but <1.99) | Close to consensus (<1.59 but >1.5) |
|---|---|
| • Societies will become increasingly authoritarian. | • Information technology will promote communication and improve understanding across cultures and nations. |
| • The expansion of unregulated global markets will lower the living standards of the majority of people. | • New types of infections and epidemics such as HIV-AIDS will endanger the health of large parts of the world's population. |
| • People will participate less and less in political life due to increasing cynicism. | • Technological innovations will result in more opportunities for marginalized groups and individuals in the workforce. |
| • The labour market will be increasingly divided into a small number of high-skilled jobs, and a large number of unskilled, temporary jobs. | • There will be a rapid increase in the number and kinds of jobs that do not now exist. |
| • Investment in education will become the primary strategy for national development. | • People will increasingly recognize a common dependency and interest in maintaining the biosphere. |
| • Inter-group (eg, ethnic, regional and religious) conflict will increase dramatically within and among nations. | • People will increasingly think of themselves as both national and world citizens. |
| • The majority of the world's population will achieve basic literacy. | • There will be an increased emphasis on life-long education. |
| | • Tensions between competing concepts of human rights will eventually result in a new consensus. |
| | • The number of refugees worldwide will grow considerably due to increasing ethnic conflict and social disorder. |
| | • People's confidence in their ability to control their futures will be reduced significantly. |
| | • The influence of extremism (eg, regimes, sects, movements) will increase. |
| | • General uncertainty about employment will substantially increase personal anxiety. |
| | • The general public will become more effective in preventing their governments from using war as a means of solving conflict. |
| | • Technological innovations will significantly slow environmental deterioration. |

If we compare the opinion-differentiating power of the two evaluation aspects – desirability and probability – the first thing which stands out is that although there are more non-consensus trends in the evaluation of probability, the overwhelming majority of these are 'near' rather than 'far from consensus'. This shows that when predicting the occurrence of the trends the opinions of the experts were closer to each other than when judging their desirability. However, there were seven trends in this group that were far from consensus (first category). If we look at the reasons for this, we must first see that the scope of prediction of the non-consensus trends is not specified in the questionnaire and thus has to be understood globally and not limited to certain regions. From this it follows that when predicting the occurrence of 'far from consensus' trends the major opinion differences are rooted in the fact that most of the experts took into consideration regional differences as well as their own prognoses. If we again consider the comments of the experts involved in the analysis, it can be seen that this assumption is correct because in their comments we see that the barriers hindering the occurrence of a trend and/or reflections to the regional differentiation are present.

## Non-consensus trends from the aspect of desirability and probability

In this group of trends there is a clear difference between the opinions of the experts and there is no consensus even when we examine the two aspects separately. There are only two trends in this group:

● There will be an increasing movement away from religious institutions.
● The pressure on rich countries to integrate refugees as citizens will increase.

The evaluation of the first trend belongs to the 'far from consensus' category (>1.59 but <1.99) from both aspects while the other one belongs to this category only as regards desirability, and to the category 'near consensus' (<1.59 but >1.5) with respect to probability. Although the extent of disagreement here is not great, it is striking that the evaluation of the desirability of both trends concerns topics that have strong value-differentiating characteristics (religion, citizenship) and also that regional differentiation might play a major role in judging the probability of these trends.

## EAST–WEST DIFFERENCES 4

Looking at the differences between East and West, it is immediately noticeable that the experts from Thailand and Japan disagree on considerably fewer items following the third and final round than the experts from North America and Europe. Moreover, the spread of opinions on items over which there is no unanimous group view is generally smaller in the East than in the West. This may be an indication of a cultural difference between the East and the West. Perhaps the desire to achieve consensus is more firmly anchored in national culture in the East than in the West. The experts from the East disagreed on the probability of only two trends:

- Societies will become increasingly authoritarian.
- People will participate less and less in political life due to increasing cynicism and alienation from governments.

In addition, they failed to agree on the desirability of four trends:

- The globalization of markets will lead to more standardization in terms of economic, social, political, and cultural relations among societies.
- The pressure on rich countries to integrate refugees as citizens will increase.
- The influence of mass media on human behaviour will increase dramatically.
- The ageing of populations in developed countries will increase dramatically the stress on social services, especially health care and pensions.

In all six cases on which the participants from Asia disagreed, the North American and European experts also disagreed, and in most cases more strongly.

Given the fact that 120 responses were required for the trends category (60 with respect to desirability and 60 for probability) and the experts from Asia disagreed only 6 times in total, this is an indication of a large measure of consensus in the East. One would have to go a long way to find such unanimity among the experts from the West as they disagreed among themselves on 74 of the 120 required responses. In the majority of cases (34) they disagreed only on the probability of a trend; in 4 cases only on the desirability, and with respect to both probability and desirability in 18 instances. Thus, the greatest disagreement was on probability (52 times) and there was less disagreement on desirability (22 times). This suggests that the Western experts did not differ so much as far as their normative frame of reference was concerned (desirability of trends), but that they are much less certain and more ambivalent about the probability of future developments. This may suggest that people in the West are less quick to accept the 'natural course of events'.

The trends which caused the most disagreement among Western experts, that is those on which there was no agreement on either probability or desirability, were the eighteen items shown in Table 4.4.

Although these include a broad range of issues, varying from economic to cultural questions, it is noticeable that many of these questions have been big issues in the Western media in recent years; for instance, globalization, ethnic identities and cultural diversity, integration of refugees, the role of the mass media, growth versus the environment and the use of genetic engineering.

If we look at the three statements which show the greatest spread among Western experts, that is the least consensus, they are, in order of degree of dissent:

- the desirability of 'Capitalism becoming the dominant political and economic system'
- the desirability of 'Privatization of public social systems (eg, health care, education, social services) increasing dramatically'
- the desirability of 'The ageing of populations in developed countries dramatically increasing the stress on social services, especially health care and pensions'.

The nature of the issues at stake shows that there is still a sharp dividing line between political groups on the desirability of capitalism and collective services.

**Table 4.4** Non-consensus trends among Western panellists

Non-consensus trends – West

- The globalization of markets will lead to more standardization in terms of economic, social, political and cultural relations among societies.
- The level of tension between economic development and competition for finite resources, on the one hand, and ethical and environmental responsibilities on the other, will increase dramatically.
- In an increasingly borderless world, powerful transnational corporations will play a larger role and take over functions of nation-states.
- Regional and ethnic identities will increase dramatically, thereby encouraging decentralization of authority around the world.
- Previously marginalized groups or individuals (eg, women, ethnic minorities) will occupy more positions of power.
- The pressure on rich countries to integrate refugees as citizens will increase.
- More regional alliances will be developed as a way of achieving peace and security.
- The influence of mass media on human behaviour will increase dramatically.
- People will continue to support economic expansion even though it may increase the stress on the environment.

- The development of nuclear power will increase as an important energy source, in spite of its ecological risks.
- The ageing of the populations in developed countries will change the conditions and length of employment.
- Increasing intermarriage of people of different racial and ethnic backgrounds will result in the blurring of cultural identities.
- The increased use of genetic engineering will create more complex ethical questions.
- Cultural diversity will increasingly become a focal point for world and national politics.
- There will be an increasing movement away from religious institutions.
- The traditional two-parent family structure will be much less common.
- The family will increasingly rely on other institutions for the care and education of children.
- Control and regulation of formal educational systems will become increasingly decentralized.

## CHARACTERISTICS

Twelve of the twenty characteristics statements in the questionnaire can be put into the non-consensus characteristics group since they were chosen by less than 25 per cent of the experts on their top ten list. Because of the differences of occurrence in percentage terms, it seems reasonable to place them in the same three non-consensus categories that were used in discussing the trends in the previous section (see Table 4.5).

**Table 4.5** Non-consensus characteristics

| Very far from consensus (less than 5 per cent occurrence) | Far from consensus (more than 5 per cent but less than 19 per cent occurrence) | Near consensus (more than 19 per cent but less than 25 per cent occurrence) |
| --- | --- | --- |
| • Loyalty to one's nation | • Ability to accept a moral code and to live by it<br>• Ability to take risks and to have a pioneering spirit<br>• Willingness to make difficult decisions for the good of the community<br>• Values spiritual development | • Competency in at least more than one language<br>• Flexibility in adapting to changing demands of jobs<br>• Ability to use traditional and evolving (electronic) technologies of communication<br>• Ability to actively adapt to rapid, unpredictable change<br>• Possessing sufficient problem-solving knowledge that can be implemented in everyday life<br>• Ability to create and sustain meaningful personal relationships<br>• Be broadly and liberally educated, possessing knowledge of history, social and natural sciences |

We suggest that these data, as regards one-sided national commitment and characteristics with moral or spiritual connotations – the rating of which is strongly value-dependent – show there was no consensus among the experts. However, those characteristics which can be associated with cultural literacy, socialization and communicative skills, and are thus less value-differentiating from the aspect of being generally necessary, are found closer to consensus.

## EAST–WEST DIFFERENCES 5

We also differentiated between the group opinions of the experts in Japan and Thailand (East) and those in North America and Europe (West) on the characteristics which future citizens ought to have. Comparing the group opinions, there are six characteristics on which both groups of experts agree. They are:

- ability to look at and approach problems as a member of a global society
- capacity to think in a critical and systemic way
- ability to work with others in a cooperative way and to take responsibility for one's roles/duties within society
- ability to understand, accept and tolerate cultural differences
- ability to be sensitive towards and to defend human rights (eg rights of women, ethnic minorities)
- willingness to resolve conflict in a non-violent manner.

Despite this consensus, there are interesting differences of emphasis between the two groups. For example, the characteristic 'to work with others in a cooperative way', got a much higher score in the West (almost 50 per cent) than in the East (35 per cent). A similar difference can be seen for the characteristic, 'capacity to think in a critical and systemic way', which scored quite highly in the West (45 per cent) and got a relatively low score in the East (31 per cent). In contrast, the characteristic, 'to look at and approach problems as a member of a global society', got the highest score in the East (52 per cent), and a much lower score in the West (35 per cent).

If we look at the characteristics which are unique to each group, that is the characteristics on which consensus existed only in the East or the West, then the experts in the East were in agreement more often. There were four characteristics unique to the Eastern experts, while there was only one characteristic unique to the Western experts. The four characteristics which were unique to the Eastern experts were:

- the values of spiritual development
- the ability to create and sustain meaningful personal relationships
- the ability to change one's lifestyle and consumption habits to protect the environment
- willingness and ability to participate in politics at local, national and international levels.

It is noticeable that these characteristics relate to personal lifestyle and the individual development of citizens. The characteristic that was unique to the Western experts is of an entirely different nature and concerns the well-known Western ideal of 'liberal education', that is,

- to be broadly and liberally educated, possessing knowledge of history, social and natural sciences.

## EDUCATIONAL STRATEGIES

In this section, the majority of the recommendations (16 out of 26) concerning educational development strategies reached consensus among the experts. However, it is worth examining the remaining ten recommendations in the three previously applied categories since the extent of non-consensus is rather different in some cases and it is interesting which of them were placed into the same category from the point of view of the topics (see Table 4.6).

**Table 4.6** Non-consensus strategies

| Very far from consensus (>1.99) | Far from consensus (>1.59 but <1.99) | Near consensus (<1.59 but >1.5) |
|---|---|---|
| • Allocate a large proportion of available resources to the education of gifted students. | • Place much greater responsibility for education on other social institutions (eg, family, business, community organizations, religious institutions, NGOs). <br> • Encourage radical redesign of schooling. <br> • Allocate a large proportion of available resources to the education of disadvantaged students. <br> • Increase dramatically the levels of support and financing of the formal school system. <br> • Increase opportunities for learners to shape their own education (eg, to decide what they learn, how they learn, and when and where it is learnt). <br> • Organize schools in small units that provide supportive environments for students. | • Offer second language instruction to virtually all students beginning at the primary school level. <br> • Implement education programmes that respect and preserve cultural traditions. <br> • Ensure that Western and non-Western cultures and languages receive attention in the school curriculum. |

The examination of non-consensus recommendations in each category suggests that the experts were motivated by some kind of search for equilibrium when choosing priorities. In other words, they did not go to extremes. This is supported by the fact that contrary recommendations such as whether gifted or disadvantaged students should be given the larger amount of financial support from educational investments were either 'very far' or just 'far' from consensus (see the first and the second category). Recommendations about the radical reform of the school (eg, social institutions should have more responsibility in education, much more money should be invested in institutional education, students' influence in education should increase, schools should be reorganized into smaller units) were all put into one category and were also 'far from consensus' (see the second category). But even the evaluation of the importance of recommendations in the third category (see 'close to consensus') suggests that there is a search for equilibrium. These can be interpreted in the topic of globalization (second foreign language, the teaching of Western and non-Western cultures and languages) versus cultural diversification (cultural traditions) and are still in the same category.

## EAST–WEST DIFFERENCES 6

The general pattern that we have already seen with trends repeats itself with strategies: a large measure of consensus among experts in the East against limited consensus among experts in the West. However, this difference is even more pronounced with strategies. The Eastern experts disagree on only one strategy, and then not markedly:

●   to increase dramatically the levels of support and financing of the formal school system.

The Western experts, however, disagree on all but four of the twenty-six strategies. These four strategies are to:

●   support the teaching of subject matter in a manner that encourages children to think critically
●   ensure that all social institutions (including the family, and educational and religious institutions) have abiding respect for the basic rights of children and contribute to their well-being
●   increase attention in the curriculum to global issues and international studies
●   emphasize students' ability to critically assess information in an increasingly media-based society.

The recommendations about which there was the greatest measure of dissension among the Western experts were to:

●   encourage radical redesign of schooling
●   allocate a large proportion of available resources to the education of disadvantaged children.

Here too, the pattern with trends noted earlier repeats itself. It is clear that there is still a dividing line between political groups in the West on these issues.

## CONCLUSION

Behind every form of enquiry into the future lurks a perception of social reality as it currently exists. Selecting a variety of experts (by profession and country) enables a degree of objectivity, or rather globalization, to be achieved, but all images of the future refer to existing reality. This is also true of the present study. With the help of 182 expert panellists spread throughout Europe, North America and Asia, an attempt has been made in two written rounds to answer three essential questions:

- What major global trends are likely to have a significant impact upon the lives of people during the next twenty-five years?
- What will be the characteristics required of individuals in order to cope with and/or manage these trends?
- How might these characteristics be developed, ie, what approaches, strategies or innovations might best implement these citizen characteristics?

The consensus reached among the experts following these two rounds produces a varied picture of trends, characteristics and strategies. The general conclusion is that a number of important challenges lie ahead, challenges which concern our natural environment and the economic and social order. The respondents in this study believe that the gap between those who have access to material resources and information technology and those who do not will increase. At the same time our natural resources are becoming increasingly scarce, the rate of population growth will increase, there will be more migration and more children will be living below the poverty line. Progress in science and technology will have a major influence on economic growth, but will, at the same time, raise new and complex ethical issues.

In some respects, one might speak of a gloom and doom scenario, although hopeful developments can also be seen. In general terms the developments outlined mean that high demands must be placed on future citizens. Future citizens will be required to think critically and globally, and they must have the will and the skills to work with others, take responsibility, resolve conflicts by peaceful means and defend human rights. They will also have to be prepared to change their lifestyle and participate actively in politics. In order to develop these characteristics in future citizens, education and schooling will have to improve. Pupils need to learn how to think critically. At the same time, the international component of the curriculum needs to be developed, the link between school and the local community strengthened and the educational role of the school enhanced through better cooperation with institutions outside the school.

It is interesting to compare the global trends on which consensus was reached in these particular spheres with those on which the 182 expert respondents failed to reach a consensus. Examining the non-consensus trends we can see that it was mainly issues relating to social rights, globalization versus cultural diversification, economic development versus environmentalism, religion and citizenship where, due to value differences, global consensus cannot be expected in the evaluation of the desirability of these trends. On the other hand, we can conclude that regional differences cannot yet be avoided in the prediction of most global trends. The findings on the non-consensus characteristics section also support the view that there is less chance of global consensus in value-sensitive areas (national loyalty, development of characteristics with moral or spiritual connotations) than on characteristics based mainly on rational consideration. Examining the non-consensus recommendations, it is clear that some kind of equilibrium politics are starting to emerge in education development strategies, and this is not only supported by the recommendations on which there is consensus but, strangely enough, by the findings on the non-consensus recommendations as well.

When we look at the differences between consensus and non-consensus trends in more detail, a number of important topics emerge. First, in the economic field, it is conspicuous that although agreement existed among the experts that the economic gap between countries, and between people within countries, will widen, consensus was not achieved in areas such as employment, the labour market, or the globalization of markets.

Second, although the experts considered the development of more regional alliances as a way to achieve peace and security to be highly desirable and moderately likely, the data give no indication that powerful transnational corporations will play a greater role in the future, taking over functions of nation-states. This means that the experts still see nation-states as the organizing structure of societies for the next twenty-five years. Neither was there any consensus among the experts that the public will become more effective in preventing their governments from using war as a means of solving conflict.

Third, findings on both the consensus and non-consensus trends regarding the environment point towards the importance of helping people become more knowledgeable about, and willing to protect, the environment. The data suggest that concern for the environment is a factor that must figure largely in any education policy for the 21st century. Citizens must be educated to see the relationship between protecting and enhancing the environment and the quality of their own lives and well-being.

Fourth, on technology, the only negative trend statement on which the expert respondents agree is on the potential threat to individual privacy posed by technology. There was no consensus among the experts on more positive trend statements about technological innovations, such as the ability of technology to slow environmental degradation, or to create more opportunities for marginalized groups and individuals in the workforce.

Fifth and finally, the role that conflict will play in the future also seems to be an area of uncertainty. There was no consensus, for example, on whether intergroup, ethnic, regional and religious conflict, will increase dramatically within and among nations over the next twenty-five years. Neither was there agreement on whether the influence of extremism, for example, regimes, sects, movements, will increase. Nor was there any clear indication from the experts that cultural diversity will increasingly become a focal point for world and national politics.

The strategies on which no consensus was reached among the experts also provide some interesting insights. First, there was no agreement on whether a large proportion of available resources should be allocated to the education of disadvantaged or gifted students, suggesting that the distribution of available resources should be based on egalitarian principles, as opposed to increasing provision based on particular learning needs.

Second, no consensus was achieved among the experts as to whether there should be increased opportunities for learners to shape their own education, for example to decide what they learn, how they learn, and when and where they learn. This finding suggests that the expertise of educators, policy makers and other professionals should be brought to bear on school curricula, pedagogy and governance, as opposed to giving more opportunities to learners themselves to make decisions about their own education.

Third, there was no indication from the data that schools should be organized into smaller units to provide supportive environments for students, or that a radical redesign of schooling should be encouraged. These findings suggest that classroom units, and schools in general, are still viewed as favourable arenas for fostering atmospheres conducive to learning, and that schools are still places where formal education for citizenship should take place.

Fourth, although the experts highly recommend that increased attention be given to global issues and international studies, consensus was not reached as to whether both Western and non-Western cultures and languages should be given attention in the school curriculum, or whether education programmes that respect and preserve particular cultural traditions should be implemented.

A single instrument was used in our study, with the items being translated for all non-English-speaking countries. Despite this, the findings show that there are interesting cultural differences in the nature and content of the responses. The first noticeable difference is that the Asian panellists in Japan and Thailand show a stronger tendency to reach consensus than their Western counterparts in Europe and North America. In the final round the European experts agreed on twenty-three items and the North Americans on only sixteen, while the respondents in both Asian countries agreed on three times as many items. The experts from the East only disagreed on the probability of two trends and on the desirability of four trends.

Second, there were also differences on content. It is noticeable that the Western experts mainly agreed on items relating to technological developments and the environment. The most obvious cultural differences could be seen in the character-istics which were felt to be desirable. There were four characteristics unique to the Eastern experts relating to personal lifestyle and the individual development of citizens (eg, 'spiritual development' and 'sustaining meaningful personal relationships'). There was only one characteristic unique to the Western experts and concerns the well-known Western ideal of 'liberal education', that is: 'to be broadly and liberally educated, possessing knowledge of history and the natural sciences'. The Eastern experts only disagree on one strategy, and then not markedly; that is, 'Increase dramatically the levels of support and financing of the formal school system', while the Western experts disagree on all but four of the twenty-six strategies. The recommendations about which there was the greatest measure of dissension among the Western experts were:

- Encourage radical redesign of schooling;
- Allocate a large proportion of available resources to the education of disadvant-aged children.

In summary, the experts' opinions present a picture of significant trends which people will have to face over the next twenty-five years, and specific characteristics citizens will have to possess to manage and cope with these trends. Finally, they recommend a number of key educational strategies to help develop and foster these characteristics in the citizens. By gathering the informed opinions of experts from a variety of fields, it is our hope that policy makers will use these findings to create policies that encourage the desirable trends, characteristics and strategies identified in this chapter, and seek to change the direction of the undesirable trends, bearing in mind their own particular national and cultural contexts.

## REFERENCES

Turoff, M (1970) 'The Design of a Policy Delphi', *Technological Forecasting and Social Change*, **2**, pp 149–71.

# 5

# MULTIDIMENSIONAL CITIZENSHIP: EDUCATIONAL POLICY FOR THE 21ST CENTURY

## Patricia Kubow, David Grossman and Akira Ninomiya

### MULTIDIMENSIONAL CITIZENSHIP: AN INTRODUCTION

Analysing the findings presented in the previous chapter, the researchers in this study sought to identify themes, concepts or constructs that would translate the data into policy recommendations, the intended outcome of this research. What struck the research team was that there was no single approach, theme, concept or idea that could successfully capture the breadth of these findings. Citizenship and an educational programme which aims to develop it are a wide-ranging concept and this is reflected in the CEPS data. The insight that finally emerged from an extended dialogue among the researchers was that the key was to be found in the complexity of the findings themselves. On the one hand, there is perhaps no single finding that is unique to the study. Although its scope across nine nations provides this study with remarkable strength, many, if not most, of the findings can be found elsewhere in the literature. On the other hand, almost without exception, in other studies such findings are isolated, or treated in isolation, as the key to citizenship. Our data suggest the need for a much more complex conception of citizenship and citizenship education. What was unique to this study was the variegated picture of citizenship that emerged from the data. The researchers concluded that citizenship education for the 21st century called for a more holistic approach marked by comprehensiveness and consistency in both depth and breadth.

In the subsequent struggle to identify a more holistic image of citizenship and citizenship education, the researchers formulated a model which they came to describe as *multidimensional citizenship* (MDC). This term is intended to describe the complex, multifaceted conceptualization of citizenship and citizenship education that will be needed if citizens are to cope with the challenges the panellists suggest we will face in the early decades of the 21st century. It is, in fact, a reminder that in the case of citizenship education, we found the sum to be greater than the parts. It was the integrating, the bringing together which was different and powerful.

Multidimensional citizenship can be best understood as comprising four key dimensions: the personal, the social, the spatial and the temporal. These dimensions, explained in detail below, are abstractions from a more complex picture of citizenship emerging from this study that allow us to categorize and classify our recommendations for policy makers. The dimensions thus fulfil an important need. They provide us with an easily accessible model and provide conceptual categories for policy analysis and recommendations.

## THE KEY GOAL FOR EDUCATIONAL POLICY FOR THE 21ST CENTURY

The overall recommendation of this study is that our vision of multidimensional citizenship must be central to educational policy if our students are to meet effectively the challenges of the next twenty-five years. Multidimensional citizenship is a broadened notion of citizenship necessary to enable citizens to respond effectively to the challenges and demands of the 21st century. The purpose of making this conception of citizenship a central goal of educational policy is to capture, in a single notion, the need to reverse the direction of the undesirable global trends and cultivate in citizens the essential characteristics for 21st century citizenship. Before the specific dimensions of the model are elaborated, it is important to highlight the eight citizen characteristics which the panellists believed required urgent consideration and attention by policy makers during the next twenty-five years. These characteristics constitute what the panellists believe to be the nature and qualities of successful citizenship during the first part of the 21st century and provide the foundation upon which our model is based. Recall that the eight characteristics are:

1.  the ability to look at and approach problems as a member of a global society
2.  the ability to work with others in a cooperative way and to take responsibility for one's roles/duties within society
3.  the ability to understand, accept, appreciate and tolerate cultural differences
4.  the capacity to think in a critical and systemic way
5.  the willingness to resolve conflict in a non-violent manner
6.  the willingness to change one's lifestyle and consumption habits to protect the environment
7.  the ability to be sensitive towards and to defend human rights (eg, rights of women, ethnic minorities, etc), and
8.  the willingness and ability to participate in politics at local, national and international levels.

These eight characteristics are indicative of the type of world in which the expert panellists envision citizens living. In an increasingly interconnected world where the issues affecting people's lives are global and, hence, cross-cultural in nature, the concept of citizenship itself becomes more complex. This complexity necessitates that citizens possess a particular set of attributes that will enable them to function successfully in the years ahead. According to our panellists, it will be increasingly important that citizens are able to approach problems as members of a global society. Citizenship understood as membership in an interconnected, global world challenges us to define ourselves in a much broader context, to expand our concept of citizen identity to include a global identity, as well as our local, state and national ones.

Membership in a global, multicultural world places emphasis on the need for citizens to understand, accept and tolerate cultural differences if citizens are to work in a cooperative, non-violent manner to confront the most pressing global trends and issues. Moreover, to understand the complexity of the issues, as well as to decide what courses of action to follow, citizens will need to think in a critical and systemic way, questioning assumptions and considering the implications beforehand of particular courses of action. The type of responses of citizens to global challenges, in turn, will be indicative of the direction in which the world heads.

Thus, the primary task then is to help citizens recognize that global challenges affect each of us personally and are part of our individual and social responsibility to address. Put simply, global challenges cannot be left for someone else to deal with; rather, the responsibility lies with each of us to safeguard global well-being. As our data suggests, a concern for the rights and needs of others, as well as one's individual concerns, will need to be developed and nurtured in citizens. If the social inequities that operate in multiple spheres (eg, the economic, political, technological, etc) are to be confronted, then citizens must be sensitive towards and defend human rights and be willing and able to participate in public life at the local, national and international levels. Twenty-first-century citizenship will require active citizen participation – citizens who view themselves as actors in the world, who take responsibility for fighting injustices, and who assume at least some burden for addressing persistent global challenges.

In order to help develop in our students these eight characteristics, we strongly endorse a programme of education built around a model of multidimensional citizenship. Multidimensional citizenship must become the central focus of educational policy. To provide a more operational model for policy makers, we have developed four interrelated dimensions: the personal, social, spatial and temporal (see Figure 5.1). Each dimension is described in more detail in the paragraphs that follow.

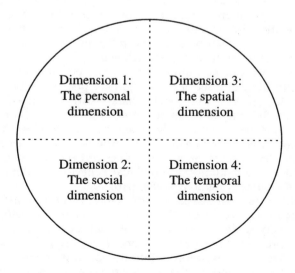

**Figure 5.1** The four dimensions of multidimensional citizenship

## MULTIDIMENSIONAL CITIZENSHIP: THE FOUR DIMENSIONS

### The personal dimension

The personal dimension of multidimensional citizenship involves developing a personal capacity for and commitment to a civic ethic characterized by individually and socially responsible habits of mind, heart and action. As citizens, we must enhance:

- our capacity to think critically and systemically
- our understanding of and sensitivity to issues of cultural differences
- our repertoire of responsible, cooperative and non-violent conflict resolution and problem-solving, and
- our willingness to protect the environment, to defend human rights, and to engage in public life.

None of these will be possible unless individual citizens are personally committed to this way of living in the world and govern their personal lives accordingly.

Of the four dimensions, the personal one is perhaps the most elusive because it links internal and private processes with external and public ones. Although as a research team we are primarily concerned with the public life of citizens, we recognize that effective citizenship first requires the internalization of a set of civic ethics or values. Thus, the personal dimension must explicitly address the areas of ethics and values, even though these are contestable across cultures and nations. The research data are clear, for example, that the panellists from Asia were more comfortable with the inclusion of notions of explicitly moral, ethical and spiritual elements in the mix of citizenship elements than were some European and North American panellists, although some did express concern about the lack of an ethical or spiritual dimension to underpin citizenship in the 21st century. In the end, there was no disagreement about the importance of personal character-istics in the development and actualization of effective citizenship. The question was how to operationalize this notion. Ultimately, the researchers in this study found a consensual approach built around the eight key citizen characteristics drawn from the data to be the most productive path.

In this context, we can best conceptualize the personal dimension as the presence or acquisition of a set of dispositions or predispositions to behave in the civic sphere in concert with the eight characteristics described earlier. In this we acknowledge with Parker and Jarolimek (1984) that fortunately or unfortunately people's behaviour is guided more by the beliefs they hold than by the information they have and that when beliefs change so does the behaviour of citizens. Informa-tion can contribute to the formation of values or even to changing values or beliefs already held, 'providing the individual believes that the information is valid and that its source is credible' (1984, p10).

In this regard, we are reminded of the remarkable case of the Canadian teenager, Craig Kielburger, who learned about the use of child labour in developing countries and launched a very successful worldwide awareness campaign directed against companies and products linked to child labour. This is a good example of the interaction between the acquisition of information and underlying dispositions to behave or act responsibly in the public arena. At the same time, there are many more negative examples of cases where information led to no action whatsoever. In summary, the neglect of the personal dimension in citizenship education could mitigate or interfere with efforts to influence behaviour in the civic sphere.

To actualize this personal dimension of citizenship, education must develop and strengthen in all students the determination to shape their personal lives in ways that enable them to attain the eight characteristics while also being sensitive to traditional values. This requires an attention to the teaching and learning of appropriate knowledge, skills and values which must be the task of the schools as a whole, both in their explicit curricula and courses of study and in the many other ways, direct and indirect, that they influence students.

While recognizing the importance of the curriculum in achieving our vision of citizenship, the researchers did not regard attention to the curriculum and pedagogy *per se* as sufficient. In particular, it was felt that the entire structure of the school must be subject to examination for its contribution to the development of multidimensional citizenship. In this regard, the researchers were concerned that educators understand that students, in working on tasks in schools, develop certain beliefs, values and preferences which, over time, are generalized to their civic life. Dreeben (1968), for example, argues persuasively that by coping with the sequence of classroom tasks and situations within schools with certain structural properties, students are likely to emerge having learned certain attitudinal orientations, or in our language, dispositions, on the basis of their experiences. Irrespective of the content or pedagogy in classrooms, such factors as authority relationships in the school and classroom, decision-making processes, or principles for grouping students, can have significant impact on behaviour in the civic realm. By coping with the sequence of classroom tasks and situations within schools with certain structural properties, students are likely to emerge with a set of dispositions towards behaviour in civic life. In other words, students develop norms that will be applied to task situations within civic life under appropriate conditions of perceived similarity.

While previous studies of citizenship education have tended to emphasize aspects of the formal content and instruction in the development of citizenship, our findings suggest that multidimensional citizenship is not something that can be confined to a specific course, or to classes in civics, or to exhortations to behave properly. Rather, it must infuse the whole atmosphere – the 'social climate' – of the schools and be identified as a priority by everyone involved in the conduct of education in that context. We feel that this is a particularly important and neglected area in what we have called the personal dimension.

Because this is a study of needed educational policy, we have naturally chosen to emphasize the role of schools and educational agencies in the development of multidimensional citizenship. At the same time, the researchers in this study fully realize that schools can achieve only so much on their own, no matter how hard they work, if they work in isolation from other institutions responsible for the socialization of youth. Thus, society at large, and especially those social institutions that influence the lives of students, must reinforce the schools' work in developing the practice of the model, and in particular, the development of dispositions to behave in the public sphere in ways that are consistent with the eight citizen characteristics described earlier.

## The social dimension

The social dimension of citizenship recognizes that, although personal qualities are essential, they are not sufficient in themselves for developing the multi-dimensional citizen. Citizenship in its very essence is a social activity. It involves people living and working together for civic purposes. Thus, citizens must be able to work and interact with other people in a variety of settings and contexts. They must be able to engage in public debate and discussion, to participate in public life, to deal with the problems and issues that face them in ways that, at the same time, equip them to deal respectfully with people whose ideas and values differ from their own. Social involvement is an important element of citizenship. In our view, the strictly political arena of political issues, elections and political parties is only one element of this social dimension of citizenship, which also encompasses the wide variety of activities and engagements usually described as 'civil society'.

With regard to the notion of 'civil society', let us emphasize the point that in our construction of the social dimension of multidimensional citizenship, we are adopting what Parker and Jarolimek (1984) have called the 'broad view' of citizen participation. The classic and more narrow view of citizen participation focuses only on behaviours that affect or intend to affect the decisions of governments, for example voting, joining a political party, or running for office. In this configuration, all non-governmental organizations are excluded from attention or analysis. This restrictive view of participation is not consistent with nor supportive of this model.

Recent literature on citizenship and civic education, particularly that arising from the transformation of many countries in central and eastern Europe towards more democratic behaviour, has revived an old and once seemingly obsolescent idea, that of the importance of this notion of 'civil society'.

Patrick (1996) has given us a lucid description of the importance of the civil society and its role in citizenship education. Civil society is a public domain that private individuals create and operate in order to promote civic purposes free from unreasonable interference from government. One classic example of the emergence of civil society is the case of Solidarity in Poland; the global proliferation of non-governmental environmental awareness and action groups is another. From a civil society perspective, the widespread exercise of social and civic freedom by citizens across many domains is an essential component or building block for political freedom. The basis of a flourishing civil society is a network of freely formed voluntary organizations that, although limited by law, are not part of the formal institutions of state. Some observers see this network of organizations as providing a kind of social equivalent to capital investment, or 'social capital'.

From a multidimensional perspective, citizenship cannot be confined to speculation and contemplation; rather, all citizens must be participatory if we are to cope with the challenges of the 21st century. Social involvement must also be combined with a commitment to action, that is, a predisposition to act. In this regard, multidimensional citizenship draws on the tradition that good citizens are actively involved in the social life and public affairs of their communities. At the same time, this participation is not an end in itself. Activity for its own sake is not the goal. Rather, citizen action must be the result of reflection and deliberation and be undertaken with full respect for the rights of others in an effort to address the increasingly significant challenges identified by our panellists.

With respect to citizenship education for the social dimension, the model eschews the narrower definitions of the 'good citizen' as either the loyal servant of the state or the informed voter, both of which are largely passive roles. Educational programmes based on this very narrow view of citizenship are not likely to be personally meaningful for students. Such programmes tend to treat students as passive learners who are not yet active participants in civic life. By contrast, multidimensional citizenship embraces those more recent approaches to citizenship education which view citizenship as entailing a commitment to participation in public life across a wide range of domains, both governmental and non-governmental. The researchers in this study concur with Parker (1996) that participatory democracy, that is 'direct involvement in public life' rather than 'spectatorship' (1996, p121), is the type of citizenship required. This broader view of participation creates, in turn, a spectrum of participatory opportunities for students and thereby recognizes a greater number of situations in which citizenship participation can be practised and examined before reaching adulthood.

In this context, citizenship education programmes could include any number of activities requiring direct social/political action, such as involvement in political campaigns, community projects, volunteer service, community study and internships. A growing number of schools worldwide have incorporated this type of activity into their educational programmes. In the United States, individual states have added community service as a requirement for graduation. The expansion of these activities has led to the creation of a new field of inquiry and activity, commonly called 'service learning'. The adoption and expansion of service learning would support the social dimension of the model. It is our belief that such experiences hold great potential as effective ways to develop the social dimension of citizenship in students.

In light of the present decline in political affairs and involvement in civic organizations, the development of the social dimension is viewed as necessarily urgent. We call for educational programmes that are experienced-based in which students are provided opportunities to connect with and engage in their communities through reflection, 'community service, social action, and deliberation' (Parker, 1996, p121).

## The spatial dimension

At the dawn of the 21st century, our panellists suggest that citizens must see themselves as members of several overlapping communities – local, regional, national and multinational. We refer to this as the spatial dimension. What emerges from this study, and indeed from the relevant literature, is that the world is becoming increasingly interdependent and the world of the 21st century will be even more so. This is, in part, the result of changes in technology, in communications, in trade patterns, in immigration and so on. It means that the challenges of the 21st century transcend national boundaries and will require cross-national solutions. Our panellists also advise us that at the same time the world is becoming increasingly interdependent, people's sense of identity is and will remain rooted in the local and the personal, in terms of nation and culture. In the spatial dimension, we try to deal with this characteristic, albeit contradictory, feature of modern life.

One of the ironies of the process of modernization and globalization that has confounded those social scientists of the 1950s who predicted the emergence of a single global culture is that, in the face of these processes, local and regional identities, whether based on community, ethnicity, race or religion, have proved remarkably resilient. Where once smaller communities and languages seemed doomed to extinction in the face of national, regional or global pressures, they have survived and, in some cases, have even prospered. Citing Japan as a case in point, Gusfield states that traditional Japanese culture has been well able to coexist with modern culture and that 'traditional forms of labour commitments seem to have contributed to economic growth while the same commitments were seen to be an impediment in the West' (cited in Fägerlind and Saha, 1989, p17).

Like Gusfield, Rau (1980) has also challenged the assumption that modern value orientations are incompatible with more traditional attitudes and conventional valuing. In a five-country analysis of Brazil, Ghana, India, Japan, and the US, Rau argues that people can 'adopt modern values with respect to certain dimensions of their lives but retain traditional values with respect to others' (cited in Fägerlind and Saha, 1989, p114). This global diversity amidst local and regional identities was noted by our study panellists, both in terms of retaining a positive sense of one's identity, and on the negative side, regarding the potential that the juxtaposition of competing ethnic, racial and religious groups has for local, regional and even international conflict, as currently is the case, for example, in Bosnia, Central Africa and the Middle East.

While the world is and will be increasingly interconnected and interdependent, it will retain a high level of diversity. While the basic world system will continue to be framed by nation-states and their governments, within them there will be strong local and regional systems and identities, the devolution for Scotland and Wales in the UK being a case in point. There will also be emerging regional alliances that transcend national boundaries, as illustrated by the European Union (EU) and Association of Southeast Asian Nations (ASEAN). Thus, the task is not to dismiss the claims of patriotism and national identity but to ensure that citizenship education also includes the realization that we live in an interdependent world and that nations, and the communities within them, must work together if the challenges of the 21st century are to be successfully overcome.

Multidimensional citizenship requires that citizens should be able to live and work at a series of interconnected levels, from the local to the multinational. At the most basic level, it requires that citizenship education include what Hanvey (1976) called perspective consciousness, 'the recognition or awareness on the part of the individual that he or she has a view of the world that is not universally shared, that this view of the world has been and continues to be shaped by influences that often escape conscious detection, and that others have views of the world that are profoundly different from one's own' (1976, p4). At the most advanced level, it would ask that citizens understand how one or more other cultures feel from the standpoint of an insider.

If we combine our analysis of the spatial dimension with our personal and social dimensions, we would want to create citizens who – in René Dubos' famous dictum – think globally, while acting locally. Citizenship education in this context would call upon schools to, on the one hand, explore and celebrate the diversity they find within them, and, on the other, provide opportunities for students to have experiences beyond the boundaries of their school. In the case of the latter, one well-known programme is the pairing or twinning of schools across local, regional or national boundaries in an organized pattern of exchange via mail, phone or video, and, in some cases, reciprocal visits. The new technologies have allowed for the rapid expansion of contacts of this type via the Internet at relatively low cost.

At the same time, the researchers in this study are under no illusion that the overlapping identities of modern life and the rapid increase of cross-cultural contact will be free from problems or conflict. Multiple identities can lead to role conflict and hard choices for individuals. And history is too full of examples of the disasters resulting from cultural contact, particularly to the smaller, weaker or poorer community or nation to be sanguine about the results of increasing cultural contact. Multidimensional citizenship would require that we provide a deliberative and reflective framework for students to understand their multiple roles at all levels and provide them with the skills to cross boundaries, whether they be geographical or cultural. To this end, the concept of education for international understanding and cooperation should be developed and expanded so that students view themselves as members of several overlapping communities.

## The temporal dimension

By the temporal dimension of citizenship, we mean that citizens, in dealing with contemporary challenges, must not be so preoccupied with the present that they lose sight of the past and the future. Anthropologists have made us aware of our tendency to see the world through a limited cultural perspective – what they call an ethnocentric view of the world. In fact, this cultural nearsightedness has a lesser known analogue in our tendency to have a limited time perspective – a 'tempocentric' view of the world. Just as our ability to deal across cultures can be hindered by ethnocentrism, our ability to deal with time dimensions can be limited by what some have called 'tempocentrism', or a tendency to limit our vision to present circumstances. On the one hand, our students' own age limits their perspective. It is hard to think across decades or centuries when one hasn't lived even twenty years. On the other hand, the conceptualization of time is part of the cognitive development process, and is culturally bound as well. We should be wary of our students' grasp of notions of time, subject as they are to age and previous experience.

The personal and social dimensions of multidimensional citizenship are, in large part, historically conditioned. Heritage and tradition are influential in helping citizens understand what citizenship entails. Thus, multidimensional citizenship requires that we pay appropriate attention to the past. Citizens need a rich knowledge of their own and the world's history to give them the sense of connectedness and rootedness, and the depth of understanding, that are essential to the practice of the model. At the same time, in dealing with contemporary challenges, citizens must also remember that their actions will have an impact upon the citizens of the future. This has led some, like Longstreet (1997), to advocate a futures-oriented curriculum. Multidimensional citizenship, however, requires that the present and its challenges be located in the context of both past and future, so that purely short-term solutions to problems can be avoided wherever possible. As we move into the 21st century, it will be important to formulate our citizenship education curriculum in as broad a timeframe as possible, enhancing our knowledge and understanding of the present with that of the past and the future. As citizens, we will be called upon to balance our readiness to explore and innovate with respect for the knowledge and values that constitute our heritage and with the realization that we are also stewards for the future. In classrooms, this means that students are encouraged to think about the future and past in relation to the contemporary issue being taught and discussed. In this way, the temporal dimension can be developed and nurtured in students.

## THE INTERCONNECTEDNESS OF THE DIMENSIONS

Although the four dimensions of citizenship – the personal, social, spatial and temporal – have been discussed separately above, in reality they are all closely interwoven, and educational policy must address them more or less simultaneously. Four vignettes are elaborated below to help illustrate the interconnectedness of the dimensions and to show how teachers can take advantage of classroom events to teach the concept and practice of multidimensional citizenship.

### Vignette 1: the rainforests

The first example comes from a class of 13-year-old students studying geography in Canada. The geography students were studying the rainforests of the world and had learned that the rainforests play an important role in regulating the world's climate and that the forests contain many valuable and unique flora and fauna, some of them still unknown. They had also learned that rainforests were being cut down at a rapid rate and, with the certainty of 13-year-olds, they quickly reached the conclusion that this was a selfish and thoughtless action on the part of the people in the countries involved. What they did not take into account was that those people who were cutting down the rainforests were doing so not because they were silly or selfish, but because often they had little choice. Poverty, the need for land, patterns of international trade, and economic development constraints all serve to increase pressure on the rainforests. The students' teacher pointed out that Canada had largely destroyed its own forests, and indeed was continuing to do so, and suggested that Canadians' own standard of living was implicated in the destruction of the rainforests of other countries. As the students absorbed this information and thought about it, the teacher also suggested that perhaps Canadians and others should pay a rainforest tax, say on coffee, imported timber products and cheap beef grown on pasture from cleared rainforests for fast food restaurants, in order to protect the rainforests. This led to further student discussion. The students did not resolve the problems involved, but they had been encouraged to think about some of the challenges they face as citizens, and to do so in ways that were appropriate to their age and level of maturity.

This everyday example illustrates how the four dimensions of citizenship can be integrated in a classroom. The students had been led to think about the present in the context of past and future; to think about how their everyday, personal lives intersected with a much broader problem; and about how their living in Canada, many miles away from the tropical rainforests, none the less still involved them in the problems of the world. In the process, the personal, social, spatial and temporal dimensions of citizenship were all addressed. This example is taken from a geography class, but every subject in the curriculum contains possibilities for this kind of learning.

## Vignette 2: the historical development of religious conflict and three religions

A second example comes from a lesson conducted by a world history teacher in Asia. Shortly before beginning a unit on the historical development of Judaism, Christianity and Islam, the assassination of Israel's Prime Minister Rabin took place. The teacher brought in newspaper reports and TV news clips, using the immediacy of the event and the news articles and reports to set a context for understanding the feelings that underlie the conflicts among and within these religions. Normally, it would be a considerable challenge to teach about these religions to a class of twenty-five students, where only 10 per cent or less have a personal knowledge of Christianity, Judaism, and Islam and where the majority of students do not belong to an organized religion. However, by attaching the study of the three religions to actual events and people in the news, the abstract-ness and remoteness of the subject were greatly mitigated. The current event provided a catalyst for student enquiry and discussion of the three religions. After reviewing the events surrounding the assassination and the key role of the city of Jerusalem (ie, its historical and religious significance), the teacher introduced the historical origins of the three religions and encouraged the students to explore the commonalities and differences among them. The teacher then asked the students to speculate on the implications of the assassination for future events in the Middle East, the possibility of their peaceful resolution, and the global implications of not choosing peaceful solutions to deal with conflict.

In this example, the teacher used a current event to provide a context for meaningful student deliberation and reflection about conflicts rooted deeply in history. The fact that the assassin in this instance was of the same religion as Rabin, Judiasm, only added to the intensity of the debate. In particular, the current event provided an opportunity for development of the temporal and personal dimensions, as the students were encouraged to explore existing belief/ethical systems and compare them with their own, as well as being encouraged to mentally move across time and space.

## Vignette 3: the issue of poverty

The third example comes from an English junior school classroom of 10- and 11-year-olds studying the issue of poverty. The teacher in this scenario planned a series of year-long, interdisciplinary activities to help the children learn about poverty in developing countries, as well as in their own community. In class, the students learned how poverty has been addressed past and present – through citizen volunteerism, civic and church groups and governmental programmes. As a class activity, the students created collages depicting the conditions in which children around the world live. The students then presented their collages on parents' night to raise consciousness about and heighten concern for children in need. Throughout the year, the students also engaged in a variety of service-oriented projects. In the autumn, the students collected canned goods and other non-perishable items from students and teachers in their own school, assembled their 'care packages', and distributed them at the local homeless shelter and to in-need families. During the winter months, students took turns serving soup and sandwiches to senior citizens.

The students also investigated the issue of poverty worldwide by conducting their own research and creating a 'quality of life index' depicting the living conditions according to major geographical regions. Upon completion, the class chose one particular region, Africa, for further study. In an attempt to contribute to the learning needs of African children, the students found used books in good condition in their homes and community to support the Books for Africa initiative they had learnt about from their own research. Personal reflection on the issue of poverty was recorded by the students in their journals. In this way, the students were able to process their thoughts and feelings in relation to what they were learning through the activities they participated in. The teacher also debriefed each activity through small and large group discussions.

Throughout this year-long study, the students became aware of and helped others become aware of poverty. The students developed a personal ethic of concern and social responsibility and addressed stereotypes associated with poverty, learning that people in their own communities as well as in other countries have serious needs. Moreover, the students learnt to interact and work with people of different ages and diverse socio-economic backgrounds.

## Vignette 4: air pollution

The fourth example is taken from a social studies lesson taught within a unit entitled *Contemporary Issues*. During this unit, a class of Asian students examined the topic of the environment through the use of technology and experienced-based instruction. To introduce the issue of environmental quality, with a particular emphasis on air pollution, the teacher drew upon the recent August–September 1997 fire-produced ecological disaster that occurred in Southeast Asia. The causes and effects of air pollution were studied in an interdisciplinary manner through the use of global documents the students and teacher retrieved primarily from the Internet. The Internet was also used to link the students to classrooms in the countries most affected by the air pollution disaster: Malaysia, Singapore and Indonesia. Via the Internet, the students carried on a dialogue about the ecological event in real time, exchanging information and opinions. After dialoguing across geographical and cultural borders, the students learnt about how their local air pollution index was constructed, listened to a talk from a science teacher about the problems of measurement, and took a field trip to both the environmental protection agency and one of their local measurement stations. After conducting their own research on the various positions held by governmental and non-governmental organizations on the problem, the students role-played a meeting of policy makers trying to deal with the ecological crisis. The students then wrote their own position papers on how air pollution problems should be addressed and presented their papers in their local community.

The four vignettes depicted above show how the four dimensions of multi-dimensional citizenship can be effectively interwoven across disciplines and class units with differing age groups. In the next section, we turn to the issue of assessing our present educational systems in order to create environments conducive to this model of citizenship.

## MULTIDIMENSIONAL CITIZENSHIP: ASSESSING PRESENT EDUCATIONAL SYSTEMS

The task before us is to begin to assess the capacity of our societies to implement a multidimensional citizenship model appropriate for the 21st century. What follows is a framework of questions that might assist educational policy makers to initiate a process of identifying both strengths and weaknesses of present educational systems relative to the model. This is then followed by a series of *Citizenship Education Self-Assessment Checklists* (CESAC) aimed at specific levels within the educational system to enable individuals working at those levels to judge the effectiveness of their current programmes and ascertain where changes need to be made in order to realize the goal of multidimensional citizenship.

As our research suggests, citizenship is not created in a vacuum. Our vision of multidimensional citizenship requires an acceptance of the dynamic nature of the interaction between the school and the larger society. Policy confined to one or the other of these domains will not be sufficient for the creation of multi-dimensional citizens for the 21st century. Each domain (ie, the schools and the larger communities within which schools exist) must be examined as well as the interaction between the two. Therefore, when we refer to the 'educational system' below, we mean this term to include both schools and their larger societal contexts.

Using the four dimensions described earlier, the following questions provide a broad framework for initiating an analysis of the extent to which multidimensional citizenship is or can be realized within a particular educational setting; namely, a ministry or department of education, a school district, a school, a classroom or teacher education institutions.

## The core dimensions with key questions

*The personal dimension*

To what extent is multidimensional citizenship reflected in an educational programme aimed at developing students with a personal commitment to socially responsible habits of mind, heart and action? That is, to what extent does the educational system create students with:

- a capacity to think critically and systemically?
- an understanding of and sensitivity to cultural differences and issues of human rights?
- a repertoire of responsible, cooperative and non-violent problem-solving and conflict resolution skills?
- a commitment to protect the environment, to defend human rights, and to engage in political processes?
- a commitment to shape their personal lives in ways that enable them to attain these qualities?

*The social dimension*

To what extent is multidimensional citizenship reflected in an educational programme aimed at developing students with the ability to participate effectively and thoughtfully in civic life? That is, to what extent does the educational system create students with:

- the ability to act in a reflective and deliberative manner in a variety of civic settings, including the economic, cultural, educational, social, political, spiritual and aesthetic domains?

*The spatial dimension*

To what extent is multidimensional citizenship integrated into all aspects of the system, ie, the curriculum, pedagogy, governance, organization and school-community relations? That is, to what extent does the educational system:

- create students with the ability to think and act as members of several overlapping communities, ie, local, regional, national and multinational?
- require or promote multinational linkages?

*The temporal dimension*

To what extent is multidimensional citizenship reflected in an educational programme aimed at developing in students the ability to take account of both the past and the future, as well as the present? That is, to what extent does the educational system create students with:

- the ability to think and act within a broad timeframe that encompasses both past heritage(s) and the potential impact of their present actions upon the future?

## CITIZENSHIP EDUCATION SELF-ASSESSMENT CHECKLISTS

In attempting to give policy makers and other educators a tool to assess their current education programmes in light of our recommendation that such programmes in the future need to emphasize multidimensional citizenship, we propose the use of *Citizenship Education Self-Assessment Checklists* or CESAC. The effective use of CESAC depends upon three conditions:

- that all education personnel, from the most senior governing board members and administrators through classroom teachers, are familiar with the concept of multidimensional citizenship, as described in this chapter
- that these personnel support the concept of multidimensional citizenship, and
- that they are prepared to review what they now do in order to see if it is congruent with the attainment of multidimensional citizenship and to revise existing practices where necessary.

It is impossible to formulate a CESAC of questions that would cover every contingency and circumstance at all levels of the education system across the nine nations. Such a checklist would be too detailed for successful use and would, in any case, fail to take into account local circumstances. Moreover, the research on the implementation of education programmes demonstrates that effective implementation depends upon the support and cooperation of all those involved. As Michael Fullan (1991, 1993) has noted, change is a process. It takes time, effort, persistence and mutual goodwill and understanding on the part of all involved. Simple prescription or command does not work. Thus, it seems most useful to offer a self-assessment checklist composed of questions that can be used by people involved in schools so that they can survey their existing practices and change them, where necessary, in order to achieve the goal of multidimensional citizenship. Needless to say, the questions suggested in the following might well need further refinement in particular circumstances and should certainly be seen as suggestive rather than prescriptive. They are aimed at five levels:

- national or state/provincial level educational governance bodies, eg, ministries or departments of education
- regional or local level governance bodies, eg, North American school boards
- school level
- classroom level, and
- teacher education levels, including both initial licensure and inservice continuing professional development.

Policy makers, administrators and teachers are encouraged to shape this CESAC to their own purposes according to their local circumstances. It is offered as an aid to establishing multidimensional citizenship (MDC) as the central goal of education. How this is done in any particular setting is a matter that is best decided at the local level. This CESAC, for the five levels below, is intended only as a guide.

## The national ministry/department, provincial or state department of education level

- To what extent is the concept of MDC identified as the goal of education (eg, in policy documents, goal statements, etc)?
- Are ministry/department officials at all appropriate levels aware and supportive of MDC?
- Is MDC taken into account when policy is discussed and formulated?
- What is done to ensure that the key elements of national/provincial/state policy are consistent with and supportive of MDC, specifically: curriculum, pedagogy, textbooks and resources, financing, student evaluation, teacher education and access to education?
- What is done to ensure that all levels of the education system are aware and supportive of the goal of MDC, specifically: regional and local officials, school heads/principals, teachers?
- What is done to inform the community-at-large (eg, parents, employers, the media, etc) of the importance of MDC as the central educational goal?

- What is done to alert relevant policy makers and officials in ministries/ departments other than education of the importance of MDC?

## The local or regional levels

- Are all relevant personnel (eg, school superintendents/directors, inspectors, regional authorities, etc) aware and supportive of MDC?
- Are local/regional policies, priorities and practices consistent with the achievement of MDC (eg, in such cases as curriculum, selection of learning resources, teachers' professional development, allocations of resources among schools, personnel policies)?
- Are non-teacher groups informed about the importance of MDC as the central goal of education (eg, parents, employers, local media, etc)?
- To what extent are existing policies and practices consistent with the goal of MDC (eg, curriculum, pedagogy, selection of learning resources, student evaluation, school-community linkages, etc)?
- Where these existing policies are not consistent with the goal of MDC, what can be done to change them?

## The individual school level

- Is the school head/principal, deputy/vice-principal, etc, aware and supportive of MDC as an important educational goal?
- Are the teachers and the school staff as a whole aware and supportive of MDC as the central school goal?
- To what extent are school practices supportive of the attainment of MDC (eg, in local curriculum decisions, instructional strategies, selection of textbooks and resources, student discipline, links with parents and the community, links with future employers, etc)?
- If school practices are inconsistent with the attainment of MDC, what can be done to change them?
- When school policies are established or revised, is their impact on the attainment of MDC kept in mind?
- Does the school as a whole model the concept of MDC? If not, what can be done to ensure that it does so?
- What can be done on a continuing basis to ensure that the concept of MDC is constantly kept in mind by teachers, students, parents and the wider community as a whole?

## The individual classroom level

- Is the classroom teacher aware and supportive of MDC?
- Does the classroom model the practice of MDC (eg, in teaching strategies, use of learning resources, student evaluation, rules of discipline and conduct, establishment of classroom climate, etc)?
- What is done to make students aware of the importance of MDC?

- To what extent does the teacher act as a model of MDC?
- How can students be required to practise MDC at whatever level is appropriate to their age and maturity?

## The teacher education level

- Are teacher-education institutions/programmes aware of how other levels of the education system are organized to attain MDC?
- Is MDC an explicit part of teacher-education programmes for all teachers?
- Is there a regular, two-way flow of information between teacher-education institutions and the rest of the educational system regarding MDC?
- In what ways do teacher-education personnel act as models of MDC?
- Do the research and development programmes of teacher-education institutions pay systematic attention to MDC?
- Is MDC a component of professional development inservice education programmes for teachers?
- Is evidence of a focus upon MDC one of the key areas/components in the criteria of agencies responsible for the accreditation of teacher-education institutions?

## THE CASE FOR MULTIDIMENSIONAL CITIZENSHIP

Based on our research, we believe that a more comprehensive conception of citizenship and citizenship education is needed to help citizens address the major challenges confronting the world and to enable them to function successfully in the years ahead. Although nation-states will still constitute the organizing structure of societies during the first part of the 21st century, the challenges themselves (eg, social and economic inequalities, unequal access to information technologies, reduced privacy, environmental deterioration, and threatened peace and security) are global in nature. The challenges cross national boundaries. Consequently, a broadened understanding of citizenship, which incorporates a multinational component, must be a significant part of educational policy. By making multi-dimensional citizenship the focus of educational policy, it is our desire that students will be able to critically assess global challenges and act on them with wisdom.

Citizenship, of course, is not a new concept. As noted earlier in this book, schools have, from their beginnings, been assigned a citizenship function. However, most conventional approaches to citizenship and citizenship education have been unnecessarily narrow. For example, they have emphasized national priorities to the neglect of multinational; they have often been confined to formal instruction in certain subjects, such as social studies and history, rather than being infused throughout the schools as a whole; and they have often taken too passive a view of what citizenship entails. Instead, to meet the challenges of the 21st century, we need a more comprehensive view of citizenship, which we describe as 'multi-dimensional', because it conceptualizes citizenship as addressing a series of interconnected dimensions of thought, belief and action. We have described these dimensions of citizenship as the personal, social, spatial and temporal dimensions and believe that their cultivation in students is essential to preparing them for participation in public life.

In presenting this model of multidimensional citizenship, we are well aware that over the years there have been many attempts to educate citizens who would be active participants in social and political life. The history and philosophy of education contain many discussions of the nature of democratic citizenship. To take only a few examples of curriculum projects over the past two decades, there have been approaches to 'political literacy' in the United Kingdom (Crick and Porter, 1978); to 'environmental competence' in the United States (Newmann, 1975); to 'anticipatory learning' in the Club of Rome (Botkin *et al.*, 1979); to 'global education' in a number of countries; and so on. Our concept of multidimensional citizenship shares many of the emphases and values of such approaches, but, in our view, represents something new and distinctive in that it builds upon and goes beyond these more traditional conceptions of citizenship and citizenship education and speaks directly to what are anticipated to be the challenges of the 21st century in a multinational context.

It is also perhaps worth noting that the four dimensions of citizenship are not dissimilar from the elements of citizenship and citizenship education described in the introductory chapter. There it was argued that, historically, citizenship education has been concerned with development of a sense of identity, usually at the national level; understanding of rights and duties; adoption of societal values; and involvement in public affairs. However, our research indicates that in the 21st century, citizens' sense of identity must be located at a variety of levels, ranging from the local through national but encompassing the multinational as well. This concept of multiple, interlocking identities clearly pervades all four dimensions of citizenship, making our model appropriate for the cultivation in students of citizenship as membership in several overlapping communities. The multidimensional model also emphasizes the rights and duties of citizenship which have obvious personal roots and social consequences, as well as being located in the context of time and space. Participation in public affairs and the adoption of appropriate societal values also cuts across all four dimensions of our educational model and must be encouraged in our schools.

If multidimensional citizenship is to become the central goal of educational policy in our schools, then it cannot be relegated to certain subjects or addressed only at the curricular level. It is our recommendation that multidimensional citizenship infuse the whole atmosphere of the school, shaping and pervading all aspects of education, including curriculum and pedagogy, governance and organization, funding and the allocation of resources, teacher education and school-community relations.

Although our research reveals that classrooms, and schools in general, are still viewed as favourable arenas for creating atmospheres conducive to the learning of citizenship, the school is not alone in this task to educate citizens who will be willing and able to function successfully during the next twenty-five years. Education must be a key part of the solution, but significant involvement of other social institutions and community and government agencies will be required as well. If the negative global trends detailed in Chapter 4 are to be reversed and the desirable citizenship participatory competencies developed, then collaborations between education and other social institutions are essential.

For multidimensional citizenship to be fully realized, the education of citizens must be seen as a responsibility shared among schools and other institutions within society. Thus, the concept of multidimensional citizenship must be articulated and accepted outside the professional education community by other decision makers whose policies and actions impinge upon education – by government leaders, opinion makers and the community at large. Successful implementation of multidimensional citizenship requires dynamic interaction between the school and the larger society. In order to provide a fruitful ground in which effective policy can be rooted, continued, vibrant public debate on the nature and qualities of successful citizenship for the 21st century is essential and must be examined anew by each generation.

## MULTIDIMENSIONAL CITIZENSHIP: A CONCLUSION

The thoughtful responses of the panellists provide the foundation for a rich, complex and coherent vision of citizenship necessary to prepare people to respond effectively to the challenges and demands of the 21st century. We describe this vision as multidimensional citizenship and believe that its development must become the central priority of educational policy. Although significant challenges confront us in the 21st century, our panellists in this study did not believe that these are insurmountable. However, men and women, in their capacity as citizens, must be prepared to anticipate, grapple with and overcome the challenges they will face, and in this task education will play an essential role. Only an education that incorporates the four dimensions of citizenship – the personal, social, spatial and temporal – will equip them for this task.

## REFERENCES

Anderson, C, Nicklas, S and Crawford, A (1994) *Global Understandings: A framework for teaching and learning*, Association for Supervision and Curriculum Development, Alexandria, Virginia.

Botkin, J W, Elmandjira, M and Malitza, J (1979) *No Limits to Learning*, Pergamon Press, Oxford.

Center for Civic Education (1994) *National Standards for Civics and Government*, Center for Civic Education, Calabasas, California.

Crick, B and Porter, A (eds) (1978) *Political Education and Political Literacy*, Longman, London.

Dreeben, R (1968) *On What is Learned in School*, Addison-Wesley, Reading, Massachusetts.

Fägerlind, I and Saha, L J (1989) *Education and National Development: A comparative perspective* (2nd edn), Pergamon Press, New York.

Fullan, M G (1993) *Change Forces: Probing the depths of educational reform*, Falmer, London.

Fullan, M G, with Stiegelbauer, S (1991) *The New Meaning of Educational Change* (2nd edn), Teachers College Press, New York.

Gusfield, J R (1987) 'Tradition and Modernity: Misplaced polarities in the study of social change', *American Journal of Sociology*, **72**(4), pp 351–62.

Hanvey, R (1976) *An Attainable Global Perspective*, The American Forum on Global Education, New York.

Longstreet, W (1997) 'Alternative Futures and the Social Studies', in R Evans and D Saxe (eds), *Handbook on Teaching Social Issues*, National Council for the Social Studies, Washington, DC, pp 317–26.

Newmann, F (1975) *Education for Citizen Action*, McCutchan, Berkeley.

Parker, W (1996) 'Advanced Ideas about Democracy: Toward a pluralist conception of citizenship education', *Teachers College Record*, **98**(1), 104–25.

Parker, W and Jarolimek, J (1984) *Citizenship and the Critical Role of the Social Studies*, National Council for the Social Studies, Washington, DC.

Patrick, J (1996) 'Civic Society in Democracy's Third Wave: Implications for civic education', *Social Education*, **60**(7), 414–17.

Rau, W C (1980) 'The tacit conventions of the modernity school: An analysis of key assumptions', *American Sociological Review*, **45**(2), pp 244–60.

# 6

# MAKING IT WORK: IMPLEMENTING MULTIDIMENSIONAL CITIZENSHIP

## Walter Parker, David Grossman, Patricia Kubow, Ruthanne Kurth-Schai and Shuichi Nakayama

The rapid pace of change throughout this century in both developed and developing societies has made forecasters of educators the world over. They are joined across the decades and across national and cultural boundaries with the belief that children should be educated for what is always a combination of existing and anticipated states of affairs. They are continually 'updating' and 'modernizing' the school curriculum.

This is no easy task. First, the rate and volatility of modern social change make school renewal an endless task. The job is never done. Second, the difficulty of forecasting makes school renewal inevitably off-target. The job is never done 'just right'. Third, value conflicts within societies make the school a hotly contested social space. Stakeholders argue vehemently over aims and procedures. In Japan, for example, educators struggle to internationalize the curriculum, which they believe has been insular and chauvinist; at the same time, nostalgia for homo-geneity and exceptionalism is palpable.

Amid the perennial updating, school renewal efforts have been largely national and local as distinct from international. The tools and perspectives employed by educators in these nations thereby have been limited in perspective and reach. The national and intra-national cast of their work has accomplished some goals, of course, among them nation-building, employment-training geared to the local political economy, and military-industrial competition with other nations. Other goals, however, are removed from consideration or placed so far out on the periphery of concerns as to be taken seriously by almost no one, even if they are included with some regularity in official school documents. Chief among these concerns is shared problem-solving on international and cross-cultural problems and, thereby, the cultivation of multidimensional citizenship.

Even today's reform efforts aimed at 'global education' or 'internationalization' often proceed in ways that are heavily nation-bound. Local and/or national committees, along with textbook authors, do most of the actual school decision-making work, and, because they are no more able than the rest of us to transcend their vantage points, their work is constrained by local and/or national conceptual frameworks. It could not be otherwise. No one works on neutral ground.

In this chapter we report the research team's attempt to draw implications for educational practice from the consensus findings of the nine-nation expert panel. Our work shares some similarities with the conventional approach to school renewal: mainly, our effort was a continuation (for better or worse) of the instrumentalist tradition of 'updating' schools for the purpose of achieving educational relevance to extant and forecasted social realities. However, our effort was multinational rather than national. Both the forecasts and the set of recommendations tailored to them were developed by international groups – the expert panel and the research team, respectively. Furthermore, our focus was education for *citizenship*, which has been predominantly a national concern in virtually every nation. By definition, modern citizenship is closely aligned to national borders and national identities and, in federated nations, to localities as well. By contrast, our work broached the subject of 'multidimensional' citizenship as a basis for educational change. The consensus findings from the expert panel suggested to us that the time had come for the next generation of school renewal to be in some respects a shared world project, developed, at least in part by a multinational team, since the future to which our schools must be made relevant is increasingly a shared future.

Our purpose, then, was to consider what the Delphi findings implied for educational practice in terms of recommendations that are multinational in origin and intent. They were developed by a multinational group (the research team) using multinational data (the Delphi findings), and their purpose is to influence teaching and learning in several nations – the same nine nations from which the expert panellists and researchers were drawn. By this route, we aim to encourage the desirable world trends identified by the expert panel and obstruct or manage the undesirable trends. We proceed here in four sections: implications for the school curriculum, for classroom life, for school function and organization, and finally for teacher education.

## IMPLICATIONS FOR CURRICULUM

We recommend that the development of multidimensional citizens become an important goal of the school curriculum. Multidimensional citizens are men and women who exhibit the consensus characteristics described earlier and are thereby enabled somewhat to anticipate and grapple with the trends that make these characteristics necessary in the first place. With the term 'multidimensional citizenship', we mean to capture the personal, social, spatial and temporal aspects of the citizen identity that are necessary for meeting the shared challenges of the early 21st century. Particularly, we mean the new requirement that adults function as citizens not just of some local place or group but of a seriously more complex network of mutually dependent places and groups, within, but more important beyond, the borders of their own nations.

The proposed curriculum is multinational in two ways. First, its core subject matter is explicitly organized around pressing worldwide problems. The essential subject matter of the curriculum derives from a set of six ethical questions that the research team sees as arising from the consensus trends, characteristics and strategies. These questions are augmented by a set of related concepts, skills and attitudes that are pertinent to considering the ethical questions knowledgeably, critically, cooperatively, and as members of a 'global public'. We will have more to say about this last category shortly. These six questions are:

1. What should be done in order to promote equity and fairness within and among societies?
2. What should be the balance between the right to privacy and free and open access to information in information-based societies?
3. What should be the balance between protecting the environment and meeting human needs?
4. What should be done to cope with population growth, genetic engineering, and children in poverty?
5. What should be done to develop shared (universal; global) values while respecting local values?
6. What should be done to secure an ethically based distribution of power for deciding policy and action on the above issues?

Second, the curriculum is multinational by virtue of the fact that its implementation is intended to occur across national boundaries. That is, the research team recommends that curriculum committees in the nine nations specify primary and secondary grade course experiences that have students join these questions, form these concepts, and develop these skills and attitudes over a number of years. It recommends, further, that specific courses be designed as capstone experiences in which students address this subject matter squarely as the core focus of the course. A common syllabus dealing with these four components could unite sections of, for example, a high-school Contemporary World Problems course in each nation. This course could share a broad syllabus that is elaborated locally and shared by electronic or other means with course participants in other nations. Students' work on the questions could be shared as well and discussed internationally.

## Deliberation

The proposed curriculum is 'deliberation-based'. This means that the core practice in the curriculum is discussion of the ethical questions themselves with the intention of recommending suitable public action. The English word deliberation derives from the Latin word 'libra' for 'scale'. Deliberation means 'to weigh, as in weighing which actions will best address a common problem'. Deliberation, then, is making choices about what to do about issues a group is facing in common. Neither negotiation nor debate, deliberation is making decisions together about the kind of world a 'we' wants to forge.

The research team understands that goals are transformed right within the process of public discourse. For this reason, deliberation is not only an instructional means but a curriculum outcome itself, for it creates a particular kind of democratic public culture among the deliberators: listening as well as talking, sharing resources, forging decisions together rather than only advocating positions taken earlier, coming to disagreement. Because the issues being deliberated in the curriculum are international issues, and because students are interacting in some way with one another (eg, face-to-face; electronic), actually conjoining on these common issues, this curriculum has the potential to contribute to the development of what Elise Boulding (1988) called a 'global civic culture' or what today might be called a transnational civil society.[1] That is, by moving purposefully towards an international perspective on 'citizenship' and citizenship education, this project loosens somewhat the conventional meaning of citizen as one who has member-ship in a political entity, such as a nation or province, and raises the concept *world citizen*. There is no world political entity in which an individual might have membership, of course, and this study is not interested in advocating such an entity (eg, a world government); rather, world citizen comes to mean, as in the spatial dimension of citizenship discussed in Chapter 5, one for whom the commonwealth is not only a local or national civic community, but alongside these a transnational community concerned with transnational problems and problem-solving.

## Ethical questions

We are not recommending an 'international relations' curriculum here. Rather, it is an international *problems* curriculum featuring the six ethical questions noted earlier in this chapter as the core subject matter. But why *ethical* problems? The research team was struck by the ethical implications embedded in the consensus characteristics and strategies. The Thai and Japanese members of the research team repeatedly brought the team's attention to one of the consensus educational strategies: 'Ensure that all social institutions (including the family and educational religious institutions) have an abiding respect for the basic rights of children and contribute to their well-being.' Keeping children uppermost in mind – not just 'our' children but all children – keeps the global responsibilities of citizenship in the foreground, and focusing on children's 'well-being' requires the continual enactment of an ethical imagination – seeing what can be done that is not now being done, anticipating conflict and preventing it, planning ahead for coming crises (eg, water shortage), and, most of all, paying close and continual attention to the lives of children.

We look more closely now at why the team decided on questions and why deliberation was selected as the pedagogic vehicle for the curriculum.

First, why *questions*? There were two reasons. A consensus item on the strategies list, 'Support the teaching of subject matter in a manner that encourages children to think critically', suggests that students should be helped to join questions rather than merely learn answers. More basic than this pedagogical reason, however, is a substantive one: the team did not believe that 'answers' were available. The consensus trends identified by the international expert panel pose extraordinarily complex social, cultural and environmental problems. These are messy, real problems of the sort that, in John Dewey's words, are 'set by actual social situations which are themselves conflicting and confused' (1939, p498). 'Actual' problems, particularly world civic problems, are inherently complex and controversial. They do not fit easily into disciplinary conceptual frameworks taken from the inven-tories of knowledge amassed in each academic field. Such frameworks are important to problem-solving, to be sure, and are one of the four components of the recommended curriculum, but they are resources to the problem-solving activity and no substitute for it. In fact, concepts are revised during the activity of problem-solving. In this vein, Neil Smelser (1996), an American sociologist who has attempted to identify the range of world problems that will press forward early in the next century, argues that the main task is not problem-solving but 'a serious revamping of our *modes* of understanding social problems and the social policies that are responsive to them' (1996, p285).

The six questions, then, present for students' consideration 'ill-structured' problem arenas.[2] Scholars and practitioners today are barely able to define them let alone understand or solve them. Consider the trend, 'Conflicts of interest between developing and developed nations will increase due to environmental deterioration'. Much of the information that would be helpful in an attempt, first, to understand this problem and then to reason towards a course of action is absent from the presentation of the problem, and competing perspectives and value orientations can and will be brought to bear on it. Numerous solutions are possible, assuming one ever grasps the problem itself, and citizens are bound to disagree on the best course of action. In brief, these are both serious and difficult problems. The recommendation is that students in diverse nations be taught to tackle them together, striving to forge decisions together and to communicate with one another and officials their understandings of the problems.

Why *deliberation*? When a group deliberates, it is trying to decide on the most appropriate course of action from among the alternatives. Deliberation ends, therefore, not in action itself but in a decision to take a particular course of action. Forging that decision together, reasoning together, generating and weighing alternatives, is the main activity of deliberation. It is, practically speaking, discussion with an eye towards decision-making. It is thus a prudential, moral and circumstantial activity. Before it begins, the parties to it have experienced a problematic situation together which motivates the deliberation in the first place. Of course, in heterogeneous societies, deliberation is done with persons who are more or less different from one another in political views, culture, social status, income, power, etc; we recommend for pedagogical purposes, therefore, that the deliberative groups – schools and classrooms – be as diverse as possible in these ways. What the participants have in common is the problem they experience together and must work out together. It is the problem situation that has brought them together; it is the common ground that makes of them a single public, at least for the time being.

There are other ways for publics to make decisions, that is, to decide the question 'What should we do?' *Voting* is one way. In a plurality, the alternative that receives the most votes wins; in a majority system, a decision is not reached until one of the options wins at least 51 per cent of the votes. Either way, the give-and-take of discussion is not required. In the electronic at-home systems being considered in numerous societies, the decision could be made by individuals having absolutely no interaction with one another. *Debate* is another way for groups to make a decision without discussion. The proposals being debated were not themselves forged by the group that is debating them, but by subsets (eg, debate 'teams') of the group or by parties outside the group. Either way, it is an adversarial process; one proposal wins and another loses. *Negotiation* is a third way. Here discussion is involved, to be sure, but the group is assuming competing interests and the discussion is guided by calculating constantly the gains and losses of each interest. As in debate, there is not actually one group, but at least two groups present in the same forum engaged in a contest. Deliberation, by contrast, involves everyone in the group forging together the alternatives and making a decision.[3]

Of course, 'everyone in the group forging together the alternatives' is highly problematic in actually existing democracies where power and status control participation in deliberation as well as the topics considered appropriate for deliberation. The poor, women and oppressed ethnic, religious and racial minorities are the first to be excluded from deliberative forums in most nations. Measures to assure access and equity must be in place, therefore, before any pretence to deliberation can be taken seriously. Both Jane Mansbridge (1991) and Nancy Fraser (1995) have produced insightful critiques and made helpful suggestions along these lines, including the idea that multiple deliberative forums are desirable because they allow a range of access points. A church basement, a parliament, a union hall, a farmers' cooperative and a classroom, for example, each affords a particular style of public talk. None of them assures that all voices and topics are welcome, however. A vigilant commitment to equity and to hearing multiple perspectives is needed by participants, whatever the setting. Let us summarize now the several reasons why deliberation was selected.

First, deliberation is a democratic way for a diverse group to grapple with shared problems and try to reach a shared decision about what to do. It is thus an authentic democratic activity and arguably the single most important activity in which democratic citizens must engage. Second, deliberation is a form of pedagogy that is bound up with the problems being deliberated. In fact, it is absolutely meaningless when separated from problems worth deliberating; therefore, it cannot be linked – not logically at least – to the process-without-content pedagogies roundly criticized by cognitive psychologists, educational researchers and parent groups worried about lowered expectations for their children in the name of 'progressive education'. Third, disciplined deliberation by students on pressing international problems should produce two socially valued results. On the one hand, students are learning by experience the democratic problem-solving ability at which they are expected to be skilled as adult citizens of their various communities. This is an important curriculum outcome. On the other hand, they are helping actually to sort out and solve, or at least think about, the pressing global problems they are asked to deliberate. This is an important community outcome. Fourth, deliberation on common problems is a public-building activity. 'Publics' are groups that come together to decide what to do about common problems (eg, Dewey, 1927). Within a nation's schools, deliberation helps bring students together as public citizens for public purposes, tackling pressing public problems. When students within classrooms in several nations are deliberating the same set of cross-culturally felt problems, then a larger international public – a global civil society – is encouraged. This strikes us as the major contribution of our curriculum recommendations.

## Other components

There are three components of the curriculum in addition to deliberation on shared ethical problems. The first of these are great, generative ideas or, more specifically, concepts.[4] Instruction on well-chosen concepts related to the six ethical questions is recommended for two reasons: so that deliberation is enriched by knowledge and so that the knowledge fund is in turn revised and refined by the deliberation. The concepts should be decided locally and shared eventually with course participants in other nations. Examples drawn directly from the questions might be equity, fairness, privacy, access to information, population growth, genetic engineering, children in poverty, distribution of power and wealth, and tensions such as the tension between protecting the environment and meeting human needs and the tension between shared universal values and particularistic local values. There are also concepts that undergird these but are not specifically stated in the questions themselves, for example human rights, democracy, social class and status, culture and cultural diversity, nationalism, political economy, ecosystem and sustainable future. Deciding the concepts locally should add a dynamic tension to the overall multinational project, encouraging discourse and disagreement and increasing the likelihood that a range of local voices and viewpoints is brought forward.

A small group of concepts should be targeted for intensive study. The research team recommends this so that meaningful learning might occur (eg, in-depth, sustained study on a limited number of topics) and so that faculty can focus limited resources on key instructional materials. More than these instructional reasons, however, the push for a limited set of key concepts begs the all-important curricular question, Which concepts are of most worth? Curriculum deliberation among students and faculty on this question is precisely what we hope to achieve. Such deliberation could well lead to a revision of the set of ethical questions. The revisions and the rationale for them can be shared with course participants in other nations, thus contributing substantively to the overall multinational public-building project.

In addition to instruction on key concepts, we recommend instruction on skills. Specifically, the team recommends instruction on skills related to researching and deliberating the six issues. By research, the team means scientific inquiry and critical thinking: finding worthy problems, making and testing hypotheses, judging the strength of arguments and conclusions, and judging the quality of evidence. By deliberation, as defined above, we mean cooperative discussion with an eye towards decision. Related skills include data-gathering and data-analysis procedures, participating in and moderating discussions of controversial issues, seeking opposing points of view, expressing positions and the reasoning that supports them, searching for missing voices and perspectives, weighing altern-atives, and predicting consequences of alternatives. The skills, as with the concepts, should be locally decided then shared internationally.

Particular attitudes should be singled out for fostering as well. Key are those attitudes that support research and deliberation on the ethical questions, formation of related knowledge, and development of a global perspective. Not merely tolerating diversity, but respecting it, is one attitude. Respecting evidence over prejudice and disciplining oneself not to jump to conclusions are others. The willingness actually to listen to opposing points of view and to be sceptical of one's own position and reasoning are two more.

## IMPLICATIONS FOR CLASSROOM PRACTICE

In the previous section we proposed a deliberation-based curriculum built around a set of six ethical questions that the research team derived from the consensus trends, characteristics and strategies. These questions and the requisite concepts, skills and attitudes necessary for their investigation hold out the promise of creating the qualities in our students that our scholar-experts say will be necessary for effective citizenship in the 21st century. Now we turn to the implications of implementing this curriculum model in the classroom.

Classrooms in a school that embodies the qualities of multidimensional citizen-ship would have deliberation as the foundation of learning. Students of all ages would be given the opportunity to examine in depth the great issues of our day which will most certainly impact their lives fully in the coming years. The qualities of multidimensional citizenship will not develop by chance. They need to be learnt through enquiry and discourse about key public issues.

Multidimensional citizenship is best served by an interdisciplinary approach to teaching. The six ethical questions are not embedded or confined within disciplines. Yet, given the wide variation in curricular frameworks across the nine nations in the study and internationally to be sure, the research team decided not to pursue a single framework for curriculum or classroom content. What seemed more important was the introduction of the deliberative pedagogy regardless of the organization of the syllabus, irrespective of whether the curriculum was discipline-based, concept-based, thematic, issue-oriented, etc. It was left to the various regional or country teams to adapt the findings to their own specific context. The shape of the curriculum need not constrain classroom practice.

What, then, would be the implications of this deliberative curriculum for classroom practice? We must begin with both an admission and an admonition. There is no doubt that the kind of deliberative curriculum and pedagogy proposed is very much at odds with the picture one gets of classrooms worldwide. In general, the evidence indicates that schools are marked by an overly rigid formalism framed by a textbook, and a syllabus- or examination-driven curriculum. There is, for example, an obvious contradiction between the deliberative classroom dealing with our framework of six ethical questions, and one driven by 'examination hell', like those found in the 'cram' schools so prevalent in some parts of the world.

Yet the problem of implementing a deliberative mode of instruction is worldwide. In the most comprehensive review of US classrooms in recent years, Goodlad (1984) found that the dominant classroom pattern was the recall of information. He reports, 'The topics of the curriculum, it appears to me, were something to be acquired, not something to be explored, reckoned with, and converted into personal meaning and development' (1983, p468). Some years earlier, a Canadian investigation of history teaching found a similar pattern in the vast majority of Canadian classrooms (Hodgetts, 1968).

Though observers were to observe as many as fifteen instructional techniques, Goodlad's study showed that some 85–95 per cent of what went on in classrooms was teachers' talk and/or student answers to teacher-directed questions. With so little variation in instructional technique, instruction was not significant in educational outcomes. Unfortunately, in global terms, there is a high probability that the kind of didactic, almost mindless, instruction described by Goodlad is the dominant or at least modal pedagogy in most classrooms most of the time.

This underpins the conclusion of the researchers in this study that in order to achieve the vision of a multidimensional citizenship, a fundamental transformation must take place in both the socialization and academic dimensions of schooling. In the area of socialization we would endorse the Engle and Ochoa notion (Ochoa-Becker, 1996) of the complementarity of socialization and counter-socialization. In their rationale, socialization is an inescapable process in all cultures in order to transmit cultural values and traditions to the next generation. By and large, socialization is highly conforming and neither reflective nor analytical. These ideas are also reflected in the work of Egan (1986). The aim of countersocialization, on the other hand, is to foster the independent thought and social criticism that is so crucial for democratic citizens. Countersocialization calls for a consciously reflective process where students learn to ask challenging questions and probe for thoughtful and responsible answers, such as:

- How do we know that a particular statement is true? (Validating truth claims; evaluating evidence)
- What must be done to improve specific social conditions such as crime, homelessness, foreign policy, inequality, etc?
- How can I justify my decisions? (What values? What evidence? What logic?)

These questions of course are completely consistent with the implementation of a deliberative curriculum because in such a classroom even the process of deliberation itself would be open to scrutiny and analysis.

How might this work in classroom practice? Let us explore one example adapting a four-step framework suggested by McLaughlin and Hartoonian (1995). Let us consider a lesson based on one element of ethical question 4: what should be done to cope with population growth? The first step or level would be to provide students with a context for the study of this issue with emphasis on student comprehension and conceptualization. In other words, the teacher helps students to conceptualize the issue of population growth in time, place and circumstance, presumably in relationship to the syllabus as well as to what they have studied before and will study in the future. Students should be able to identify the particular setting, story and context within which they will study this problem. Once this context is established, the class can move to the second level, examination of causality. Students would be able to explain the origins and implications of population growth within the context of their study. At level three the teacher and students examine the truth or validity of the claims made by demographers, NGOs, historians, economists, journalists, politicians, their community and peers as to the causes and impact of population growth. They evaluate the nature of the evidence presented, and the bias of each source. At the fourth level teachers would encourage students to create their own questions, interpretations, stories or explanation of population growth in various modalities: oral, written, visual, etc. British examples of classroom practice in community-based work and developing international understanding can be found in Edwards and Fogelman (1993) and Hicks and Townley (1982), Hicks (1995).

The larger implications of these approaches for classrooms become increasingly apparent. If we were to place classrooms along a continuum from teacher-centred to student-centred, the social ecology of a deliberative classroom puts more emphasis upon the student as a learner, or at least moves that classroom away from the teacher-centred pole of the continuum. Postman and Weingartner (1969) once suggested, in a somewhat light tone, that teachers be limited to three declarative sentences and fifteen interrogatives in any single lesson. While we (and they to be sure) would not be this prescriptive or rigid, the message is clear. We concur with Torney-Purta:

> Finally, there is no substitute for dialogue or discourse in the classroom if the goal is for teachers to understand how students organize knowledge and to encourage them to relate what they already know to what they are expected to learn by engaging in meaningful or 'deep' processing of information. In finding words to express ideas to others, either orally or in writing, those ideas are reshaped, connected and consolidated. (1991, p197)

How achievable is this vision of a 'deliberative' classroom given Goodlad's gloomy picture of the state of classroom pedagogy? Fortunately, there is room for hope.

In a considerably smaller sample of schools (13) in the San Francisco Bay Area, the American Schools and the World (ASAW) project found a greater variety of instructional strategies than were observed by Goodlad in a study focused on knowledge of and concern for global issues (Weiler *et al.*, 1987). In fact, there was considerably more variation in instructional strategies than in content. In addition to the traditional teacher-centred question-and-answer format, the researchers observed small working groups, debates and role-playing in ninth and eleventh grade social studies classrooms. The study reports a continuum of teacher behaviour that ranged from divergent questioning in a relatively open atmosphere to strictly convergent questioning in a relatively closed atmosphere.

In the 1968 Canadian survey, noted earlier, investigators found a minority of classrooms that very effectively practised what was described as a 'dialogue' approach, where teachers and students worked together in a problem-oriented fashion, closely resembling what we have described as deliberation (Hodgetts, 1968).

A pattern emerged at the two extremes of this continuum. Generally, the divergent questioning style/open climate classrooms prompted students to think, to share ideas, and to respect the process of sharing those thoughts. The more a teacher tended towards a strictly convergent style of questioning, combined with a tight control over the class, the less sharing of perspectives and examination of issues was observed. Instructional strategies proved to be a more important source of variation in student knowledge and attitudes towards global issues than either classroom content or formal teacher training in teaching global issues. Three factors seemed to be important in explaining the kind of classroom interactions that took place: first, the level of support that the school provided for introducing international content; second, the ability of the teacher to foster a dynamic in the classroom in which differences of opinion among students were encouraged in discussions; and third, the socio-economic and ethnic mix of students (with the diversity of student populations being a positive factor).

Other recent research supports these findings. Hahn (1996) concluded that when attention to the triple variables of content, pedagogy and climate results in presenting content from multiple perspectives, using interactive pedagogical strategies, and maintaining an open classroom climate, then the essential ingredients for effective issues-centred instruction in global education, as well as in other social studies content areas, appear to be present.

Deliberation in relation to the curriculum is not widely used in the British literature. There is, however, a long history of British work on teaching styles and their effects on students' learning. Stenhouse (1982) in the Humanities Project advocated the notion of the teacher as 'neutral chairman' when discussing sensitive social issues with students. Using this approach the teacher provided sensitive and ethical issues upon which students were encouraged to deliberate. Approaches to the teaching of sensitive issues to middle school students through history, geography and the social sciences was advocated by Blyth *et al.* (1976) and Derricott and Blyth (1979). Here deliberation was taken to mean the evaluation and interpretation of evidence. A British history curriculum project (Sylvester, 1976; Shemilt, 1980, 1983) applied similar approaches to the evaluation of evidence with older students.

Bennett (1976) reinforced the link between teaching styles and students' learning. This study was much maligned because of its inadequate sampling but the message remained strong and clear, that is, teaching styles are an important variable in the progress students make. Bennett's work was taken in some quarters as an attack on progressive primary school child-centred methods. Further work by Bennett (1984, 1992) explored the incidence of different teaching styles mainly in primary classrooms. These studies indicated that what was required in classrooms was a style and a climate in which there was a balance between teacher-directed approaches and those which provided students with structures in tackling any issue but which allowed, within limits, students choice. With the advent of the National Curriculum much of this work was taken up by the radical right and seen as a justification of whole class instruction and teacher direction (Pollard 1987, 1994). The research, however, indicates that a deliberation curriculum has three important facets – content, climate and pedagogy. Not all content can be approached through deliberation but sensitive and ethical issues are the best subjects for deliberation, if only to avoid indoctrination. A deliberation approach thrives in a social and emotional classroom atmosphere which values respect for the individual and his rights. The accompanying pedagogy has to employ an approach to evidence which encourages examining what is being taken for granted and challenges students to become confident in their own deliberations.

Beyond these issues of classroom climate and pedagogy, there are at least two other areas of concern derived from this study that have direct implications for the classroom. First, this study determined that there was both support for the potential of the new information technologies for education and liberation, and at the same time, concern that these same technologies might be sources of greater social inequities or instruments of invasive social control. Based on these findings, the researchers recommend that attention be paid in classrooms not just to developing the skills of using these new technologies, but that greater attention in schools should be devoted to questions of access to these technologies and the critical evaluation of the information that is disseminated through them. Therefore, we would argue for an enhanced role for a visual or media literacy element in classrooms.

Finally, this study identified specific concerns in the areas of equity and access, touching specifically on issues of gender, race, ethnicity and class in various social contexts. These concerns have direct relevance to both classroom organization and instruction. There is some indication, for example, that females and males have differing interests in and ways of thinking about public issues, and that teachers afford males greater opportunity than females to discuss them in class. Further, researchers have identified differing effects of race, class and ethnicity on attitudes towards democratic participation. The classroom implications of this are clear: at the very least it demands greater attention and sensitivity to the impact of these factors on citizenship education. More than this, it urges teachers to adapt their modes of instruction to mitigate any possible negative effects from these factors, or in a more positive sense, that we harness the diversity within the classroom to achieve our vision of multidimensional citizenship.

## Classroom recommendations

In summary, what would be the underlying characteristics of classrooms that emphasized teaching in a deliberative mode? Based on our interpretation of the consensus findings and augmented by ideas suggested by Evans *et al.* (1996) and Newmann *et al.* (1995), we suggest that the following elements would be found in classrooms using the deliberative mode:

- intellectually challenging and developmentally appropriate content organized around or integrated with our six ethical questions
- accurate and up-to-date materials reflecting multiple perspectives on the question at issue
- content that accepts and reflects upon the richness of the human experience in all its diversity and variety
- pedagogy that emphasizes deliberation on the six questions in which students experience influence and control over the deliberation itself
- pedagogy that emphasizes depth of understanding over superficial exposure
- pedagogy that links the classroom to the community, the nation and the world, at least electronically, and whenever possible, also through direct contact via field trips, exchanges and guest lecturers
- a classroom climate that is characterized by open discussion, divergent questioning, and freedom to express opinions contrary to that of the instructor
- a classroom climate that harnesses the diversity of the classroom, community, region or nation (eg, gender, class, ethnicity, race) to enhance the deliberative process while mitigating any potential for the negative impact of these same factors, and
- classroom climate that uses the potential of information-based technologies but also emphasizes equity in access to and critical evaluation of these same sources of information, whatever the technology or media.

## IMPLICATIONS FOR THE STRUCTURE AND FUNCTIONS OF SCHOOLING

Educational institutions must promote the development and expression of multidimensional citizenship. They should be explicitly designed in a way that the school organization fosters ethical deliberation, environmental stewardship, and principled uses of information technology; while demonstrating justice and compassion in the distribution of power and resources. Schools must also respect the unique potential of each individual and her/his rights, culture and history, while maintaining awareness of larger issues of mutual concern to the world community.

With this in mind, and in the spirit of deliberative, question-centred, curriculum and pedagogy, we encourage experts, community leaders, concerned citizens, educators and students to join together in assessing the quality of their educational institutions through consideration of the following questions:

1. To what extent are school policy and practice responsive to the basic needs, rights and interests of children? Have local schools established, and do they act decisively on the basis of, clearly defined procedures that protect children from physical, emotional and sexual abuse? Do schools contribute broadly to the well-being of all young students?
2. To what extent do school policy and practice ensure equitable access, participation and opportunity for locally marginalized or disadvantaged groups? Do school programmes respectfully and effectively support diverse learners? Do the schools sponsor community outreach programmes to prepare all citizens to respond to the needs and interests of traditionally marginalized segments of society?

3. To what extent do school policy and practice model sound environmental thought and action? Have local educational institutions formally adopted a code of environmentally minded behaviour, and do they then abide by this code with respect to the use of their own resources? Do local schools play an active role in promoting community awareness and action to support sustainable development?
4. To what extent do school policy and practice model varied and effective processes of conflict resolution? Is the use of violence, in all of its forms, effectively opposed? Do local schools function as safe and inclusive sites for the expression of diverse opinions and collective deliberation regarding timely, significant and controversial issues confronting the community?
5. To what extent do school policy and practice demonstrate principled use of technology – particularly those technologies used to collect, process and share information? Do the schools promote careful evaluation of societal implications of new information technologies in order to address such issues as equal access and personal privacy? Are local schools involved in establishing and maintaining extensive technologically enhanced connections that support the development and exchange of information on local, national and global levels among students, teachers, experts, researchers and community members; among people from diverse cultural backgrounds; among social institutions; and across varied bodies of knowledge?
6. To what extent do school policy and practice support diverse and generative collaborations among schools and the many and varied communities of which they are a part? Do the schools serve as centres for vibrant and principled public life? Do schools provide resources for the community as the community provides resources for the schools? Does the entire community assume shared responsibility for the education of its citizenry?
7. To what extent do schools strive to model for their communities processes of self-reflection and renewal? Do local schools demonstrate effective use of varied modes of assessment to evaluate the quality of their programmes in relation to the areas listed above? Are local schools provided the necessary resources and then held accountable for demonstrating progress towards social, cultural, economic, political, environmental sustainability worldwide?

For these questions to be asked and considered seriously, participation in decision-making processes that shape and support educational systems must be broadened and diversified. Movement towards comprehensive implementation of the recommendations proposed here cannot be the task of a single set of actors. Neither the vision of an extraordinary leader, nor top-down decision-making by a small group, nor grass-roots community initiation, will be sufficient to provide the educational opportunities necessary for multidimensional citizenship. Authentic power-sharing in educational settings can be achieved only if we are willing to join together in moving not only with, but also beyond, contemporary approaches to educational politics. Such movement might include:

- moving from reliance on highly professionalized processes of negotiation and bargaining towards attempts to facilitate more inclusive policy conversations
- de-centralizing educational decision-making whenever possible to ensure full participation of those likely to be most directly affected

- decreasing the size of educational programmes and institutions, where appropriate, to create learning communities small enough to support meaningful exchange
- encouraging the reaching of sensitive and informed judgements concerning the acquisition, configuration, use and accessibility of information technologies
- transcending the emphasis on narrowly pragmatic and technical concerns in education policy-making to deliberation that is informed also by ethical and aesthetic standards.

Schools can model the creative and adaptive dynamics of power. How we learn, decide, act and assess together in our schools should assist us not only in developing responsible adaptations to global change, but also in anticipating and shaping such changes. The curricular and policy challenges implied are significant but not insurmountable. Our research has identified major areas of agreement on what contemporary educational policy activists find urgent and feasible.

## TEACHING THE TEACHERS OF MULTIDIMENSIONAL CITIZENS

Teachers will be among the chief stewards of this transformation. Without them, it is impossible. Teachers cannot act alone, of course, for in democracies they labour on behalf of the publics that create and fund (and often ignore) the schools, and their thought and action are constrained by the economic forces, cultural traditions and power relations that form the institution of schooling in the first place. Yet they are key change agents in the school system. How they are (and are not) supported in their work, therefore, is a matter of central concern. In this final section, we consider the implications of our study for teacher education.

It is enormously helpful if the teachers of multidimensional citizens are themselves multidimensional citizens. This is not likely to be the case, however. Teacher education begins with the preschool through high school education of persons who later choose teaching as a vocation, and teachers in any nation have not generally been (no more than the rest of us) the recipients of the sort of education we outlined above. Furthermore, teacher-education programmes at colleges and universities are but a small piece of a teacher's life-long education. Consequently, we cannot be overly optimistic about what can be accomplished in a teacher education programme. With that caveat, we recommend the following.

Multidimensional citizenship needs to become a central focus of teacher-education programmes, both preservice (new teacher preparation) and inservice (continuing professional development). We recommend, generally speaking, a form of teacher education that is focused on the recommendations discussed in the three sections above regarding the school curriculum, classroom practice, and school function and structure. Towards this goal, we recommend four initiatives for teacher education programmes: cultivation of a global/cross-cultural outlook, emphasis on the development of a critical perspective, emphasis on democratic pedagogies, and improved community collaborations. While these overlap considerably, we sketch them one by one.

## A global/cross-cultural outlook

Teacher-education faculties need to develop means by which preservice and inservice teachers take seriously the six global ethical questions that form the core of the recommended school curriculum. The contents of these questions encourage the needed cross-cultural style of inquiry while deliberation provides the method for joining them.

Deliberation within teacher education should function in at least two ways. First, deliberation should focus on an ethical question in a broad, international context that includes multiple cases and perspectives. Teacher-education faculty can help their students clarify the question, gather material from several sources, examine cases from numerous societies, and compare divergent policy approaches that have been proposed to address the question at hand. Second, deliberation should involve placing the question under consideration in a local educational context. For example, if the first question is being deliberated, teachers should be encouraged to consider equity and fairness in relation to what happens within the school's walls. That is, how does equity and fairness manifest itself within particular classrooms and schools? Who has access to a multidimensional citizenship education and who does not? What are the barriers and obstacles to equity and fairness in classrooms? What action is needed?

We recommend, further, that teacher exchanges and study-abroad programmes be made routinely available to teachers. Such experiences need to become the rule rather than the exception for future and current teachers for they help develop an understanding of cultural differences, challenge teachers' own assumptions, and foster renewed observation of one's taken-for-granted practices. Such is the 'reflective mirror' of international travel. A global outlook can also be developed in teacher-education by reading multicultural literature, recruiting cultural minorities into teacher education programmes (both as students and faculty), visiting cultural resource centres and inviting guest speakers who supply differing viewpoints.

## A critical perspective

Due to the complexity of the challenges facing citizens during the next twenty-five years, teacher-education programmes must foster a critical perspective, which involves the consideration of multiple philosophic traditions and diverse cultural practices when deliberating civic problems, broadly, when thinking about the world and one's place in it. We believe a critical perspective is best encouraged by the activity of deliberating with diverse others on controversial questions faced in common. The questions themselves must be situated in actual local instances if they are to make sense, and these local instances are likely to be different from one another, thus assuring multiple perspectives on the problem. Moreover, deliberation itself, as we saw earlier, is the activity of weighing alternatives in order to decide what 'we' should do. The formation of a critical perspective, then, may be supported by instituting a teacher-education programme that includes deliberation on cross-cultural ethical questions.

As well, teacher-education faculty can challenge teachers to evaluate current schooling practices and their relationship to the development of multidimensional citizenship. Without such evaluation, future and current teachers may not scrutinize the conditions and assumptions of the present education establishment. Critique, then, is a gateway towards curricular, classroom and school transformation. This requires that rote learning not be the dominant pedagogical orientation of teacher-education programmes and that opportunities to contemplate and practise critical thinking be made routinely available.

## Democratic pedagogy

The third initiative we recommend for teacher-education programmes is a curricular concentration on democratic forms of pedagogy. As the challenges of the 21st century require active citizen participation in the public affairs in several overlapping 'publics' (local, national and international), future and present teachers need to be exposed to instructional practices that build democratic publics (Harber, 1987; Harber and Meighan, 1989). As we suggested above, deliberation on ethical questions is a pedagogy matched well to this goal. When a group deliberates, it is engaged in democratic self-government, trying to decide on the 'best' course of action from among the alternatives. Deliberative groups – large and small – need to be as heterogeneous as possible, as we saw; and what the participants have in common is the problem they experience together and must work out together – a school bully, a regional water shortage, a community crisis. Deliberation, then, involves everyone in a group forging together the alternatives and making a decision. *Multiple* deliberative forums, you recall, are desirable because they allow a range of perspectives and access points, ensuring broader participation and a wider array of ideas. Deliberation, then, is an authentic democratic activity and arguably the single most important activity in which democratic citizens must engage. Students are learning by experience the very democratic problem-solving ability they need as citizens of their various communities. Deliberation, in brief, is a non-violent conflict resolution technique that fuels civic life while solving problems.

Attention must also be given to the hidden curriculum in teacher education, that is, the implicit messages carried by the environment or climate of the teacher-education programmes. These messages concern power and influence, rules of conduct, ways of thinking, and attitudes appropriate and inappropriate for educators. Teacher-education faculty need to examine together the hidden messages of their programmes and consciously build the type of environment they want teachers to create in their own schools and classrooms, such as openness to divergent philosophical and cultural perspectives, respect for human rights, and attitudes and behaviours that are non-sexist and non-racist. Teacher education, in other words, must strive to foster classroom climates that are conducive to and model the practice of multidimensional citizenship.

## Community collaboration and information technology

The fourth initiative is a community-oriented concept in which teachers are encouraged to take part in community affairs by incorporation of a community action component in teacher education. This should serve three purposes. First, a community action component can develop in teachers a sensitivity to community issues and diverse populations. Working on a rural farm or an urban jail or shelter can create awareness of problems in one's own community, heighten concern for the rights and needs of others, and incite action that is grounded in knowledge and a more elaborate understanding of the context in which the problem exists. Second, a community action component provides teachers with personal experience from which to deliberate the six ethical questions and the concepts underlying them (ie, equity, power, access, human rights, the relationship between the individual and his/her society/world). Third, community participation during a teacher-education programme provides teachers with concrete examples of how to orchestrate service programmes and community projects inside and outside the school. A desired outcome is that teachers will be willing and able to promote schools as active centres of community life and as agents for community development. Thus, it is recommended that teacher-education programmes require a substantial record of community action for admission to preparatory institutions and for completion of teacher certification.

Like community action projects, information technologies can play an important role in facilitating collaboration and providing opportunities for teachers to engage in problem-solving activities. Information technologies should be harnessed, therefore, to enhance teachers' and students' abilities to communicate through 'virtually diverse' forums. Teacher-education programme participants need routinely to converse with one another across national boundaries – sharing perspectives, the results of their deliberations, school descriptions and stories, and curriculum resources. Additionally, computer-based networks can be used to establish extensive international links among educational institutions at all levels to support international studies.

## CONCLUSION

The schools of each of the nations included in this study have many things in common. Children do schoolwork, they play together, they behave and misbehave according to locally meaningful norms, and they participate in numerous ritualized activities; adults attempt to teach them a curriculum that is updated from time to time in order to better match contemporary concerns and circumstances; the function of the school and curriculum is geared towards some combination of vocational, academic and political purposes; and so on. The similarity in which we were mainly interested here, however, is this: all these schools educate citizens. Our concern: what if we were to *plan* this citizen education rather than leave it to habit, convention, tradition or some other authoritative but perhaps unexamined mode of doing things? What then would it be?

This was the question on our minds as we – the international research team – sat down to interpret the consensus findings of the international expert panel and draw implications for educational practice. We did this work together over several days in Hiroshima. Our method was to deliberate the consensus findings on trends, citizen characteristics and educational strategies until we ourselves reached consensus on the recommendations presented in this chapter. Through deliberation, then, in which the consensus findings served as a shared data base, we arrived at a deliberation-based curriculum focused on ethical problems, a characterization of classroom practice that would support this curriculum, broad criteria to guide school restructuring efforts, and broad initiatives for teacher-education programmes.

We do not believe these recommendations are complete. Surely they are only a piece of a wider puzzle that must include liberal studies, namely the humanities, in which students engage in rigorous cross-cultural enquiry and learn the variety of ways in which different peoples understand everyday life and learn to justify political judgements in the context of diversity. We see our recommendations collectively, therefore, as a springboard. We hope they will stimulate numerous additional conversations – local and international – about the nature of multi-dimensional citizenship and the educational practices that might support it. We are confident that through such efforts more creative and sensitive recommendations than ours will obtain, and we welcome them.

The stakes are high, we believe. Without such efforts, and without the cultivation of multidimensional citizenship, we face the prospect of becoming a world of economically developed and technically competent people who have lost, or who never gained, the ability to be citizens not just of some local place and group but of the world – to situate ourselves in multiple communities, to reason cross-culturally, to think critically, to cooperate on shared problems with people who may be very different from ourselves, and to love the humanity and diversity of others all around the globe.

## ENDNOTES

1. Civil society is a different public realm from government. It counterbalances government and is therefore important to preventing government tyranny. See Jeffrey Alexander's (1997) sociological (versus economic) account of civil society as a realm of non-governmental solidarity.
2. On the 'informal' reasoning needed for addressing 'ill-structured' problems, see Perkins (1985) and Simon (1973).
3. This taxonomy is from Dillon (1994).
4. We define concepts as the attributes shared by members of a class; the class is formed as shared attributes among things are identified. This identification is a social activity.

## REFERENCES

Alexander, J C (1997) 'The Paradoxes of Civil Society', *International Sociology*, **12**(2), pp 115–33.
Bennett, N *et al.* (1984) *The Quality of Pupil Learning Experiences*, Erlbaum, London.
Bennett, N (1992) *Managing Learning in the Primary Classroom*, Trentham Books, Stoke-on-Trent.
Bennett, N (1976) *Teaching Styles and Pupil Progress*, Open Books, London.
Blyth, W A L *et al.* (1976) *Curriculum Planning in History, Geography and Social Science*, Collins and ESL Bristol for the Schools Council, London.
Boulding, E (1988) *Building a Global Civic Culture: Education for an interdependent world*, Teachers College Press, New York.
Derricott, R and Blyth, W A L (1979) 'Cognitive Development: The social dimension', in A Floyd (ed.), *Cognitive Development in the School Years*, Croom Helm and Open University Press, London, pp 284–316.
Dewey, J (1927) *The Public and its Problems*, Swallow, Chicago.

Dewey, J (1939) *Logic: The theory of inquiry*, Holt, New York.

Dillon, J T (ed.) (1994) *Deliberation in Education and Society*, Ablex, Norwood, N J.

Edwards, J and Fogelman, K (eds) (1993) *Developing Citizenship in the Curriculum*, Fulton, London.

Egan, K (1986) *Individual Development in the Curriculum*, Hutchinson, London.

Evans, R W, Newmann, F M and Saxe, D W (1996) 'Defining Issues-Centered Education', in R Evans and D Saxe (eds), *Handbook on Teaching Social Issues*, National Council for the Social Studies, Washington, DC.

Fraser, N (1995) 'Politics, Culture, and the Public Space: Toward a post-modern conception', in L Nicholson and S Seidman (eds), *Social Postmodernism: Beyond identity politics*, Cambridge University Press, Cambridge.

Galton, M J (1995) *Crisis in the Primary Classroom*, Fulton, London.

Goodlad, J I (1983) 'Study of Schooling: Some Findings and Hypotheses', *Phi Delta Kappan*, **64**(7), pp 465–70.

Goodlad, J I (1984) *A Place Called School*, McGraw-Hill, New York.

Hahn, C L (1996) 'Research on Issues-Centered Social Studies', in R Evans and D Saxe (eds), *Handbook on Teaching Social Issues*, National Council for the Social Studies, Washington, DC.

Harber, C (1987) *Political Education in Britain*, Falmer Press, London.

Harber, C and Meighan, R (1989) *The Democratic School: Educational management and the practice of democracy*, Education Now Publishing Co-operative Ltd., Ticknall.

Hicks, D W B (1995) *Visions of the Future: Why we need to teach about tomorrow*, Trentham Books, Stoke-on-Trent.

Hicks, D W B and Townley, C (1982) *Teaching World Studies: An introduction to global perspectives in the curriculum*, Longman, London.

Hodgetts, A B (1968) *What Culture? What Heritage?*, Toronto, OISE Press.

Mansbridge, J (1991) 'Democracy, Deliberation, and the Experience of Women', in B Murchland (ed.), *Higher Education and the Practice of Democratic Politics*, Kettering Foundation, Dayton, OH.

McLaughlin, M A and Hartoonian, M H (1995) *Challenges of Social Studies Instruction in Middle and High Schools: Developing enlightened citizens*, Harcourt Brace, Fort Worth, Texas.

Newmann, F M, Secada, W G and Wehlage, G G (1995) *A Guide to Authentic Instruction and Assessment: Vision, standards and scoring*, Wisconsin Center for Educational Research, Madison, Wisconsin.

Ochoa-Becker, A S (1996) 'Building a Rationale for Issues-Centered Education', in R Evans and D Saxe (eds), *Handbook on Teaching Social Issues*, National Council for the Social Studies, Washington, DC.

Parker, W C (ed.) (1996) *Educating the Democratic Mind*, State University of New York Press, Albany.

Perkins, D N (1985) 'Reasoning as Imagination', *Interchange*, **16**(1), pp 14–26.

Pollard, A (1987) *Children and their Primary Schools: A new perspective*, Falmer Press, London.

Pollard, A (1994) *Changing English Primary Schools: The impact of the Education Reform Act at Key Stage One*, Cassell, London.

Postman, N and Weingartner, C (1969) *Teaching as a Subversive Activity*, Dell, New York.

Shemilt, D (1980) *History 13–16 Evaluation Study*, Holmes McDougall, Edinburgh.

Shemilt, D *et al.* (1983) *The Philosophy of History Teaching*, Wesleyan University Press, Middletown, Conn.

Simon, H A (1973) 'The Structure of Ill-Structured Problems', *Artificial Intelligence*, **4**, pp 181–201.

Smelser, N J (1996) 'Social Sciences and Social Problems: The next century', *International Sociology*, **11**(3), pp 275–90.

Stenhouse, L *et al.* (1982) *Teaching about Race Relations: Problems and effects*, Routledge and Kegan Paul, London.

Sylvester, D W (1976) *What is History?: Teachers' guide*, issued by Schools Council History 13–16, Holmes McDougall, Edinburgh.

Torney-Purta, J (1991) 'Theory and Cognitive Psychology: Implications for social studies', *Theory and Research in Social Education*, **19**(2), pp 189–210.

Torney-Purta, J and Lansdale, D (1986) *Classroom Climate and Process in International Studies: Qualitative and quantitative evidence from the American schools and the World Project*. Paper presented at the annual meeting of the American Educational Research Association, San Francisco.

Weiler, H *et al.* (1987) *Final Report: American schools and the world*, Stanford University: Study of Stanford and the Schools, Stanford.

# 7

# THE CHALLENGE OF MULTIDIMENSIONAL CITIZENSHIP FOR THE 21ST CENTURY

## *John J Cogan*

We now come to the true test of what we have done over the past four years: the task of seeking to implement the findings and the resulting recommendations of this study. This requires those in policy-making and decision-making positions, as well as practitioners in classrooms and teacher educators in colleges and universities, to put into place the framework for the development of multi-dimensional citizens in the 21st century. This is a complex undertaking, but if it is not done, all that has been accomplished to date is simply an academic exercise. For in policy research, the only true successful outcome is the improvement of practice.

The concept of multidimensional citizenship is elaborated elsewhere in this book. It is a powerful, overarching set of ideas which have implications for all those involved in policy-making about education at local, regional, national and international levels. The concept of multidimensional citizenship has some obvious messages for policy makers but if the phrase is used rhetorically, as a form of words which trip off the tongue easily, the values behind the concept can be lost and ignored. If the ideas and values behind such phrases are not examined and made explicit, then they have as much impact as the warning 'fragile' has to luggage handlers in a busy international airport.

This chapter will discuss the implementation of the model of multidimensional citizenship based upon the findings of this study. It will explore the challenges and difficulties of implementing the study recommendations within existing systems of education and schooling, both centralized and decentralized. It will examine some of the difficulties of translating the key concepts of the multi-dimensional model cross-culturally and the applicability of the model in other parts of the world which were not a part of this study. Finally, it will identify additional research which needs to be carried out since this study is only the beginning of a research endeavour which needs to be carried out and extended in other regions of the world.

## CHALLENGES OF IMPLEMENTATION

Both the opinions of our policy experts and the global trends literature reviewed in Chapter 1 indicate that children and youth in schools today can expect to live and work in a century very different from ours in many respects. The list of challenges facing those who will be the adult citizens of the early 21st century is long and challenging. As noted in Chapter 4, they include significant environmental issues, economic conflict and disparity, and access to and appropriate use of modern technologies. Further, our data raise the prospect of the loss of a sense of shared community and a declining commitment to the common good, as well as a loss of a sense of political efficacy. Students, for the most part, will not have been the ones to have caused these problems, but they will most assuredly be the ones to have to find the solutions to them.

Also, the pace of change is accelerating and the seriousness of the problems facing the world are manifested in local settings. These will no longer be someone else's problems that can be ignored but will affect people in their everyday lives. We believe that these challenges can be confronted only through a fundamentally different approach to citizenship education, one centred in the multidimensional citizenship model presented in Chapters 5 and 6.

This transformation is unlikely to be accomplished quickly. It took a very long time to get to the present condition; it will take time and a strong commitment to the goals and the processes of multidimensional citizenship to implement the needed changes. We shall need the help of everyone, especially policy shapers such as those who participated so actively in the conduct of this study, to ensure that our will does not falter. We have some ideas regarding *what* must be done which are explicated below; but most important now is the *will* to do it.

Thus, in this chapter we suggest a number of implementation strategies which are critical to ensure that the multidimensional citizenship model outlined in the previous chapters becomes a reality. It is true that by and large schools are not transformative institutions, but rather tend to reflect the existing values and socio-economic structures of their societies. However, the findings of this study indicate that schools now face a variety of formidable challenges across the countries we have studied and beyond. They are challenges which must be addressed, not by schools alone, but rather by a concerted and mutual effort of schools and their communities.

The underlying premise of any set of implementation strategies is that the school, first and foremost, must embody the conception of multidimensional citizenship we propose in this book. Further, the school must become a centre for change.

## THE SCHOOL AS A MODEL COMMUNITY

The task of preparing multidimensional citizens can best be addressed by organizing the school itself in such a way that it becomes a model of multidimensional citizenship, ie, that its whole atmosphere and functioning model equitable policies and practices, environmental stewardship, ethical uses of informational technologies, and global awareness. The school structure and organization, its faculty and staff, the curriculum, assessment measures and the general ethos within the school, must be focused upon the:

- development of cooperative working relationships
- development of critical and systemic thinking

- development of appreciation, tolerance and respect for multiple perspectives and points of view
- defence of human rights for all
- development of the ability to view problems and issues from a global perspective
- development of a willingness to change one's lifestyle and consumption habits in order to protect the environment
- development of the willingness and ability to participate in civic and public affairs at multiple levels, ie, local, provincial or regional, national, international.

The study findings suggest that what is needed is a redefinition of both the socializing and academic functions of the school. Although schools have always played a socializing role, generally understood as the maintenance of traditional values and norms for societal continuity and stability, they must also encourage students, as well as adults, to critically evaluate societal norms and to develop the attitudes, skills and abilities to cope with, and to counteract, undesirable global trends. Schools must become the democratic institutions they purport to be in preparing children and youth for their important citizen roles in the larger society.

One of the most disturbing study findings was the panellists' prediction that it would be increasingly difficult in the future to develop a shared belief in the common good. Yet civil society depends so heavily upon this covenant, that any possibility of its weakening must be cause for serious alarm. Without it, people's sense of community and social responsibility will decline significantly.

The school must be reorganized into a number of learning communities within the whole. Schools must be organized from sets of individually graded classrooms to clusters of learners working with a group of teachers over an extended period of time, perhaps two or three years at a stretch, who embody the citizen characteristics outlined in Chapter 4 and as outlined in the seven principles at the beginning of this section. Schools as currently structured, for the most part, are not designed nor equipped to meet the challenges and demands of the coming century. They must be changed to model the kind of multidimensional citizenship education outlined in this book.

These changes will not come easily for they first and foremost involve power-sharing and those who have power usually give it up or share it very reluctantly. But this must occur if significant movement is to be made towards the development of citizens who are multidimensional. It is here where policy shapers, both those who were involved in this study, as well as others who were not, can be of the most important help. They have the power to influence change at a variety of levels from ministerial and legislative bodies to the governing boards of individual schools.

If we are successful in this first step, making the school a model of multidimensional citizenship, then the others to follow will be much easier to implement. This is not to suggest that the task will be easy; only that it is essential that the school models what is to be expected from the rest of the community.

## THE SCHOOL WITHIN THE LARGER COMMUNITY

The data from this study suggest that schools cannot be the sole source of citizenship education within their communities or within the larger societies.

Indeed, this has never been the case. Traditionally, families, societal agencies and institutions, churches and religious institutions and the community-at-large have played a significant role in the overall development of citizens. More than ever, if multidimensional citizenship is to become reality, then the entire community in which schools exist must become involved in the educative process. Everyone from family members to business and labour, government, spiritual and civic leaders must play their part. Citizenship education for the 21st century requires that political and social institutions, including families and schools, work together.

In part this is so, because our expert panellists suggest that the most significant challenges facing citizens in the early 21st century will be those of increasing economic disparities, social inequities, information access and privacy issues, and environmental concerns, and these can be addressed only in part by the schools through revised educational policies and practices. Added to this is the need to empower these citizens to become knowledgeable about and active in civic and public affairs. That is, they must not confine their learning only to schools but must increasingly apply what they have learned in their communities. This must be done through meaningful, relevant, well-planned and implemented community-based learning activities.

One possibility is to challenge learners in school to examine and research the kinds of issues and problems identified by the panellists in this study with an emphasis upon possible solutions. This would put relevance into their learning as they would be working on solutions to problems which they must face in their lifetime. Who knows what novel or innovative answers these students might generate and thus help in resolving some of these issues in the process.

Given the need for increased linkage between schools and communities, we recommend that they recognize and act upon their shared responsibility to contribute to the education of citizens with a global and future-oriented vision by developing a school culture in which students experience and participate in an environment that embodies the values, knowledge, skills, and attitudes necessary for the development of multidimensional citizenship. In this context, schools and their communities should assess their educational culture with respect to the following questions.

To what extent does school policy foster and/or demonstrate:

- sound environmental practices?
- sensitivity to and respect for human rights?
- respect for the opinions and ideas of others?
- cooperative, collaborative working relationships?
- open communication and the peaceful resolution of conflict?
- a respect for past traditions and practices but an orientation towards the future?

Historically, schools in most nations, and certainly in the ones participating in this study, have been an important part of their local communities. While the locus of control may not be local, but rather at the provincial, state or even national level, schools have been viewed as an important part of the locale in which they are situated. They have often been the focal point, the centre of communities. Citizens talk about 'our schools' demonstrating a very personal stake in them. But over the past thirty to forty years in some places, this has changed and we need to reclaim this local or community sense of schooling. The successful implementation of the multidimensional citizenship education model requires that citizens, whether or not they have children in the schools, view themselves as stakeholders in the education of the citizens who will in time direct the futures of their communities. Citizens must take some responsibility for ensuring that the school where its citizens are educated is the best possible school it can be, that it has the best prepared teachers, the best curriculum, the best teaching materials to deliver that curriculum, that it has the resources, financial and otherwise, to do the job properly, and that it has the best possible leadership both from the professional cadre within the school and from the community-at-large in their governing or advisory capacity.

The community-at-large must also reassume many of the social and familial responsibilities which have historically been within its domain, but which have often been transferred intentionally or *de facto* to the schools. The most significant thing that communities can do in this regard is to ensure the health of families within their locale. Nothing will strengthen the link between schools and their communities faster than having parents, be they single, two-parent or extended families, involved fully in the schooling of their children. The message conveyed both to their children and to their teachers is unbelievably powerful. The most disturbing aspect of the findings of this study was their bearing upon children, especially those living in poverty.

Again, the policy experts who participated in this study, and policy shapers in general, can play a powerful role in achieving this goal. They are the individuals in their local communities to whom others look for guidance and direction. They can lead by example, by becoming actively involved themselves and by encouraging, prodding, challenging others to do so as well. This will improve the educational environment in the community-at-large as well as the school dramatically. There can be no more significant investment towards the long-term health, vitality and stability of a community than this.

## THE SCHOOL AS AN ENVIRONMENTAL MODEL

Four of the seven most significantly challenging trends facing us in the next twenty-five years, in the view of the panellists, were related to the environment. It follows, therefore, that schools should formally adopt and abide by a code of environmentally minded behaviours including the careful use of water, energy and other resources, as well as appropriate waste disposal and recycling procedures. The school, through its policies and its personnel (including students) must model appropriate environmental behaviour not only for the long-term benefit of their own local community, but for the region, the nation, and the planet. Teachers and students within schools must play active roles in their communities in promoting action to support sustainable development to protect the future of the planet. The environment provides multiple opportunities to become actively involved in projects in the community. And, as witnessed in many parts of the globe, including the nine nations participating in this study, it is often children and youth who take the lead in educating their parents about the importance of environmental awareness and stewardship. They become the teachers and develop leadership abilities in the process.

Those involved in work to protect and restore the environment are constantly seeking the involvement of new citizens, and environmental work provides a natural avenue for community activists and experts to be brought into school activities. This would expedite community dialogue regarding key environmental issues and how they might be resolved. It would further the process of deliberation within the formal school curriculum and thus help to develop critical thinking and analytical skills. And the school could become a place where community-based activities could be planned and piloted before being disseminated more broadly.

## A DELIBERATION-BASED CURRICULUM

As outlined in Chapter 6, this study's findings suggest that a deliberation-based curriculum be implemented within schools. This would apply to all grade levels and, as appropriate, to all subject areas. If young citizens in our schools are to develop the requisite eight major citizen characteristics outlined in Chapter 4, then they must engage in the kinds of learning activities which will nurture and develop these characteristics over time. We believe that the most promising way to accomplish this is to involve children and youth in the debate and discussion, in deliberation, of the problems which will face them and their communities both now and in the future. As noted in Chapter 6, this deliberative curriculum should be organized around six major ethical questions or issues which cut across the curricular subjects and enable us to address the key global trends identified by the panel experts simultaneously.

These questions are best addressed in multiple learning environments and through discipline-based and interdisciplinary studies both in school and in the wider communities in which students live. The underlying foundation of this learning, however, must be deliberation. Students of all ages must be given the opportunity to examine in depth the great issues of our day which will most certainly impact their lives fully in the coming years. The kinds of knowledge, skills and attitudes noted above do not develop by chance; they must be learnt through enquiry and discourse about key civic and public issues. And they must have the opportunities to put their learning to practical application, again within the school and/or in the wider community. Thus, we strongly recommend a deliberation-based curriculum within a school learning environment which models the attributes of multidimensional citizenship.

This underlines the need for a fundamental transformation not only in the socialization role of schools but in the academic role as well. The established disciplines will continue to occupy central roles within the curriculum, but they must be taught in an increasingly interdisciplinary manner. The kinds of global trends which our panellists identified are not necessarily the domain of single disciplines but rather, in general, cut across a number of them. Thus, in order to truly get to the resolution of these issues and problems, they often cannot be studied through just one discipline but rather in an interdisciplinary manner which draws upon the key concepts and processes of each and every relevant field of study. This is the way the world really is and the way in which it works. One of the major stated reasons by youth for their lack of interest in civic and public issues is that in their school learning, the relevance of in-school work is never brought to bear upon the real issues of the day in their own communities. Students don't feel they are really studying things which will impact them, or at least the relevant linkages are seldom pointed out or made obvious. This must change, and a deliberation-based curriculum which is interdisciplinary and gets students actively involved in projects in their communities is the direction we strongly recommend. We believe that the six key ethical questions raised above should be the advanced organizers for this deliberation.

Again, this deliberation, while centred in the school and the curriculum, must not become the sole domain of the school. Rather, the school must become a learning community *within* the broader community within which the children live. While children and youth learn the knowledge and skills of deliberation within the context of schooling, in order for this to have meaning and relevance to the community-at-large, the issues being studied are most likely to be found in their own local communities as well as in those across the planet. It becomes essential, therefore, that deliberation is based upon the six organizing ethical questions noted in Chapter 6 and occurs within the community-at-large. This brings the worlds of the school and home together into one extended community where all can partake. In doing so, the bridge between home and community is built and barriers fall.

## TEACHERS AS EXEMPLARS

Education for multidimensional citizenship requires that teachers be appropriately prepared in its theory and practice. Without teachers as living models of what the students are to embody, it will be difficult, if not impossible, to succeed. Teacher preparation institutions, both at the initial licensure and inservice professional development levels, must reorganize and restructure their programmes to ensure the development of the knowledge, skills and attitudes of multidimensional citizenship as outlined in this book. Without teachers who are themselves examples of multidimensional citizens, it will be impossible to develop the four dimensions of multidimensional citizenship in students.

Specifically, we recommend that professional development programmes for teachers be based upon and model the application of the following:

- deliberation-based curriculum and pedagogy
- information- and media-based curriculum and pedagogy
- multiple uses of technology for teaching, learning and researching
- focus upon environmental issues and problems of a global nature which possibly reveal themselves locally
- a globally oriented curriculum, that is to say one which uses examples, readings, illustrative pedagogical activities, learning materials, media, etc, from other parts of the world
- democratic decision-making processes and values
- the development of cooperative, collaborative working relationships, and
- practice in the application of one's learning in the wider community.

Only with teachers prepared in this manner can the multidimensional citizenship model be implemented. Students must see their teachers as living examples of what they are professing, as people who are personally involved in their communities, working on projects of a civic or public nature, knowledgeable about developments in other parts of the nation and the world, able to debate key civic and public issues with other colleagues in the school as well as those in the community at large, aware of the historical antecedents of these issues so that they have a context for their discourse, and possessing a vision of what might be done to resolve or at least improve the situation.

This requires that those who prepare teachers are themselves imbued with a sense of the importance of community-based learning and understand the concept and practice of multidimensional citizenship. Teacher educators must model multidimensional citizenship in their own lives.

## THE CHALLENGE TO DEVELOP MODELS

Finally, we need some models of what we are proposing above. It would be desirable to develop several pilot projects in the respective nations participating in this study to get the process of implementing multidimensional citizenship under way. Large-scale projects with lofty goals and ideals seldom achieve the kinds of success anticipated at the outset. But if we expect entire communities to become involved in this reconceptualization of the 21st century citizen, then we should begin appropriately with models developed in local communities from which others might learn and replicate.

What are required are not large national programmes, although these should not necessarily be ruled out if they are deemed appropriate in any given situation. Rather, we suggest beginning with partnerships between individual schools or school districts, their communities and a teacher preparation institution(s). Small, carefully planned, locally based models have the best chance for success in the long term. They need to be designed, implemented and evaluated so that others might possibly replicate them in communities nearby or faraway. The documentation of the process will be very important as only through full disclosure of the successes as well as the failures and problems incurred along the way will any one project be of substantial use to others as they seek to build their own model. To be sure, no two models will be exactly alike as no two communities are exactly alike. But the model must be grounded in multidimensional citizenship and include the elements noted above. That is, it must:

- view the school as a model community from which the larger community can learn
- view the school as a community within the community-at-large and draw upon its many resources in order to develop multidimensional citizenship
- view the school as a model of sound environmental practice and behaviours
- utilize a deliberation-based curriculum as the primary pedagogical focus within the school and within this context
- organize the curriculum around six major ethical questions to be implemented through teachers who are exemplars of the multidimensional citizenship model.

## IMPLEMENTATION IN CENTRALIZED AND DECENTRALIZED SYSTEMS

One of the key challenges facing those in the nine nations participating in this study is that of getting the respective national systems of education to examine and reconsider education for citizenship that is multidimensional. The first problem, of course, is that the systems of education and schooling in these nine nations differ, in some cases considerably. They differ in their organization and structure, in their curricular scope and sequence, in their preferred methods of teaching, in their assessment measures, and in their initial and continuing professional development of teachers. Some are highly centralized systems where power and authority are vested in national ministries; others are very decentralized and control is located at the state or provincial level, or even in some cases locally. Thus, one of the major challenges for those attempting to implement multidimensional citizenship as educational policy will be to determine the locus of control and to work most intensively at first with officials at that level.

While it might seem on the surface that this is done more easily in systems that are highly centralized, this is not always the case. National ministries of education can be large, unwieldy and sometimes firmly entrenched bureaucracies that have developed a life of their own and do not respond easily to change, especially change which is initiated from the outside. But they do have the advantage that once, or perhaps better if, that wall is penetrated, they can put authority and momentum behind a policy decision which will likely ensure its implementation.

Working in decentralized systems can embody another set of problems. Finding the person(s) who can influence change within such systems is often very difficult because they are spread out over provinces, states or regions and have developed networks and power bases of their own. In some respects, external pressure for change is responded to more directly in decentralized systems since one is working with people much closer to the point of implementation. But this is not always the case. Again, it is important to carefully identify these policy shapers and work to enlist their support.

But, in either case, or some combination of the two, the critical element in implementing the concept of multidimensional citizenship will be to work on a number of fronts simultaneously. That is, while working with key figures at the ministerial level, be it national, regional or state/provincial, one must also work with people in local communities, in local school districts or even in a school, with the public media, with teachers' unions and organizations, with leaders in labour, business and industry, and with those in colleges and universities to ensure a multifaceted approach to implementation of multidimensional citizenship as educational policy.

In addition to educators, there is a whole range of other individuals and groups who may not have been as fully involved in educational policy development and implementation in the past, eg, government officials, journalists, corporate, business and labour groups, parent and teacher organizations, as well as others. Multidimensional citizenship requires the formation of new coalitions of persons interested in the education of present and future generations while at the same time maintaining working relationships with those who have historically been involved in policy issues.

## CROSS-CULTURAL/CROSS-NATIONAL ISSUES AND WIDER APPLICABILITY

One of the problems always faced by those doing research which is both cross-cultural and cross-national is the question of wider applicability beyond the participants involved. Even in the case of the nine nations which participated in this study this issue exists. In Chapter 4 we discussed the differences between what we have termed East and West, that is Japan and Thailand which represent a more Eastern perspective, and the remaining nations, Canada, England, Germany, Greece, Hungary, the Netherlands, and the United States which are more Western in their orientation. As noted in Chapter 4, there was far greater agreement on many items among the Japanese and Thai expert panellists at the end of the third round than was the case with those in the West. Perhaps this is an indication of a greater desire on the part of Asians, or at least these experts from these two Asian nations, to work towards greater consensus.

Any study involving a specific set of participants runs a risk in suggesting the applicability of its findings beyond the original population. This said, however, it is important for all nations to examine the findings and resulting recommendations of this study in terms of their own settings. Indeed, we would challenge educators in other nations and parts of the world to take our questions and our survey instruments and test them for applicability in their own environments.

## CONTINUING THE RESEARCH

It was never our intent that this was to be a comprehensive research project. From the beginning, we have viewed this as the testing of the viability of a network of universities in several parts of the world and their ability to work together on a common research project. We viewed this as a pilot or groundbreaking effort which would be extended in time to other nations. To be sure, it was hoped that this could be merely the initial stage of a longer-term project which would include participant nations in other regions of the world. We believe that we have developed a research framework which could be utilized by others either in the same or some modified form and applied to their own situations. The expert panellists in our study responded to the three original questions which we posed regarding the identification of emerging global trends, the citizen characteristics required to cope with and/or manage those trends, and the necessary educational strategies to develop the characteristics as well as the resulting 106 item survey instrument that was developed. Would other policy experts in other nations and regions of the world share these views? We simply don't know without replicating what we have done elsewhere. Would other kinds of participants have generated the same kinds of data in response to our original questions? We don't know. But we certainly hope others will replicate this and add to the knowledge base accordingly.

A study which builds upon this one has in fact already been undertaken in the area of teacher education (Kubow, 1996). This study utilized the survey instrument developed for the original study reported in this book with university students in post-baccalaureate initial teacher education licensure programmes in the three English-speaking nations in the original study, ie, Canada, England and the United States of America, in terms of comparing their views with those of the panel experts in our study. A follow-on from Kubow's dissertation project is currently under way. It involves the use of the original research questionnaire as a survey to be utilized with college and university-level students from England, The Netherlands, Japan, Taiwan, Hong Kong (SAR), China, Thailand and Singapore. These findings will be compared with those of the policy experts in this initial study, as well as with Kubow's findings. Publication of this second stage work is expected in late 2000. A third stage of the project work involving secondary school teachers and their students is in the early planning phase at the time of this publication.

Another study which could be done would be a more or less direct replication of this one with volunteer participant nations in as many of the world's regions as is feasible. This would allow us to continue to work with policy experts as they attempt to influence citizen education policy in their respective nations and regions of the world. The original survey instrument could be utilized as the starting point but respondent panellists from these new nations would be strongly encouraged to add new global trends, citizen characteristics and educational strategies to the framework to extend the scope of the findings and recommendations.

Another possibility would be to choose an entirely different group of 'experts' altogether. As noted above, in this instance we chose policy experts because the focus of the study was upon developing policy. But other groups could be utilized as well. For example, what if we utilized a more typical or ordinary group of respondents, the person in the street so to speak, or the poor and disenfranchised. How might our data differ? Assuming that it did, what about comparing these responses with those of our policy experts?

And still another possibility, the recipients of the educational policy in this original study, students. What kinds of future would the children and youth in our schools envision over the next twenty-five years? How might it be the same or different than that characterized by our policy expert panellists in this study? Children in particular are often neglected in these kinds of research endeavours largely because adults don't think they are interested in the future or even if they were, don't have much to say about it. This has proven not to be the case (Kurth-Schai, 1988, 1991).

Still another possibility would be to attempt to do a more broadly based Delphi survey, based upon the original instrument as a starting point, but to try and do it electronically, ie, via e-mail or the Internet. One of the most costly aspects of the study reported herein was the annual international meetings of all twenty-six researchers. On the one hand, we deemed this to be absolutely essential in establishing the kind of trusting, respectful working relationships which emerged as the study proceeded. However, we also became very aware that the cost of replicating this on a larger global scale would become cost prohibitive. Thus, the issue has been raised regarding the use of technology, perhaps even involving teleconferences, as a means to cut the costs of personal travel and meeting face to face. This needs exploration to be sure.

Another option being explored as this book is being written is to bring key educational policy leaders together at some site to brief them on the study which we have undertaken and to train them in the method so that they might then go back to their own countries and replicate it for their own uses. In other words, there would be no further research carried out by the original researchers but rather they would inform and prepare others to carry on the work in their own nations or regions on their own. There are clearly strengths and drawbacks to this proposal. The major strength is that it would cut costs considerably since these would be borne in the main by the participant policy leaders and their respective nations. The drawback would clearly be the loss of opportunity to develop a much more comprehensive and global picture of the needs and policy directions regarding citizenship education as we enter the 21st century.

There are undoubtedly other options as well but we shall leave them for future discussions. We simply wish to note that what we have accomplished here should be viewed as only the beginning of a continuing process of research and policy development as well as the follow-on development of curriculum materials, innovative methods of teaching and assessment and most assuredly a restructuring of the manner in which teachers are prepared for their work. There is much work to be done.

## CONCLUSION

Earlier in this final chapter we outlined the challenges of implementing the multidimensional citizenship model we have developed based upon the findings and recommendations of this study. We wish to close with a reminder of those challenges.

First, we need to begin with the restructuring of the school as we currently know it into one that is a model community of the concept and practice of multidimensional citizenship. This is fundamental.

Second, we must ensure that the school is no longer the sole source of citizenship education within societies. It must be viewed as playing a primary role certainly but in concert with the communities at large within which it exists. Families and other institutions within communities need to reassert their role in the development of the children and youth, their future leadership cadre, into knowledgeable, critical-thinking, participatory citizens.

Third, given the enormous environmental problems and issues raised by these study findings, it is essential that schools become models of the kind of environmental sustainability which they profess. They must become lighthouses to their communities in this regard; the children must be prepared to be the teachers of their parents.

Fourth, the multidimensional citizen, above all, must be a thoughtful, reflective, deliberative individual. Thus, the school curriculum and the instruction and assessment measures utilized to implement it must be deliberation-based. Deliberation does not just happen; it is developed, nurtured, taught. It requires practice over a long period of time, the whole of one's school life to be sure. And it must be focused upon the most critical issues and questions of our time. We have listed six major ethical questions as a starting point but those implementing curriculum need to be constantly challenged to add others to the list as well.

Fifth, if all of the above are going to fall into place and work towards the development of the multidimensional citizen, then we have to seriously re-think the kinds of teachers required to do the job. They must be exemplars. They must be models themselves of what we mean by multidimensional citizens. Their students and their communities must view them as the kinds of persons which they wish to emulate. This is a major, perhaps *the* major challenge we face in the implementation of the multidimensional citizenship model.

Sixth, and finally, we need to have models. We must begin somewhere if we are to indeed ensure that multidimensional citizenship becomes the educational policy for the early 21st century. We believe that these models can emerge from any community, in any state or province, region or nation. We have suggested small locally based projects but these are by no means the only possibilities. Each situation will be different and call for different solutions. So we leave this to others. The only prerequisite is that the multidimensional citizenship model as outlined in this book must be the basis for the implementation. We encourage communities to make local adaptations as appropriate but to give the model as conceived the best possible chance for success. This will be a long-term process.

Those who expect quick solutions should turn elsewhere. For this is nothing less than an investment in the future of our communities and we can think of nothing better than that.

## REFERENCES

Kubow, Patricia K (1996) *Reconceptualizing Citizenship Education for the Twenty-First Century: A study of postbaccalaureate social studies students from Canada, England and the United States*, An unpublished doctoral thesis, University of Minnesota, Minneapolis, USA.

Kurth-Schai, Ruthanne (1988) 'Collecting the Thoughts of Children: A Delphic Approach', *Journal of Research and Development in Education*, **21**(3), pp 53–9.

Kurth-Schai, Ruthanne (1991) 'Educational Systems Design by Children for Children', *Educational Foundations*, **5**, pp 19–39.

# APPENDIX

## CEPS PROJECT RESEARCH TEAM MEMBERS

### Japan*

Mizoue Yasushi, Naruto University of Education, Co-Team Leader
Ninomiya Akira, Hiroshima University, Co-Team Leader
Nakayama Shuichi, Hiroshima University
Otsu Kazuko, Hokkaido University of Education
Uozumi Tadahisa, Aichi University of Education

### Thailand

Somuwung Pitiyanuwat, Chulalongkorn University, Co-Team Leader
Chumpol Poolpatarachewin, Chulalongkorn University, Co-Team Leader
Arunsi Anantrasirichai, Ministry of Education
Walai Panich, Chulalongkorn University
Chanita Rukspollmuang, Chulalongkorn University
Suchin Visavateeranon, Sukhothai Thammathirat Open University

### Europe

Sjoerd Karsten, University of Amsterdam, the Netherlands, Team Leader
Raymond Derricott, University of Liverpool, UK
Athan Gotovos, University of Ioannina, Greece
Zsuzsa Matrai, National Institute of Public Education, Hungary
Hans Merkens, Frei Universität, Berlin, Germany

### North America

John J Cogan, University of Minnesota, Project Director and Team Leader
Patricia K Kubow, University of Minnesota, Project Research Coordinator
Patricia Avery, University of Minnesota
Roland Case, Simon Fraser University, Canada
Fred Finley, University of Minnesota
David Grossman, Hong Kong Institute of Education, Hong Kong, SAR, PRC**
Ruthanne Kurth-Schai, Macalester College
Kenneth Osborne, University of Manitoba, Canada
Walter C. Parker, University of Washington
Kathy Skau, University of Calgary, Canada

* Japanese names appear with family names listed first as is customary.
** Dr Grossman began the CEPS project with the North American team in his position as Director of the Center for Teaching Asia and Pacific Studies at the East-West Center in Honolulu. He subsequently moved to his present post in Hong Kong in late 1995.

# AUTHOR INDEX

# SUBJECT INDEX

**NB:** italicised page numbers = figures, tables, etc

*191*

# Subject Index

# Subject Index